Retrofitting Sprawl

EDITED BY EMILY TALEN

Retrofitting Sprawl

Addressing
Seventy Years of
Failed Urban Form

THE UNIVERSITY OF GEORGIA PRESS   Athens and London

© 2015 by the University of Georgia Press
Athens, Georgia 30602
www.ugapress.org
All rights reserved
Designed by Kaelin Chappell Broaddus
Set in 10.4/12.75 Minion Pro Regular by Graphic Composition, Inc.
Printed and bound by Thomson-Shore, Inc.
The paper in this book meets the guidelines for
permanence and durability of the Committee on
Production Guidelines for Book Longevity of the
Council on Library Resources.

Most University of Georgia Press titles are
available from popular e-book vendors.

Printed in the United States of America
19   18   17   16   15   P   5   4   3   2   1

Library of Congress Cataloging-in-Publication Data

Retrofitting sprawl : addressing seventy years of failed urban form / edited by Emily Talen.
    pages cm
    Includes bibliographical references and index.
    ISBN 978-0-8203-4544-4 (hardcover : alk. paper) — ISBN 978-0-8203-4545-1 (pbk. : alk. paper) —
ISBN 978-0-8203-4819-3 (ebook) 1. Urban renewal—United States. 2. Cities and towns—United
States—Growth. 3. City planning—United States. I. Talen, Emily, 1958–
    HT175.R473 2015
    307.3'4160973—dc23

                                                                              2014042987

British Library Cataloging-in-Publication Data available

Contents

Retrofitting Sprawl

Retrofitting Sprawl

EMILY TALEN

This book grew out of a "Retrofitting Sprawl" symposium held in April 2012 at the Phoenix Urban Research Laboratory (PURL), an urban design center at Arizona State University. We were in the right place for this discussion, as Phoenix ranks high on the list of most sprawling places in the United States. It is, as one observer put it, "a thousand-square-mile oasis of ranch homes, back yards, shopping centers, and dispersed employment based on personal mobility."[1] To anyone hoping to reform the way we occupy the land, it is exactly the kind of place in need of retrofitting.

We were all well aware of the enormity of the problem and the intractability of proposed solutions. But, as this book testifies, these hurdles have not stymied creative thinking on the topic in terms of both analysis and proposed remedies. The chapters in this book consolidate multiple perspectives to provide a state-of-the-art overview of current thinking about ways to fix—or, as it's also called, "repair" or "retrofit"—sprawl.

We know a lot about sprawl, having spent decades measuring and defining it, quantifying its costs and effects, and unraveling its underlying causes.[2] A pragmatic definition of sprawl is "low density, noncontiguous, automobile dependent" development—although, some would argue, sprawl can occur anywhere, even in the very heart of a city.[3] This simple, concise definition means that "sprawl" is not synonymous with "suburb." Some suburban places—mostly of the pre–World War II variety—are transit-served, walkable, more affordable than dense urban cores, and constitute some of the best human settlements now existing in the United States. Where the term "suburb" is used in this book, it refers specifically to suburbs that lack those qualities. Since much of suburbia is in the form of sprawl, it is easy to understand how the terms have come to be used interchangeably.

Since sprawl accompanies urban growth, it has always existed (on this point, there is no disagreement with *Sprawl: A Compact History,* which painted sprawl as something benign).[4] The problem with sprawl as it currently exists—and more specifically, in a twenty-first-century American context—is its magnitude. It became an acute problem following a "perfect storm" of twentieth-century conditions: the rise of automobiles and expendable income, highway building, housing subsidies, accelerated depreciation, cheap land, Real Estate Investment Trusts (REITs), zoning, subdivision regulations, production builders, and social intolerance. All of these factors and more created the perfect context for the land-consuming, dispiriting landscape we call sprawl.

Sprawl is blamed for some of the most serious problems facing American society: global warming, social inequity, environmental degradation, exorbitant energy use, economic inefficiency and waste, job loss, and the decline of public health. Recently, sprawl has been blamed for exacerbating the deindustrialization of American cities, leading to a decline of not only a once-robust and growing middle class but also an increasingly mythical American dream.[5]

Perhaps these attributions are exaggerated. But the need to do something proactive to address the problem of sprawl resonates widely. In effect, the twenty-first century ushered in its own "perfect storm" of conditions that necessitated the reverse of sprawl: (1) the need to reduce energy consumption and "live local" (climate change); (2) the need to build incrementally and in small-scale ways (the global recession); and (3) the need to provide smaller and more centrally located housing types (demographic change). These conditions fundamentally conflict with the scale, pattern, and consumption that accompanies sprawl, mandating a radically different approach to human settlement.

While there is a now a consensus regarding what sprawl is and why it's a problem, there is also general agreement about what a world without sprawl would be like: compact, walkable settlements in a variety of forms, including villages, towns, and cities, transit-served and diverse where possible. Rural, low-density settlement is not excluded from this vision, but balance is required. Car dependence that is innocuous—that is, where urban amenities are given up in exchange for access to nature—is tolerable. But car dependence that pays no attention to its negative effects is not.

So what can be done about sprawl? Taking to heart that we no longer need to obsess over the question of whether compact, diverse, less car-dependent living is better for the planet, fixing sprawl focuses on what the specific policy and design responses should be. The question before us now is whether government subsidies and funding priorities, market incentives, new kinds of codes, transportation systems, or urban design schemes are achieving or are likely to achieve what is needed.

Retrofitting sprawl will require not only new kinds of tools but also new ways of conceptualizing. Until recently, planners have been mostly focused on sprawl restriction (e.g., growth boundaries), not repair—which requires a different kind of thinking. A recurrent point is the need for spatial triage: not every place can reinvent itself as a walkable, mixed-use neighborhood surrounded by connecting boulevards. There is a need to prioritize places and tactics, leveraging future investment in ways that stimulate better urbanism in strategic locations.

The idea of fixing sprawl is relatively new, but enough material has accrued to document and learn from efforts so far. Most approaches are novel if not Herculean: failed malls converted to main streets, McMansions transformed into apartment buildings, and big box stores reenvisioned as agricultural land. Ellen Dunham-Jones and June Williamson, with their book *Retrofitting Suburbia*, were trailblazers in the documentation of retrofitting strategies. Galina Tachieva's book *Sprawl Repair* was similarly path-breaking with its accessible offering of creative design strategies for transforming car-dependent suburbia into something more livable.[6]

The urgency of the issue has resonated with the general public and the popular press: "recycling suburbia" was recently rated by *Time* magazine as the #2 "Idea Changing the World"; *Dwell* magazine sponsored a design competition called "Reburbia" devoted to "re-envisioning" suburban growth (www.reburbia.com); Long Island, New York, launched its Build a Better Burb website and design contest (http://buildabetterburb.org/); and the Urban Land Institute has been sponsoring events and publications aimed at finding ways to redirect investment toward retrofitting sprawl.

Drawing on this momentum, this book presents the latest thinking on sprawl retrofitting. Chapters are grouped into three sections with self-explanatory titles: "Existing Realities," "Case Studies," and "Imagined Possibilities."

The first section uncovers some essential baseline realities about the prospects of retrofitting sprawl, viewed from four different angles. It begins with a chapter by Julia Koschinsky and me where we use a unique dataset—Walk Scores for the entire United States—to show just how far off we are from an urban pattern composed of walkable, high-access neighborhoods (the opposite of sprawl). We find that only 4 percent of neighborhoods in suburban areas can be characterized as accessible, that is, having Walk Scores of 70 or higher. When suburbs and cities are combined, only 18 percent are accessible. The implication of this is that, perhaps unlike other economic and social problems Americans are currently facing, sprawl is omnipresent and highly visible. Most of us live or work in sprawl and experience it daily.

Brenda Case Scheer next looks at just how difficult the task of fixing sprawl is going to be from a structural point of view. She hones in on the possibilities of transforming the "strip," a sprawl element that is a problem "as much for what it represents as for how it operates." Her exploration shows how it is essential to look further than signage, landscaping, and other "Band-Aids" to address structural flaws, especially the relationship between sprawl elements (in her case, between the strip and its surrounding residential subdivisions). As it turns out, the unloved, seemingly chaotic commercial strip and the orderly housing suburb are "necessary corollaries" of each other. Using the tools of morphological analysis, she shows that there is in fact an underlying order to the strip that explains its character and evolution. It is a geometry that emphatically resists change. For landowners, the morphology provides no imperative to contemplate the relationship of any given parcel to the public realm or to the street. It is an "interlocking system" of lots, formulaic building types, and financial systems that make fixing it a huge challenge.

Next is an exploration of the political hurdles involved in sprawl repair. Gerrit-Jan Knaap, Aviva Hopkins Brown, and Rebecca Lewis detail the case of code reform—a staple of efforts to fix sprawl. Although Montgomery County, Maryland, is a place well known for cutting-edge planning and a highly engaged constituency, the ongoing effort to replace a sprawl-inducing, Euclidean zoning ordinance with something more conducive to building walkable, compact, and diverse communities (i.e., form-based coding) has been "long, tedious, and contentious." Important changes allowing mixed-use and accessory dwellings went through, but planners estimate that the revised code "will have little impact on 95 percent of property in the county." The authors document a failed process and show us what can happen when future visions are not well presented.

Matthew Salenger explores the complexity of individual living preferences, tackling the question: If sprawl is so terrible, why do so many people seem to want to live there? His quest is to uncover individual choices as they relate to sprawl, and how these choices "combine to create the culture, politics, economy, and aesthetics of sprawl." He uses a survey of 101 people living in Phoenix to tease out some hypotheses that might help us make sense of the apparent contradictions. He proposes some interesting connections between the zones of a city and the connection people have to "place." In far-out locations people find a connection to "nature," while in closer-in, denser locations people connect to people and facilities. People in the middle sprawl zone are connected to neither.

Section two presents a series of case studies—"real world" examples of how sprawl is actually being transformed. The section opens with June Williamson's overview of essential "urban design tactics" that are being used in the quest to retrofit sprawl. She provides case studies relating to eleven different kinds of tactics, including adaptive reuse of big box stores, restoration of wetlands, placement of liner buildings, and mixing of housing types. The installation of "new urban morphologies of walkable blocks and interconnected streets" would be a radical adjustment indeed, but an important point is the need to prioritize and selectively seed. The "strategic deployment" of tactics is a recurrent theme.

David Dixon looks at the case of new suburban downtowns through three examples. He argues that in these places there is evidence of a remarkable shift in thinking. These new downtowns are a new brand, an approach deeply critical of the "privatized nature and anonymity" of "lifestyle centers" and other past attempts that only mimic authentically diverse places. They are not, however, spontaneous—they are "consciously planned" and dependent on backing and funding from local government. Dixon likens them to the early railroad suburbs: in both versions, economic value is created by paying attention to social value—that is, "community."

Ellen Dunham-Jones and Wesley Brown offer a case study of Atlanta, Georgia, another city that often ranks near the top on sprawl indicators. They show how crucial the public sector was in transforming a "zombie" subdivision, leveraging capital, and playing the role of master developer. Strategic partnerships, public financing, a strong plan, a committed staff—these elements are what rescued a subdivision headed for desertion. The message boils down to the importance of a strong community vision and the need to position sprawl retrofits firmly within that larger conception.

Nico Larco documents the unsanctioned pedestrian pathways being foraged by the beleaguered suburban pedestrian. This is suburban retrofit in its most elemental form—trails cut here and there in constant pursuit of a shorter route between home and shopping or workplace. The dilemma for urban planning is whether to "leave well-enough alone" and turn a blind eye to the problems of safety, equity, and liability these ad hoc pathways create, or whether to try to legitimate them at the risk of undermining a cobbled-together-but-nevertheless-improved form of pedestrian access. Tactical as they are, a government-backed planning response could have the effect of backfiring and ultimately creating even more blockage.

Section three includes chapters that explore new and as yet untested ideas—the "imagined possibilities"—of retrofitting sprawl. The section begins with a study of suburban streets and how they might be repurposed. Marc Schlossberg and Dave Amos document a profound mismatch: the incongruous situation that 41 percent of paved suburbia consists of on-street parking that is only minimally used. With an average vacancy rate of 89 percent, they ask, why not find a better use for this leftover, underutilized pavement, leveraging it for environmental management, urban agriculture, or civic space? This proposal is perhaps more politically saleable than other retrofitting proposals, as it involves repurposing public land for both private and public gain (via increased tax revenue).

Gabriel Díaz Montemayor and Nabil Kamel explore the possibilities of reconceptualizing the spaces between public and private realms. Their proposal is to better connect single-family detached houses to the surrounding public realm by loosening up these intermediate, transition spaces of "ecotones." Their definition of the "sprawl problem" is one of rigidity, and fixing sprawl requires moving beyond an "obsession with property rights" toward thinking about sprawl as something better suited to urban evolution. They make the case that communities locked in sprawl can "renegotiate" urban space by thinking of transitional areas as ecotones that allow flexible uses, the redefinition of boundaries, and the loosening up of "the rigid spatial delineations of sprawl."

Two final chapters focus on the repurposing of cul-de-sacs, a form often equated with sprawl. Benjamin W. Stanley, Aaron Golub, Milagros Zingoni, Whitney Warman, and Christian Solorio show how cul-de-sacs can be retrofitted into something much more sustainable. The intent is to stimulate "place-based economic activity" by again calling for spaces that are flexible and adaptable and thus able to "squeeze more value out of existing urban configurations." These include strategies not only for mixing uses and building types but also for encouraging on-site production of capital in all forms (human, social, natural, financial). The "physical capital" of the cul-de-sac allows this to happen, the authors contend, "without market exchange."

Galina Tachieva uses the "occupy Wall Street" analogy to propose the occupation of sprawl in incremental fashion, "one sprawl element at a time." As in the previous chapter, the element to be fixed is the ubiquitous cul-de-sac. The goal is to document innovative but straightforward strategies that could have a catalytic effect on sprawl. She proposes the insertion of buildings that will rebalance and diversify the homogeneity of the cul-de-sac. In her graphic examples, buildings are grouped to produce new centers of activity, but the groupings are not fixed blueprints. They represent the components of a toolkit: modular, flexible, and adaptable.

While the tone of the book is critical in terms of its assessment of sprawl, it is also hopeful in terms of what the future holds. The authors address head-on the most controversial aspects of sprawl—issues of power and control, justice and equity, and the intractable nature of American attitudes about controlling private development. But they also contextualize these issues in a practical, grounded way, bringing in examples of redesign that are already occurring around the country, from the retrofitting of corridors to the repurposing of cul-de-sacs.

Whether retrofitting sprawl requires a cultural shift in thinking or a coordinated effort on the part of local government, the essays in this book testify to the fact that some combination of forethought and creative thinking will be needed. Sprawl will never fix itself on its own—we need creative ideas, best practices, and continuous study of the successes, failures, and lessons learned. My hope is that this book will be useful to those engaged in any part of that effort.

NOTES

1. Grady Gammage Jr., *Phoenix in Perspective: Reflections on Developing the Desert* (Tempe, Az.: Herberger Center for Design Excellence, 2003).

2. A few sources for understanding the impacts of sprawl include: F. Kaid Benfield, Jutka

Terris, and Nancy Vorsanger, *Solving Sprawl: Models of Smart Growth in Communities across America* (New York: Natural Resources Defense Council, 2001); Robert Burchell, Anthony Downs, Barbara McCann, and Sahan Mukherji, *Sprawl Costs: Economic Impacts of Unchecked Development* (Washington, D.C.: Island Press, 2005); Marcy Burchfield, Henry G. Overman, Diego Puga, and Matthew A. Turner, "Causes of Sprawl: A Portrait from Space," *Quarterly Journal of Economics* 121, no. 2 (2006): 587–633; Reid H. Ewing, *Endangered by Sprawl: How Runaway Development Threatens America's Wildlife* (Washington, D.C.: National Wildlife Federation, Smart Growth America, 2005); Jason Freihage, Stephen Coleman, Royce Hanson, George Galster, Harold Wolman, and Michael R. Ratcliffe, "Wrestling Sprawl to the Ground: Defining and Measuring an Elusive Concept," *Housing Policy Debate* 12, no. 4 (2001): 681–717; Howard Frumkin, *Urban Sprawl and Public Health: Designing, Planning, and Building for Healthy Communities* (Washington, D.C.: Island Press, 2004); Edward L. Glaeser and Matthew E. Kahn, *Sprawl and Urban Growth*, NBER Working Paper no. w9733,SSRN, 2003, http://ssrn.com/abstract=412880; George A. Gonzalez, *Urban Sprawl, Global Warming, and the Empire of Capital* (Albany: State University of New York Press, 2009); Joel S. Hirschhorn, *Sprawl Kills: How Blandburbs Steal Your Time, Health and Money* (New York: Sterling & Ross, 2005); Rolf Pendall, "Local Land Use Regulation and the Chain of Exclusion," *Journal of the American Planning Association* 66, no. 2 (2000): 125–42; Gregory D. Squires, *Urban Sprawl: Causes, Consequences and Policy Responses* (Washington, D.C.: Urban Institute Press, 2002); Thad Williamson, *Sprawl, Justice, and Citizenship: The Civic Costs of the American Way of Life* (New York: Oxford University Press, 2010).

3. D. N. Bengston, J. O. Fletcher, and K. C. Nelson, "Public Policies for Managing Urban Growth and Protecting Open Space: Policy Instruments and Lessons Learned in the United States," *Landscape and Urban Planning* 69, nos. 2–3 (2004): 271–86.

4. Robert Bruegmann, *Sprawl: A Compact History* (Chicago: University of Chicago Press, 2005).

5. Raj Chetty, Nathaniel Hendren, Patrick Kline, and Emmanuel Saez, *The Economic Impacts of Tax Expenditures: Evidence from Spatial Variation across the U.S.* (Cambridge, Mass.: Equality of Opportunity Project, 2013), http://www.equality-of-opportunity.org/; see also Paul Krugman, "Stranded by Sprawl," *New York Times*, July 28, 2013, http://www.nytimes.com/2013/07/29/opinion/krugman-stranded-by-sprawl.html.

6. Ellen Dunham-Jones and June Williamson, *Retrofitting Suburbia: Urban Design Solutions for Redesigning Suburbs* (Hoboken, N.J.: John Wiley, 2011); Galina Tachieva, *Sprawl Repair Manual* (Washington, D.C.: Island Press, 2010). See also Dan Chiras and Dave Wann, *Superbia: 31 Ways to Create Sustainable Neighborhoods* (Gabriola Island, B.C.: New Society, 2003); Julia Christensen, *Big Box Reuse* (Cambridge, Mass.: MIT Press, 2008); Congress for the New Urbanism, *Malls into Mainstreets: An In-Depth Guide to Transforming Dead Malls into Communities* (Chicago: Congress for the New Urbanism, 2005); Paul Lukez, *Suburban Transformations* (Princeton, N.J.: Princeton Architectural Press, 2007); Lee Sobel and Steven Bodzin, *Greyfields into Goldfields: Dead Malls become Living Neighborhoods* (Chicago: Congress for the New Urbanism, 2002).

Existing Realities

CHAPTER 1

From Sprawl to Walkable
How Far Is That?

JULIA KOSCHINSKY AND EMILY TALEN

Key Points and Practice Takeaways

1. A primary objective of "fixing" sprawl is to transform it into places that are walkable and mixed-use.

2. We use a national neighborhood-level dataset of 359 metropolitan areas to address the question of walkable access to amenities and also to examine the tradeoffs between walkable access and socioeconomic neighborhood characteristics.

3. The vast majority of neighborhoods (82 percent) do not have walkable access. Even within cities, the vast majority of neighborhoods (73 percent) are not accessible.

4. Living in places with walkable access involves tradeoffs, as such neighborhoods tend to be more expensive. On average, accessible suburbs are more expensive to live in than accessible cities.

5. Suburbs have several assets that could be leveraged to increase the supply of walkable neighborhoods, including a range of residential density levels, higher-quality schools, and lower segregation levels.

Conceptually, life in walkable, mixed-use neighborhoods is easily contrasted with car-dependent sprawl. Recent books have popularized the contrast, and their titles reveal the high hopes associated with urbanism. Examples include *The Option of Urbanism: Investing in a New American Dream* and *Walkable City: How Downtown Can Save America.*[1] Over 400 articles have recently been published on topics related to walkable access and walkability.[2]

A primary objective of "fixing" sprawl is to transform it into places that are walkable and mixed-use. This chapter quantifies how far we have to go: What is the extent of high-access (and therefore walkable) places in suburban and urban areas across all metropolitan areas in the United States? Are such places open to people of all income groups? In addition, we quantify the tradeoffs involved in this pursuit: Are high-access places always a good thing? What are the potential downsides?

Using a unique, comprehensive, national neighborhood-level dataset, this chapter addresses the question of what the supply of accessible neighborhoods and units looks like in urban and suburban areas, where affordable housing fits into this picture, and what the tradeoffs are between walkable access and socio-economic neighborhood characteristics. Before presenting these findings, the data and measurement of walkable access are discussed. The chapter concludes with a summary and discussion of the implications.

Growing Demand for Mixed-Use and Walkable Neighborhoods

Several recent surveys indicate a growing demand for urban and mixed-use communities. For instance, the National Association of Realtors (NAR) found that 47 percent of respondents preferred living in urban or mixed-use suburban communities compared to 52 percent with a preference for residence-only suburbs, small towns, and rural areas. These numbers were corroborated by a 2014 survey of 10,000 people by the PEW Research Center, which found that 48 percent of respondents preferred "a community where the houses are smaller and closer to each other, but schools, stores, and restaurants are within walking distance," while 49 percent preferred "a community where the houses are larger and farther apart, but schools, stores, and restaurants are several miles away." In the NAR survey, of the residents with an urban or mixed-use preference, 8 percent would like to live in the downtown area of cities, 11 percent in urban residential areas, and 28 percent in mixed-use suburbs. In comparison, 12 percent like living in residence-only suburbs, 18 percent in small towns, and 22 percent in rural areas.[3]

Living in mixed-use walkable neighborhoods is even more popular among younger households: 55 percent of 18- to 34-year-olds would like to live in such areas. This preference is stronger among lower-income households (58 percent for households with less than 80 percent of area median income) than house-holds with higher incomes (44 percent with >120 percent of area median in-come). Demand to be able to walk or bike to work (less than one mile) increased by 45 percent between 1995 and 2009 and even more so (59 percent) for being able to walk or bike to errands within less than one mile.[4]

However, despite this changing demand toward more urban, mixed-use, and accessible forms of living, the supply of these living options is still lagging be-hind: although 23 percent of households would like to walk or bike to work, the supply of such neighborhoods only consists of 4 percent. Similarly, the demand to be able to walk or bike for errands (22 percent) is met in less than half of all cases (10 percent).[5]

Arlie Adkins also found that for the residents he surveyed who expressed a preference for accessible neighborhoods, only 53 percent of higher-income respondents and 27 percent of low-income respondents were able to realize this preference and actually move to a very walkable area (as defined by Walkscore, see below). The proportion of residents with an access preference who were able to move to a somewhat walkable area is higher but still below demand: 76 per-cent of higher-income respondents and 60 percent of low-income respondents were able to move to such a neighborhood.[6]

Preferences and Compromises

Even though about half of all households express a preference for urban or sub-urban mixed-use communities, in practice households often face decisions that involve tradeoffs between this preference and other priorities, such as school quality, safety, or single-family homes, that might be more prevalent in residen-tial suburban areas. For low-income households, these tradeoffs are accentuated since finding any affordable housing is challenging, let alone in accessible neigh-borhoods. This is especially true in strong housing markets where the quality of amenities within accessible reach (such as schools, parks, and retail) is often higher but where home values also reflect this added value.

One issue is that neighborhoods can be walkable in terms of urban form dimensions like small block size and land use diversity, but such neighbor-hoods might not be the ones that offer the most employment access, the low-est crime, or the best schools. Research that is just now surfacing seems to indicate that the most important factors for residents are low poverty and low crime, and that walkable, well-serviced, "sustainable" urban form is of secondary importance.[7] In some neighborhoods, access to nearby parks and transit stops might coincide with higher crime risks, and land use mix might represent a higher likelihood of living near a variety of undesirable land uses.[8] In other words, the same indicators of walkability that are appreciated in higher-income neighborhoods do not necessarily have the same value in neighborhoods where crime, poor quality of amenities, and undesirable land uses are prevalent.[9]

Further, the goals of "walkable" and "affordable" neighborhoods are often at odds. No longer is the goal a matter of producing affordable housing wherever cheap land is found, but affordability is sought in places where land, because of its accessibility, is likely to be more expensive. A few studies have documented these tradeoffs. One study of housing prices in New Urbanist development—a development form meant to be walkable—found that most projects were priced at above-market rates. Subsequent research has continued to support the finding that developers of walkable neighborhoods or "traditional neighborhood development" have been able to command a higher price in the marketplace. A survey of housing prices in 152 nonsubsidized New Urbanist developments found that few were affordable to low-income residents. Song and Knaap's study of New Urbanist housing values found that a net 18 percent premium was being paid for design amenities like pedestrian quality and walkable access.[10]

Research is also confirming that demand for transit-served areas is rising, thus resulting in a decrease in affordability in these high-demand locations. These studies are motivated by a desire to preserve affordable housing in transit areas and employment centers, suggesting that the development of affordable housing in outlying suburbs not served by transit is problematic. With a focus on transit-oriented development (TOD), studies have found that although a substantial number of affordable apartments are located close to public transit, affordability for more than two-thirds will expire within the next five years. A recent study funded by the U.S. Department of Transportation found that many transit-oriented developments are becoming increasingly unaffordable.[11]

A new "place-conscious" federal urban policy has placed a stronger emphasis on the neighborhood context of federally subsidized housing, including a focus on so-called high-opportunity neighborhoods, walkable access, and mixed-income communities. Several new programs are supposed to promote these linkages and the location efficiency of affordable housing, for example, through HUD's new Office of Sustainable Housing and Communities, the Choice Neighborhoods Initiative, and the Sustainable Communities Initiative. Housing choice vouchers have also been associated with policy hopes of moving more tenants to high-opportunity neighborhoods, even though the results of the Moving to Opportunity (MTO) Experiment were sobering in regards to employment and education outcomes.[12]

Finally, another potential tradeoff is between locating affordable housing in more central, urban, accessible neighborhoods, which often turn out to be more segregated, versus locating it in more racially integrated but also more suburban, less accessible communities. This tension is also expressed in different priorities in the fair housing and community development advocacy communities, which are respectively prioritizing desegregation (potentially at the expense of accessibility) and accessibility (potentially at the expense of segregation). Although much applied work on the "geography of opportunity" has been characterized by this dichotomy between "poverty neighborhoods" versus "fair housing," recent studies have sought to maintain the multidimensionality of the tradeoffs between urban and suburban opportunity structures. In this context, a matrix of potentially countervailing opportunity components in neighborhoods is promoted as a better representation of this complexity than previous opportunity indices that collapse multiple dimensions into one.[13]

Data

2010 Census block groups within metro areas are the common unit of analysis (total of 174,186 block groups) in this chapter. Block groups are used as proxies for neighborhood units, with an average of 1,473 people per block group. To identify metropolitan areas, the analysis draws on the 2003 definition of Core Based Statistical Areas of the Office of Management and Budget (referred to as "metro areas" here).

To differentiate urban, suburban, and rural areas, the following definitions are applied. The 2010 Census defines 1,308 principal cities of metropolitan or micropolitan statistical areas.[14] These include cities, towns, villages, boroughs, and other municipalities. This analysis is based on the subset of 1,187 principal cities in metro areas that the 2010 Census identifies as cities (i.e., excluding towns or villages).[15] For the purpose of this analysis all other neighborhoods outside of these cities but within the metro area are identified as "suburban" if there are no housing units in rural parts of the neighborhood (i.e., any neighborhoods with rural housing units are excluded here).[16] Figure 1.1 shows examples of rural, suburban, and principal city neighborhoods within the Chicago and Atlanta metro areas. To differentiate neighborhoods at varying density levels, the number of housing units (2010 Census) is divided by the total area (in acres) in a 2010 block group, which allows for the classification of neighborhoods into five density levels: 0–1, 1–2, 2–3, 3–4, and 4+ units per acre.

Table 1.1 summarizes the variables and data sources that the analysis is based on: 16.7 million addresses are aggregated at the block group level, including employee numbers of 11.8 million businesses; 4.6 million federally subsidized housing units; school quality data for 73,600+ schools; and 215,000+ accessibility scores (Walk Scores). In addition, home values for 51,000+ Census tracts and low-income household data for 38,000 zip codes are also summarized at the block group level (since tracts and zip codes larger than block groups within the same larger spatial unit share the same values but these data are not available at smaller resolutions). Data to characterize neighborhoods' race/ethnicity and housing are derived from the 2010 Census at the block group level.

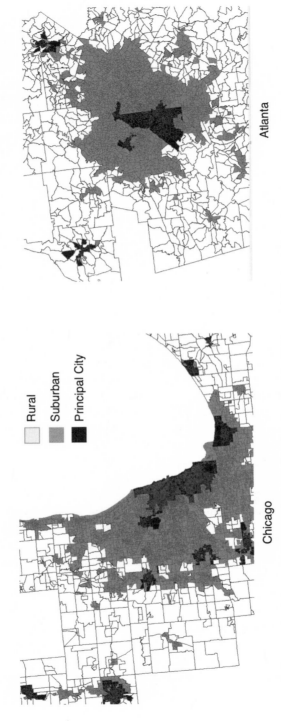

Rural

Suburban

Principal City

Chicago

Atlanta

FIGURE 1.1. Rural, suburban, and principal city neighborhoods within the Chicago and Atlanta metro areas. *Maps by Julia Koschinsky.*

TABLE 1.1. Data sources and variable description

Variable	Description	Year	Original scale	Source
Neighborhoods	2010 Census block groups in 359 metro areas (average 1,473 people)	2010	174,186 block groups	2010 Census
Regions (West, South, Midwest, Northeast)	West: Alas., Ariz., Calif., Colo., Hawaii, Idaho, Mont., N. Mex., Nev., Ore., Utah, Wyo., and Wash.; South: Ala., Ark., Del., D.C., Fla., Ga., Ky., La., Md., Miss., N.C., Okla., S.C., Tenn., Tex., Va., and W. Va.; Midwest: Ill., Ind., Iowa, Kans., Mich., Minn., Mo., Neb., N. Dak., Ohio, S. Dak., and Wisc.; Northeast: Conn., Maine, Mass., N.H., N.J., N.Y., Pa., R.I., and Vt.			U.S. Census Bureau
Walk Score and components	Score from 0 to 100 that indicates how accessible amenities are within 0.25 miles in street network distance from the center of each block group	2012	215,000+ addresses	Walkscore.com
% Low income	Percentage of tax filers who were eligible for the earned income tax credit	2008	38,000+ zip codes	Internal Revenue Service, via Brookings Institute
# Jobs	Number of employees in businesses	2010	11.8 million addresses	Infogroup/InfoUSA, via ESRI business analyst
Distance to reach better vs. worse school	Distance (meters) from block group centroid to closest high-performing school (ranking 9–10) minus distance (meters) from block group centroid to closest low-performing school (ranking 1–2)	2012	73,671 addresses	GreatSchools.com
Diversity	Simpson diversity index for race/ethnicity (larger = more diverse)	2010	174,186 block groups	2010 Census
% Black, White, Hispanic	Number of African Americans/population, Whites/population, and Hispanics/population	2010	174,186 block groups	2010 Census
Units	Housing units	2010	174,186 block groups	2010 Census
Home value	Estimated median single-family home values based on home loans	2009	51,000+ 2000 Census tracts	HMDA, via components of Urban Institute/LISC's market strength index
% HUD Housing	Number of HUD-subsidized vouchers, LIHTC, public housing, and projects (TRACS)/all housing units	2012	4.6M addresses	U.S. Department of Housing and Urban Development and U.S. Census

(continued)

TABLE 1.1. (*continued*)

Variable	Description	Year	Original scale	Source
% Renter	Number of renter-occupied units/housing units	2010	174,186 block groups	2010 Census
% Vacant	Number of vacant units/housing units	2010	174,186 block groups	2010 Census
% Tenant Vouchers	Number of tenant vouchers/ housing units	2012	2.1M units (addresses)	U.S. Department of Housing and Urban Development and U.S. Census
% LIHTC	Number of low-income housing tax credit units/housing units	2012	1.6M units (addresses)	U.S. Department of Housing and Urban Development and U.S. Census
% Public Housing	Number of public housing units (traditional and HOPE VI)/ housing units	2012	961,000+ units (addresses)	U.S. Department of Housing and Urban Development and U.S. Census
% Developers	Number of project-based units (TRACS)/housing units	2012	1.15M units (addresses)	U.S. Department of Housing and Urban Development and U.S. Census

Measurement of Walkable Access

Since this chapter is based on an analysis of national neighborhood-level data, it is only possible to measure walkable access at this scale (as opposed to the quality of the walking environment). For this purpose, we draw on data from Walkscore.com, which automatically generates a 0–100 score for every residential address in the United States based on an algorithm that measures the distance between an address and the number and types of amenities that can be reached within 0.25 miles of street network distance.[17] Amenities that are included in the score are grocery stores, restaurants, shopping, coffee shops, banks, parks, schools, bookstores, and entertainment. Grocery stores receive the largest weight while each additional amenity within walkable access (e.g., for restaurants or shopping) is weighted less. Each amenity receives an on-access score of 0–100 that is then integrated with the overall score, which is also adjusted for intersection density and the ratio of street segments to intersections. Walk Score distinguishes five walkable access categories: 0–24 = car-dependent (almost all errands require a car), 25–49 = car-dependent (most errands require a car), 50–69 = somewhat walkable (some errands can be accomplished on foot), 70–89 = very walkable (most errands can be accomplished on foot), 90–100 = walker's paradise (daily errands do not require a car). This analysis groups the lowest three categories (0–69: car-dependent and somewhat walkable) into an inaccessibility category and the top two categories (70–100: very walkable and walker's paradise) into an accessibility category.

The advantage of this approach is that it is the only data source that can provide current access scores at the address level on a national scale within an automated and current framework. Disadvantages of the approach include the fact that the quality of amenities is not taken into account (e.g., the difference between a full-size grocery store and a convenience corner store), categorization errors (e.g., industry codes for a library and school in downtown Phoenix that are located in a prison), and a prioritization of consumption amenities (such as restaurants and coffee shops), while jobs, day care, or health care services are not included. Finally, Walk Score is a unidimensional measure in contrast to multidimensional scales of walkability or the Irvine Minnesota Inventory.[18] However, since these latter tools require manual data collection, they do not scale to the national level.

Findings

Of the nonrural neighborhoods in all 359 metro areas in the United States, about half (51 percent or 70,087) are located in suburbs and half (49 percent or 67,619) in principal cities. About 4.8 million more units are located in suburbs (with a total of 43,059,923 units) than in principal cities (where the total number of units is 38,219,966).

Supply of Accessible Neighborhoods

What is the current supply of accessible neighborhoods and units in suburbs and principal cities? It turns out to be small. The vast majority of these neighborhoods (82 percent) are not accessible and only 18 percent (24,193) have walkable access to amenities. Not surprisingly, given the lower density levels and reduced mixed land use in suburbs, they are less accessible than principal cities: only 4 percent of all neighborhoods in suburbs (with 3.1M units) are accessible compared to 13 percent in principal cities (10.4M units). This translates to 5,801 accessible suburban neighborhoods and 18,392 such urban areas.

In both suburbs and cities, accessibility increases with density. All amenities except for banks are more accessible in principal cities than in suburbs. Entertainment, intersection density, and parks are particularly more prevalent in cities than suburbs. As before, higher-unit densities are associated with higher-amenity scores in both suburbs and cities. At the same time, for most of the other amenities, the difference between suburban and urban amenity scores is within 10 points.

Table 1.2 lists the twenty suburbs and cities with the highest proportions of accessible housing units. Boston, New York, San Francisco, Los Angeles, Wash-

TABLE 1.2. Percentage of accessible units, top ten metro areas, sorted by suburb

	Inaccessible (0–69)		Accessible (70+)	
	Suburbs	Principal cities	Suburbs	Principal cities
1. Boston-Cambridge-Quincy, Mass.-N.H.	63%	8%	13%	16%
2. New York-Northern N.J.-Long Island, N.Y.-N.J.-Pa.	42%	5%	11%	41%
3. Salinas, Calif.	60%	24%	11%	5%
4. State College, Pa.	89%		11%	
5. Ocean City, N.J.	69%	15%	10%	6%
6. New Haven–Milford, Conn.	77%	8%	8%	7%
7. San Francisco–Oakland–Fremont, Calif.	40%	22%	8%	31%
8. Santa Cruz–Watsonville, Calif.	57%	22%	8%	13%
9. Los Angeles–Long Beach–St. Ana, Calif.	36%	35%	7%	22%
10. Springfield, Mass.	72%	16%	6%	5%
11. Providence–New Bedford–Fall River, R.I.-Mass.	61%	20%	6%	13%
12. Lexington-Fayette, Ky.	94%		6%	
13. Washington-Arlington-Alexandria, D.C.-Va.-Md.-W.Va.	74%	11%	6%	9%
14. Scranton–Wilkes-Barre, Pa.	74%	15%	5%	6%
15. San Luis Obispo–Paso Robles, Calif.	75%	16%	5%	4%
16. St. Barbara–St. Maria–Goleta, Calif.	47%	33%	5%	14%
17. Athens–Clarke County, Ga.	95%		5%	
18. Carson City, Nev.	95%		5%	
19. San Diego–Carlsbad–San Marcos, Calif.	44%	38%	5%	13%
20. Louisville, Ky.-Ind.	95%		5%	

ington, D.C., and San Diego are among the larger metro areas with accessible suburbs, while New York, San Francisco, Chicago, Los Angeles, Philadelphia, Seattle, Portland, Boston, New Orleans, and San Diego are the larger principal cities that are accessible.

Tradeoffs

Although cities are more accessible than suburbs, households face tradeoffs like the ones mentioned above in the choice of living in suburban or urban communities. Despite the fact that poverty levels are increasing in suburbs,[19] the overall proportion of low-income households is still smaller in suburbs than cities: 15 percent of households who claimed Earned Income Tax Credits in 2008 lived in suburbs compared to 22 percent in cities (the differences in accessible versus nonaccessible areas are negligible). These urban-suburban differences are particularly strong in the Northeast (24 percent vs. 11 percent) and Midwest (23 percent vs. 14 percent), smaller in the South (26 percent vs. 19 percent), and much smaller in the West (17 percent vs. 15 percent).

The proportion of jobs is also almost split halfway between cities and suburbs, although, at 54 percent versus 46 percent, cities still contain slightly more employment opportunities than suburbs. However, in both suburbs and cities, there are more jobs in nonaccessible areas: 41 percent of all jobs (37.6M) are in nonaccessible neighborhoods in suburbs (vs. 5 percent accessible) and 34 percent (30.8M) are in nonaccessible places in cities (vs. 20 percent accessible). With 31 percent of jobs in accessible urban areas in the Northeast, this proportion is higher here than in the other three regions.

In general, the higher school quality in suburbs compared to cities also represents an important tradeoff with accessibility: worse schools are more accessible in cities than in suburbs. In suburbs the difference between being able to reach a better school versus a worse school (see table 1.1 for definitions) is negative—in other words, better schools are within shorter reach. This is also the case in nonaccessible parts of cities at density levels up to three units per acre. In nonaccessible cities at density levels of three or more units per acre, as in accessible urban neighborhoods at all density levels, worse schools are within closer reach than better ones. An analysis of school quality by region indicates that this national pattern is representative of the West except for parts of accessible suburbs with closer proximity to worse schools. In the Midwest and Northeast, there is an even clearer split between suburbs and cities. With one exception, in suburbs of all density levels, distances to better schools vis-à-vis worse schools are shorter while worse schools are more accessible in cities. Finally, in the South, worse schools are more accessible in suburbs and cities at all density levels.

On average, racial and ethnic diversity is slightly higher in cities (diversity index of 1.82) than suburbs (1.71), and accessible areas are more diverse in both places than nonaccessible ones. There is a tendency for higher-density areas to be more diverse than lower-density ones although this does not hold for accessible cities. Here neighborhoods with lower densities (1–3 units/acre) are more diverse than the densest areas (4+ units per acre), which are also the most expensive ones. African American residents are more than twice as likely to live in cities than suburbs (20 percent vs. 12 percent), which is not true for Hispanic residents where the difference of 15 percent living in cities and 11 percent in suburbs is smaller. In comparison, at 72 percent, white households are more likely to live in suburbs compared to cities (58 percent).

Home values are highest in the densest, most accessible neighborhoods ($261,400), followed by the densest parts of suburbs (4+ units/acre) ($243,628). This pattern holds in the Northeast and Midwest but not in the West and Southwest where accessible suburban locations yield higher home values than their urban counterparts (at $212,965 vs. $193,513 in the South and $307,728 vs. $305,700 in the West). In both accessible and nonaccessible parts of cities and suburbs, home values tend to go down with lower density levels and back up at the lowest density of 0–1 units per acre. In contrast to the South and West, accessible suburbs in the Northeast and Midwest have lower home values in the densest and least dense neighborhoods compared to the density levels in-between, pointing potentially to the older age of the accessible suburban housing stock in these regions.

The proportion of renters is much higher in cities (43 percent) than suburbs (29 percent) and, within both areas, more so at the highest density levels of 4+ units per acre (except in the Midwest with more renters in accessible low-density urban areas). As expected, more households rent in accessible neighborhoods in both cities (58 percent) and suburbs (52 percent) than in nonaccessible suburbs (27 percent) or cities (38 percent). This pattern is characteristic of all regions. Interestingly, vacancy rates are lowest at 8 percent in the lower-density nonaccessible suburbs (<4 units/acre) and highest in lower-density accessible cities (12–15 percent for <4 units/acre). This pattern is generally consistent throughout all regions but particularly representative of the Midwest and Northeast.

There is a strong positive (statistically significant) relationship between vacancy rates and affordable housing. Areas with a relative oversupply of housing (and thus higher vacancy rates) have higher proportions of federally subsidized housing. This means that the largest percentage of subsidized housing (16–19 percent) is located in accessible cities at the lowest density levels (0–3 units/acre). In suburbs, such units are located in accessible areas at 1–2 units/acre and 4+ units/acre. Public housing units and tenant vouchers have the largest proportions of units in very low-density urban areas (7 percent and 5 percent, respectively). Privately developed and managed affordable housing units (including project-based units and Low Income Housing Tax Credit units) have larger proportions in accessible urban neighborhoods with density levels of 1–3 units per acre.

Summary and Implications

In general, suburbs and nonaccessible neighborhoods have several assets that make them attractive, including quality schools, jobs, and lower racial segregation. At the same time, they are also less accessible, less diverse, more expensive (except for the highest-density accessible urban neighborhoods), and offer fewer subsidized housing options.

Even within cities, the vast majority of neighborhoods (73 percent) are not accessible—only 27 percent of all neighborhoods are. And of these accessible neighborhoods, 91 percent are in areas with density levels of at least 4 units per acre, that is, walkable access is concentrated in the densest pockets of cities where higher concentrations of residential housing meet greater numbers of amenities. Hence, inaccessible neighborhoods not only characterize suburban areas but also most parts of urban areas.

However, in suburbs, this gap between accessible and inaccessible areas is indeed even larger, with 92 percent of all neighborhoods being inaccessible and only 8 percent of neighborhoods having walkable access (the proportions are even lower for housing units at 93 percent and 7 percent). But those suburban walkable neighborhoods have a greater variety of density levels: 78 percent are dense (4+ units/acre) compared to 10 percent with 3–4 units/acre and 12 percent lower density levels (table 1.2). Meeting the demand gap for more accessible neighborhoods could thus be achieved through increasing density pockets and intersection density levels in suburbs, including increasing medium-density levels if higher-density levels are unpopular. Interestingly, the residential density levels in inaccessible suburban areas also vary, including higher-density neighborhoods: 25 percent of these neighborhoods already have at least 4 units/acre and 58 percent have 1–4 units/acre (table 1.2). What is missing to make these neighborhoods accessible are amenities that can be reached within walking distance from these residential units (which might require a change from residential to mixed-use zoning).

In existing accessible suburban areas, Walk Scores for grocery stores, schools, restaurants, shopping, bookstores, and coffee shops are already comparable to those of accessible urban areas (banks are even more accessible in suburbs). As mentioned, the biggest gap in accessible amenities between accessible suburbs and cities that could be a focus for retrofitting sprawled areas consists of parks and entertainment.

On average, accessible suburbs are actually more expensive to live in than accessible cities except in the highest-density category of cities (4+ units/acre or 13 percent), while inaccessible suburbs are more expensive than their urban equivalents at all density levels (table 1.3). And, as mentioned, the areas with the largest lack of demand (indicated by higher vacancy levels) turn out to be lower-density accessible urban neighborhoods. However, these areas only represent 9 percent of accessible neighborhoods—the remaining 90 percent of accessible neighborhoods have lower vacancy levels of 10 percent.

In terms of the tradeoff between accessibility and affordability, federally subsidized tenants are more likely to live in accessible urban neighborhoods compared to the overall proportion of units in these areas. However, not surprisingly given lower land values, the subsidized housing that is located in accessible urban neighborhoods is located in areas with lower demand (higher vacancy rates) and lower density levels. Further, in terms of total numbers of subsidized housing, more units are located in inaccessible urban areas (2.2M) than accessible ones (1.3M). Although about half of all neighborhoods are urban versus suburban in the 359 metro areas, subsidized housing is disproportionately (64 percent) located in cities rather than suburbs. Compared to the proportion of urban neighborhoods that are accessible (13 percent) versus inaccessible (36 percent), the percentage of subsidized housing in accessible urban neighborhoods is actually notably higher (24 percent). It is also slightly higher in inaccessible parts of the city compared to all neighborhoods (40 percent vs. 36 percent) as well as a little higher in accessible suburbs (5 percent vs. 4 percent

TABLE 1.3. Accessibility, housing, and neighborhood characteristics in suburbs and cities, by density level, units/acre (359 metros)

		units/acre				
	0 to 1	1 to 2	2 to 3	3 to 4	4+	Total
SUBURBS						
Units						
Inaccessible (0–69)	6,342,704	10,219,225	7,878,293	5,600,204	9,913,186	39,953,612
Accessible (70–100)	19,587	108,941	195,722	291,383	2,490,678	3,106,311
Total						43,059,923
% Renter						
Inaccessible (0–69)	20	22	25	28	39	27
Accessible (70–100)	39	40	42	40	55	52
Total						29
% Vacant						
Inaccessible (0–69)	8	8	8	8	10	9
Accessible (70–100)	10	10	12	10	9	9
Total						9
Home value						
Inaccessible (0–69)	$ 205,858	$ 190,986	$ 186,787	$ 185,326	$ 186,600	$ 190,753
Accessible (70–100)	$ 223,111	$ 212,020	$ 217,177	$ 229,048	$ 243,618	$ 238,885
Total						$ 194,737
% HUD housing						
Inaccessible (0–69)	3	3	4	4	6	4
Accessible (70–100)	7	9	6	7	9	9
Total						4
% Low income						
Inaccessible (0–69)	13.2	13.6	14.3	15.2	17	14.7
Accessible (70–100)	11.8	13.6	13.8	13.3	16.4	15.7
Total						14.8
# Jobs						
Inaccessible (0–69)	12,893,882	11,010,379	6,102,523	3,377,804	4,182,321	37,566,909
Accessible (70–100)	224,962	530,943	612,808	589,266	2,546,005	4,503,984
Total						42,070,893
% Jobs						
Inaccessible (0–69)	14	12	7	4	5	41
Accessible (70–100)	0	1	1	1	3	5
Total						46

Dist. better vs. worse schools	Inaccessible (0–69)	-3,508	-2,991	-2,027	-1,502	-627	-2,081
	Accessible (70–100)	-3,854	-4,341	-2,483	-1,720	-767	-1,152
	Total						-2,004
Diversity	Inaccessible (0–69)	1.55	1.61	1.68	1.75	1.88	1.70
	Accessible (70–100)	1.73	1.70	1.65	1.65	1.89	1.84
	Total						1.71
% African Am.	Inaccessible (0–69)	10	11	11	12	15	12
	Accessible (70–100)	11	9	8	8	13	12
	Total						12
% White	Inaccessible (0–69)	79	77	75	71	63	73
	Accessible (70–100)	74	76	76	74	61	64
	Total						72
% Hispanic	Inaccessible (0–69)	7	8	10	12	15	11
	Accessible (70–100)	11	14	14	14	18	17
	Total						11
PRINCIPAL CITIES							
Units	Inaccessible (0–69)	1,828,736	4,578,755	4,933,785	4,596,733	11,883,198	27,821,207
	Accessible (70–100)	20,104	121,209	248,087	361,233	9,648,126	10,398,759
	Total						38,219,966
% Renter	Inaccessible (0–69)	31	30	33	34	45	38
	Accessible (70–100)	57	57	54	51	58	58
	Total						43
% Vacant	Inaccessible (0–69)	10	9	9	9	11	10
	Accessible (70–100)	15	14	14	12	10	10
	Total						10
Home value	Inaccessible (0–69)	$ 152,179	$ 150,339	$ 146,431	$ 149,230	$ 162,926	$ 154,972
	Accessible (70–100)	$ 200,527	$ 158,847	$ 165,416	$ 182,106	$ 261,400	$ 253,654
	Total						$ 181,803

(continued)

TABLE 1.3. (*continued*)

				units/acre			
		0 to 1	1 to 2	2 to 3	3 to 4	4+	Total
% HUD housing	Inaccessible (0–69)	8	7	7	6	9	8
	Accessible (70–100)	19	17	16	12	12	12
	Total						9
% Low income	Inaccessible (0–69)	22	21.3	22	21.9	23.4	22.4
	Accessible (70–100)	20.4	22.6	21.6	20.3	22.2	22.2
	Total						22.4
# Jobs	Inaccessible (0–69)	8,613,617	8,099,456	5,298,498	3,483,731	5,323,296	30,838,598
	Accessible (70–100)	831,792	1,621,813	1,953,559	1,850,052	11,866,921	18,124,137
	Total						48,962,735
% Jobs	Inaccessible (0–69)	9	9	6	4	6	34
	Accessible (70–100)	1	2	2	2	13	20
	Total						54
Dist. better vs. worse schools	Inaccessible (0–69)	-476	-403	-78	321	933	337
	Accessible (70–100)	565	934	771	953	694	708
	Total						438
Diversity	Inaccessible (0–69)	1.72	1.73	1.74	1.78	1.85	1.79
	Accessible (70–100)	1.70	1.97	1.92	1.83	1.90	1.90
	Total						1.82
% African Am.	Inaccessible (0–69)	20	19	19	17	22	20
	Accessible (70–100)	18	17	17	13	21	20
	Total						20
% White	Inaccessible (0–69)	66	67	65	64	54	60
	Accessible (70–100)	65	64	64	67	51	52
	Total						58
% Hispanic	Inaccessible (0–69)	11	11	12	15	16	14
	Accessible (70–100)	10	16	18	17	17	17
	Total						15

overall). Inaccessible suburbs are the only areas where there are disproportionately more units overall (49 percent) than subsidized units (30 percent).

If the demand for walkable, mixed-use neighborhoods expressed by survey respondents translates to actual market preferences, then the chances for fixing sprawl are good. As this chapter has shown, suburbs have several assets that could be leveraged to increase the supply of accessible neighborhoods, including a range of residential density levels that should be sufficient to make the development of additional amenities, such as smaller-scale corner grocery stores and other neighborhood-scale retail options, economically viable. The prerequisite for such densification of amenities near existing residential density would be changes in zoning to allow for such commercial land uses. Higher school quality and lower segregation levels also represent assets. However, home values in suburbs are often higher, and since subsidized housing is still concentrated in urban areas such housing has limited impact in making suburbs more affordable for low-income tenants. Finally, the different dynamics of accessibility and related tradeoffs in the Southwest and West compared to the Midwest and Northeast indicate that different strategies to increase accessibility are required in both newer and older suburbs.

Acknowledgments

The work that provided the basis for this publication was supported by funding under an award from the U.S. Department of Housing and Urban Development. The substance and findings of the work are dedicated to the public. The authors are solely responsible for the accuracy of the statements and interpretations contained in this publication. Such interpretations do not necessarily reflect the views of the government.

NOTES

1. Christopher B. Leinberger, *The Option of Urbanism: Investing in a New American Dream* (Washington, D.C.: Island Press, 2008); Jeff Speck, *Walkable City: How Downtown Can Save America, One Step at a Time* (New York: Farrar, Straus & Giroux, 2012). See also Christopher B. Leinberger and Mariela Alfonzo, *Walk This Way: The Economic Promise of Walkable Places in Metropolitan Washington, D.C.* (Washington, D.C.: Metropolitan Policy Program at the Brookings Institution, 2012).

2. For reviews of this literature see, for instance, R. C. Brownson, C. M. Hoehner, K. Day, A. Forsyth, and J. F. Sallis, "Measuring the Built Environment for Physical Activity: State of the Science," *American Journal of Preventive Medicine* 36, no. 4 (2009): s99–123; D .Ding and K. Gebel, "Built Environment, Physical Activity, and Obesity: What Have We Learned from Reviewing the Literature?" *Health & Place* 10 (2011): 1016; G. F. Dunton, J. Kaplan, J. Wolch, M. Jerrett, and K. D. Reynolds, "Physical Environmental Correlates of Childhood Obesity: A Systematic Review," *Obesity Reviews* 10, no. 4 (2009): 393–402; C. P. Durand, M. Andalib, G. F. Dunton, J. Wolch, and M. A. Pentz, "A Systematic Review of Built Environment Fac-

tors Related to Physical Activity and Obesity Risk: Implications for Smart Growth Urban Planning," *Obesity Reviews* 12, no. 5 (2011): 173–82; R. Ewing and R. Cervero, "Travel and the Built Environment," *Journal of the American Planning Association* 76, no. 3 (2010): 265–94; J. Feng, T. A. Glass, F. C. Curriero, W. F. Stewart, and B. S. Schwartz, "The Built Environment and Obesity: A Systematic Review of the Epidemiologic Evidence," *Health & Place* 16, no. 2 (2010): 175–90; G. Elsevier, W. Heath, R. C. Brownson, J. Kruger, R. Miles, K. E. Powell, and L. T. Ramsey, "The Effectiveness of Urban Design and Land Use and Transport Policies and Practices to Increase Physical Activity: A Systematic Review," *Journal of Physical Activity and Health* 3, no. 1 (2006): s55–76; B. E. Saelens and S. L. Handy, "Built Environment Correlates of Walking: A Review," *Medicine and Science in Sports and Exercise* 40, no. 7 (2008): s550–56; Emily Talen and Julia Koschinsky, "The Walkable Neighborhood: A Research Summary," *International Journal of Sustainable Land Use and Urban Planning* 1, no. 1 (2013): 42–63.

3. National Association of Realtors, "The 2011 Community Preference Survey: What Americans Are Looking for When Deciding Where to Live," Conducted by Belden Russonello and Stewart llc, Washington, D.C., Pew Research Center for the People and the Press, 2011; *2014 Political Polarization Survey*, Table 3.1, http://www.people-press .org/2014/06/12/preferred-community/.

4. Arthur C. Nelson, *Reshaping Metropolitan America* (Washington, D.C.: Island Press, 2013); U.S. Department of Transportation, "National Household Travel Survey," Sponsored by the Bureau of Transportation Statistics and the Federal Highway Administration (Washington, D.C.: U.S. Department of Transportation, 2009); "National Household Travel Survey," Sponsored by the Bureau of Transportation Statistics and the Federal Highway Administration (Washington, D.C.: U.S. Department of Transportation, 2011).

5. Ibid.

6. Arlie Adkins, "Inaccessible Accessibility: Low-Income Households and Barriers to the 'New American Dream,'" presentation at Portland State University on June 7, 2013, http://otrec.us/events/entry/inaccessible_accessibility_low_income_ households_and_ barriers_to_the_new_am.

7. Rolf Pendall and Joe Parilla, Comment on Emily Talen and Julia Koschinsky's "'Is Subsidized Housing in Sustainable Neighborhoods? Evidence from Chicago': 'Sustainable' Urban Form and Opportunity: Frames and Expectations for Low-Income Households," *Housing Policy Debate* 21, no. 1 (2011): 33–44; Vicki Been, Mary Cunningham, Ingrid Gould Ellen, Adam Gordon, Joe Parilla, Margery Austin Turner, Sheryl Verlaine Whitney, Aaron Yowell, and Ken Zimmerman, "Building Environmentally Sustainable Communities: A Framework for Inclusivity," a paper of the What Works Collaborative, 2010, http://furman center.org/files/publications/White-Paper-Environmentally-Sustainable-Communities.pdf.

8. S. Foster and B. Giles-Corti, "The Built Environment, Neighborhood Crime and Constrained Physical Activity: An Exploration of Inconsistent Findings," *Preventive Medicine* 47, no. 3 (2008): 241–51.

9. Emily Talen and Julia Koschinsky, "Is Subsidized Housing in Sustainable Neighborhoods? Evidence from Chicago," *Housing Policy Debate* 21, no. 1 (2011): 1–28.

10. Charles C. Tu and Mark J. Eppli, "An Empirical Examination of Traditional Neighborhood Development," *Real Estate Economics* 29, no. 3 (2001): 485–501; E. Talen, "Affordability in New Urbanist Development: Principle, Practice, and Strategy," *Journal of Urban Affairs* 32,no. 4 (2010): 489–510; Yan Song and Gerrit Knaap, "New Urbanism and Housing Values: A Disaggregate Assessment," *Journal of Urban Economics* 54 (2003): 218–38.

11. L. Quigley, ed., "Preserving Affordable Housing Near Transit: Case Studies from At-

lanta, Denver, Seattle and Washington, D.C.." Enterprise Community Partners, Inc., 2010, http://www.practitionerresources.org/cache/documents/674/67410.pdf; Rick Haughey and Ryan Sherriff, *Challenges and Policy Options for Creating and Preserving Affordable Housing near Transit and in Other Location-Efficient Areas* (Washington, D.C.: Center for Housing Policy, National Housing Conference, and What Works Collaborative, 2010); B. A. Lipman, "Heavy Load: The Combined Housing and Transportation Burdens of Working Families," Center for Housing Policy, October 2006; Rodney Harrell, Allison Brooks, and Todd Nedwick, *Preserving Affordability and Access in Livable Communities: Subsidized Housing Opportunities Near Transit and the 50+ Population* (Washington, D.C.: AARP Public Policy Institute, 2009); U.S. Department of Transportation, Federal Transit Administration, and Reconnecting America, *Realizing the Potential: One Year Later, Housing Opportunities near Transit in a Changing Market* (Washington, D.C.: U.S. Department of Transportation, 2008).

12. Xavier de Souza Briggs, Susan J. Popkin, and John Goering, *Moving to Opportunity: The Story of an American Experiment to Fight Ghetto Poverty* (New York: Oxford University Press, 2010).

13. Institute on Race and Poverty, *Access to Opportunity in the Twin Cities Metropolitan Area* (Minneapolis/St. Paul, Minn.: n.p., 2007); Edward Goetz, "Opportunity Neighborhoods and Regional Equity: What Role for Community Development?" Paper presented at the AESOP/ACSP Joint Congress 2013, Dublin, July 18, 2013; PolicyLink, *Promoting Regional Equity. A Framing Paper* (Oakland, Calif.: PolicyLink, 2002); Bill Sadler, Elizabeth Wampler, and Jeff Wood, *The Denver Regional Equity Atlas: Mapping Access to Opportunity at a Regional Scale* (Denver: Piton Foundation and Reconnecting America, 2012).

14. The PCICBSA10 variable in the 2010 Census Designated Place, 2010 TIGER/Line Shapefile, U.S. Department of Commerce, U.S. Census Bureau, Geography Division, Publication_Date: 2010; 2010 Census Designated Place, 2010 TIGER/Line Shapefile, http://www.ofm.wa.gov/pop/geographic/tiger10/metadata/cdp10.html.

15. The LSAD10 variable in the 2010 Census Designated Place, 2010 TIGER/Line Shapefile, U.S. Department of Commerce.

16. TheH2 variable in the 2010 Census Designated Place, 2010 TIGER/Line Shapefile, U.S. Department of Commerce.

17. "Walkscore 2010," in *Walk Score Methodology* (Seattle: Walkscore, 2010), www.walkscore.com.

18. Christopher B. Leinberger and Mariela Alfonzo, *Walk This Way: The Economic Promise of Walkable Places in Metropolitan Washington, D.C.* (Washington, D.C.: Metropolitan Policy Program at the Brookings Institution, 2012); see also L. D. Frank, "Land Use and Transportation Interaction: Implications on Public Health and Quality of Life," *Journal of Planning Education and Research* 20, no. 1 (2000): 6–22.

19. Elizabeth Kneebone and Alan Berube, *Confronting Suburban Poverty in America* (Washington, D.C.: Brookings Institutions Press, 2013).

CHAPTER 2

Strip Development and How to Read It

BRENDA CASE SCHEER

Key Points and Practice Takeaways

1. Commercial development along arterials is a ubiquitous suburban condition that is dominated by chain stores, parking lots, curb cuts, congestion, and visual cacophony.

2. Research shows that the suburbs have three dominant kinds of "tissues": static tissues of residential subdivisions; campus tissues of large, single owners like apartment complexes, malls, schools, and airports; and elastic tissues, which line the arterials.

3. Elastic tissues are the most disordered of all, consisting of very limited road networks, highly varied and irregular lot sizes, repetitious building types that float in large parking areas, and relatively rapid change.

4. Quiet and orderly subdivisions are a necessary corollary to elastic tissues; their lack of through streets, restricted use, and need for services inspire the formation of congested arterial commercial strips.

5. The arterial commercial strip is the most difficult kind of form to change—sign controls and street landscaping only paper over the underlying disorder of the lot configurations and lack of networks.

Stretching for miles in what seems to be an undifferentiated landscape of signs, driveways, parking lots, and cheap buildings, the American commercial strip is one of the most exasperating, yet ubiquitous urban forms ever created. Occurring in nearly every settlement of any size in the country, the strip is a familiar eyesore.[1]

Beginning about 1945, with postwar development and the suburbanizing boom, the highway commercial strip became an economic engine that quickly rivaled the downtown core. Chester Liebs describes how the earliest strips were generated by streetcar routes lined with cheaply built single-story commercial buildings, generally focused on roadside uses, like motels, gas stations, and other services for travelers.[2] Even in 1963, it did not occur to planners that the strip would evolve to compete with more traditional shopping in downtown areas.[3]

With the fantastic growth in car ownership, clever builders changed the traditional type of shopping street by moving shops to the rear of lots and parking to the front, creating the familiar strip shopping center. With ample parking, roadside access, and large signs, a much wider assortment of retail moved in. The highway strip now houses a limited assortment of repetitious building types scaled and operated for the benefit of the fast lane. In their landmark study of the Las Vegas strip in 1972, Venturi, Scott-Brown, and Isenour observe how detailed architectural expression became obsolete as the buildings became simple boxes decorated with signs large enough to be read at great speeds.[4]

The urban arterial (see figure 2.1) has historically been designed with efficient, safe movement of high levels of motorized vehicles as its primary, and sometimes only, goal. Definitions for the urban arterial are typically provided by professional engineering associations such as the Institute for Transportation Engineers and the American Association of State Highway and Transportation Officials (AASTHO, 2011), as well as various U.S. federal and state organizations (e.g., the U.S. Department of Transportation and Federal Highway Administration).[5] Within street classification systems, the urban arterial typically falls between the limited access highway and the collector street. Its function is primarily mobility (rather than local access) and the carrying of vehicles between different cities and across urban areas. Urban arterials are subsequently differentiated between principal arterials (whose function is intercity and cross-city mobility and the connection of collector streets to major highways) and minor arterials (whose function is more access-oriented in connecting collector streets and major destinations). Arterials are intended for longer-distance travel between destinations, at speeds that are relatively unimpeded (except for traffic signalization, which controls both speed and entry into the arterial system).[6]

The unintended result of high traffic volume is a ubiquitous suburban nightmare of land uses that thrive only when there is a very large volume of cars. Pedestrians and bicycle facilities are extremely neglected, if not absent. The street itself is a wide, multilane cart way, with many curb cuts, and fast-flowing

FIGURE 2.1. A view down Colerain Avenue near Area 3, 2013.
Photo by Udo Greinacher.

traffic that is dangerous to cross. Next to the road, development is skewed toward a limited variety of standard commercial types. Large signs, limited sidewalks, and huge parking lots define an in-between space very different from the traditional commercial Main Street. In closer-in urban arterial locations, abandoned or downtrodden businesses line congested streets that were once intercity highways. These areas suffer from a distinct set of problems and have a very different physical feel.

This chapter is an exploration of the underlying order of strip development. It seeks to capture, through formal analysis, the question of how these places form and how these forms vary from place to place. The search for order in strip environments has been attempted before. Venturi, Scott-Brown, and Isenour sought to explain the order of the Las Vegas strip, claiming that the street (paving, the sidewalk, the light posts, and so on) has an urban order and continuity but that what happens off the street has an order only internal to the property.[7] Grady Clay, an acute observer of urban physical phenomena, attempted to explain the strip in terms of a series of "generations"—streets or highways that are parallel to one another and developed in different eras, often as bypasses.[8]

The typical American city extends out from a relatively small core, which usually has some gridded form that was laid down at its founding and extended from time to time in less regular fashion (see, for example, New Orleans, St. Louis, and Cincinnati). The grid extensions were performed by or at the behest of a private land development company, perhaps guided by early connecting roads into the surrounding farmland. At some point in the early twentieth century, this system of grid extension was abandoned due to very rapid urbanization, the flexibility of the car, and a significant change in the style of housing subdivisions.[9] As the American city exploded in size and population in the 1950s and 1960s, these roads also became the main carriers of suburban traffic to and from the city center. With the construction of the interstate highway system, their role as intercity connectors diminished significantly.

Liebs observes a rather obvious but important point: the strip is like a timeline. As you move outward from the center of town, the strip changes character because it was developed at different times. Because he is interested in building types like restaurants and motels, Liebs attributes this interesting change in character to architectural adaptation to the car, from streetcar suburbs to commercial highways. Liebs sees the strip unfolding like a movie as one moves along it, with the evolving building types as interesting characters: Now, we are in 1925, now in 1945. Liebs's investigation, while important, ends around 1970, when the interesting and unique roadside architecture ends and the repetitious fast food and plain-box commercial structures of national chains begin to dominate. This transformation is a critical one—the loss of the unique and sometimes weird identities associated with strips in specific places (i.e., giant cowboy signs in Texas and giant lobsters in Massachusetts) caused by the rise of multinational corporate roadside architecture that is the same everywhere. More recently, roadside architecture has shifted from plain boxes to "stucco muffins"—plain commercial buildings decorated to comfort people with a more traditional look: cornices, mullioned windows, wooden doors, even fake second floors.

The strip constitutes a problem, as much for what it represents as for how it operates. The strip's operations as a traffic artery are less than perfect: the movement in and out of multiple parking lots onto wide highways causes traffic congestion, accidents, and delays. As major arterials, the strip acts as the sole access to some housing developments, whose residents cannot avoid this congestion. Making matters worse, the appearance of the strip is chaotic and offensively commercial. Being forced to sit in traffic while assaulted by commercial messages and a chaotic physical environment is a difficult price to pay for living the suburban dream. Most people cannot reconcile the lovely lawns and houses of their subdivision with the chaos that lies just outside it and through which one must travel to reach it.

Historically, planners and most people will often assume that it is the roadway signs that are the main problem—causing a hodgepodge of unrelated elements vying for maximum attention. There is a history of legislation seeking to control suburban strip development through sign control and, sometimes, landscaping. This can be somewhat effective as an aesthetic Band-Aid, but it does not really address the central condition of the strip as a place that is structurally flawed and intimately tied to the form of the housing subdivisions around it. That these two very different forms (subdivision and strip) are necessary corollaries of each other is widely ignored. However, the strip really began to take on its present character when it evolved to serve the neighborhoods being built into the outer reaches of the city.

More recently, improvements to urban livability through the transportation lens are growing popular among progressive transportation planners, city planners, and urban designers. Various related movements seeking to improve the design of urban arterials include the livable street movement; the complete streets movement; context-sensitive design; the green streets movement; traditional streets research; and various street redesign programs.[10] Two shortcomings with these movements can be proposed. First, they typically focus on streets that already offer some physical indication of a livable and walkable nature (i.e., the roadway is narrow or can be visually narrowed) rather than the wide urban arterials and big-box commercial corridors that offer the greatest challenge. Second, very little of this literature focuses on surrounding land uses, signs, building types, or urban aesthetics.

The old intercity radial arterials continue to carry tremendous local auto traffic, which gives rise to their use as convenient commercial territory for the suburbs. Auto traffic acts as an attractor for all kinds of retail businesses, since it provides a high level of visibility and accessibility. High-traffic conditions are exacerbated by the new form of the subdivision, which does not provide for multiple connections to other subdivisions as the old gridded street networks did.[11] Thus, suburbanites have limited access to alternatives to the arterial and cannot easily avoid it no matter how much traffic congestion it develops. The urban arterial is the backbone of the suburbs.

Methodology

Our case study examines Colerain Avenue in Cincinnati, Ohio. Colerain Avenue (U.S. 27) extends from the edge of the nineteenth-century city of Cincinnati to the city of Oxford, Ohio, some thirty miles distant (see figure 2.2). At first it was a difficult road to travel, climbing up out of the Ohio River Valley. The early-twentieth-century streetcar along it never extended into the hills beyond the early grid development of the city. By 1950, however, it was a smoothly paved federal highway with only sporadic roadside development. By 1994, when this longitudinal study began, it was a complete highway strip—at least ten solid miles of commercial development leading out of the old core of the city, diminishing significantly a few miles beyond where it crosses the circumferential interstate.

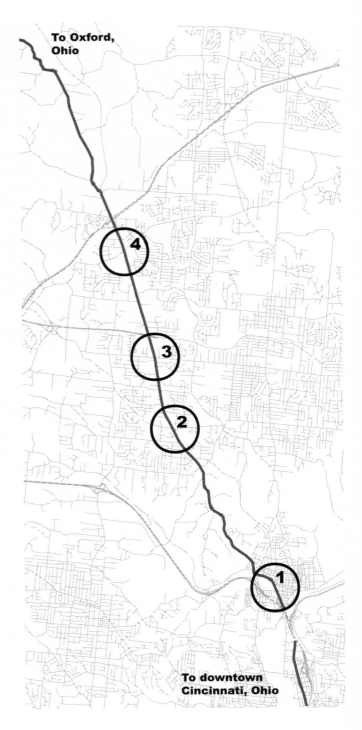

FIGURE 2.2.
The study area of
Colerain Avenue.
Map by author.

The central question of this study was whether there exists an underlying order to the strip development that can explain its current character. By discovering and analyzing this formal order, we arrive at a greater understanding of the complexity of changing the nature of the strip. Urban morphology is the study of the form of cities over time. Form has several components in this context, but most morphologists agree that buildings, streets, and lots are the basic elements. These elements come together to form blocks, districts, and entire regions.

In looking at the question of the strip from the perspective of the morphologist, we can identify at least two theories of its formation that can be used for further analysis. Caniggia and Maffei identified a kind of formation they called a "matrix route," which connects two settlements or two nodes of built activity.[12] Colerain Avenue, in its earliest phase as a route between Cincinnati and Oxford, Ohio, has the characteristics of a matrix route. According to this theory, which generally describes the development of western, European cities, a matrix route is at first built only to connect two nodes, not primarily to service development along it. Over time, however, development inevitably creeps out from the center, at first consisting of a solid frontage of buildings and lots lining the route. After a time, it becomes efficient to build additional streets and lots behind the matrix route rather than to continue to develop the matrix route frontage only. In this way, development occurs over time, eventually creating, organically, a compact and efficient urban tissue.

M. R. G. Conzen was also interested in the development at the edges of built-up urban areas.[13] He identified, in English examples, the concept of the "fringe belt"—a roughly circular area of larger buildings with relative disorder that builds up on the outside of a city but often becomes subsumed within it over time (see figure 2.3). The relative disorder and larger scale persist, however, leaving a trace of the city's historic growth like the rings of a tree.

Both of these patterns are observable in some of the oldest American cities, but both seem to rely on a slow growth rate and a strong preference for developing the closest land first. The latter, in particular, is a characteristic of a nonmotorized age. In the autotopia we have created, these patterns are obsolete, mostly because development is no longer slow and contiguous development is not advantaged.

Nevertheless, the method of study of form, morphology, can be applied to suburban areas, and the search for order in these messy places demands it. Those who have attempted formal analyses without studying this work may miss an important component that explains the processes of development very clearly. Venturi, for example, while analyzing figure ground, parking lots, and signs in Las Vegas, missed a very important force in the formal character of the particularities of the strip: namely, the property lines (lots). These alone explain a great deal about the order, relationship, and orientation of the individual properties.

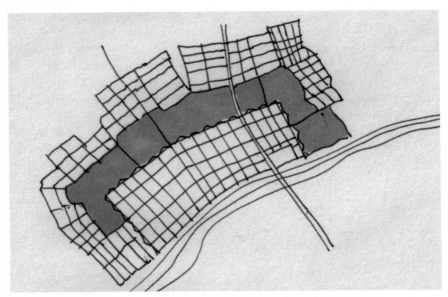

FIGURE 2.3. A fringe belt is a relatively disordered belt of land that grows up on the edge of a settlement before being subsumed in subsequent development. After M. R. G. Conzen.
Illustration by author.

In the study of car-oriented environments, the methods of analyses used to describe early settlement patterns need only a slight revamp to account for the scale and rate of change. Tissues, for example, are a formal concept used by urban morphologists, generally defined as an urban formation in which the building types, the lots, the blocks, and the streets have certain congruences. A 1970s residential neighborhood is a good example of one kind of tissue, since it exhibits formal similarities from place to place. My previous work has postulated that there are three generalizable types of tissues that are applicable in suburban contexts.[14]

I proposed that residential neighborhoods in the United States were characteristic of one generalized type of tissue, the static tissue. These are tissues that have similar lot sizes, small lots, and one building per lot. They are built over a relatively short period so that the building types are very similar as well. Most static tissues are residential, but being residential is not critical to the definition of a static type (see figure 2.4).

A second type that will not be explored much in this chapter is the campus type. This tissue type is characterized by multiple buildings on a single large lot (see figure 2.5). Examples include airports, universities, schools, apartment complexes, and office parks.

The third tissue type is somewhat controversial because it seems to have no

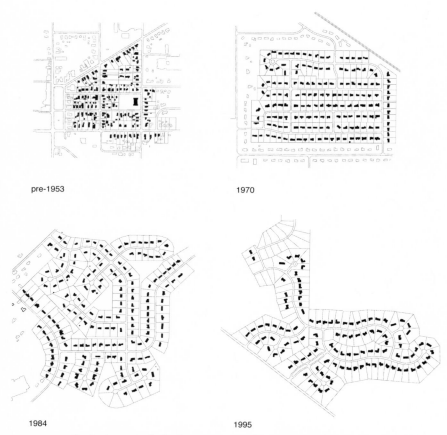

pre-1953   1970

1984   1995

FIGURE 2.4. Static tissues include these variations in residential neighborhoods. *Illustrations by author.*

formal order and thus is difficult to attribute to a "type" at all. This is the elastic tissue (see figure 2.6). I have called it "elastic" because one of its chief characteristics is that it changes rapidly compared to the other two tissue types.

Other characteristics of the elastic tissue are:

- the lots within an elastic tissue are highly varied in size and irregular in shape;
- the buildings are of different types and sizes and likely to vary widely in age due to rapid turnover and obsolescence; and
- these tissues are formed almost exclusively along an arterial road, which is the main through connector of the district.

In this study, I applied these concepts to the tissues alongside the arterial street, hoping to more clearly define the "elastic" tissue and look for its different man-

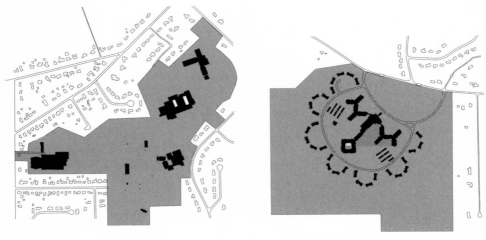

A. school complex   B. apartment complex

FIGURE 2.5. Campus tissues comprise many buildings situated on a larger lot. *Illustrations by author.*

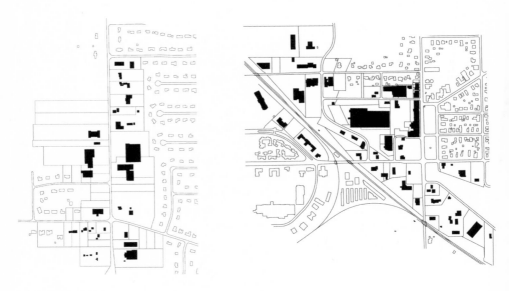

A. roadside strip   B. village center

FIGURE 2.6. Elastic tissues change rapidly and are usually found along arterial roads. *Illustrations by author.*

ifestations and origins. Morphological analysis requires that the study of places include the perspective of time, as well, ideally comparing the same place in different periods or comparing two similar kinds of places built at a sufficient time span apart so that their formal differences are clear. While this study looks at change in the same places over a span of almost twenty years (1994–2013), I also use another idea to provide comparative analysis.

Like Liebs, I see the radial highway as a timeline. The method of this study was to select points along the route that could be compared to each other. These points represent different "eras" of roadside development. Although they look alike to many people, we shall see that they are quite different and represent an interesting evolution of elastic tissue formation. In looking at these points, I also compared 2013 and 1994 development patterns to maps from the 1950s. The study looks closely at three different intersections on the road, plus a fourth area close to the origin of the arterial in the heart of the city for comparison with suburban examples (see figure 2.2). For ease of following the description, the areas are numbered one to four with the earliest example being number one.

Description of Data

The first set of diagrams show same-scale maps from 2012. The circles are 1/2 mile (800 meters) in radius in every case. The dark gray shading is the area identified as "elastic"—that is, having the physical characteristics of elastic tissue as described above. The light gray shading calls attention to a "change incident" in the buildings or land that happened between 1994 and 2013. A change incident is where the buildings or land subdivision actually changed between 1994 and 2013.

Area 1 (figure 2.7) is a close-in, traditional fabric, mostly shown for comparison of scale to later suburban areas. It grew during the streetcar era of the late nineteenth and early twentieth centuries and has since deteriorated completely into vacant storefronts and marginal uses. Redevelopment has been very slow in this district, probably owing to its proximity to two major interstate highways that have decimated the integrity of nearby neighborhoods. Note, however, that this early elastic area still has lots and buildings that are somewhat irregular, especially when compared with the surrounding residential (static) areas. The changes from 1994 are minimal and include one large new building visible from and oriented to the interstate.

Area 2 (figure 2.8) is a very interesting introduction to the ideas of suburban strip development. At the southern end of Colerain there are houses along the road, with development occurring behind them at nearly the same scale. This resembles the expected pattern that Caniggia identified for a "matrix" route. Farther north, we encounter the elastic area, which seems to have been created out of an earlier fabric of matrix-route-style development.

FIGURE 2.7. Area 1, a close-in, traditional fabric.
Illustration by author.

FIGURE 2.8. Area 2, with matrix-route development to the south and a more elastic area to the north.
Illustration by author.

FIGURE 2.9. A bungalow married to a commercial addition, 1997. The structure had been demolished by 2013.
Author's photo.

In Area 2, it is clear that commercial strip development occurred after a previous development of houses along the street. Only a single "house" actually remains from what was a row of houses close to the highway. Over time, retail demand responding to the increasing traffic inspired the reuse of some houses as retail buildings. Many of these still exist, dating from around the 1950s. These have additions to the front, most of which are unusually awkward collisions of two very different architectural and functional types. Figure 2.9, from 1997, shows a photo of the marriage between a bungalow house, possibly dating from the 1930s, and a "modern" box-like addition, probably dating from the mid-1950s. The wooden mansard roof was a decorative effect popular in the 1970s. The lot has been completely paved, with a few spaces in the front on the highway and a larger lot in the rear. In 1994 it was used as a clinic, but it had been demolished by 2013. Just next door is a lot completely redeveloped as a small freestanding restaurant. Its style indicates that it was built as a Taco Bell restaurant, but the sign is for a Chinese restaurant. More telling is the "for lease" sign: the building is ready for a new theme!

Next to this is another narrow lot with a relatively new restaurant. Like many American suburban retail buildings, this one is an architectural "logo"—a building whose awnings, style, roof, and general arrangement are corporate standards. McDonald's and then White Castle were early examples of this technique, which has become ubiquitous.

This area shows the most variety in building age (but not size), though the overall depth of the elastic development is quite narrow, responding to the original house lots. There is a striking lack of sensitivity to the public realm: an incredibly poor public right-of-way, punctuated with literally hundreds of curb-cuts, no sidewalks, and huge utility poles, with every single lot almost completely paved. Even the nonpaved areas are simply pathetic remnants. The signs are relatively sparse compared to other areas, but they seem more offensive, stuck in a landscape of cracked asphalt and a wide variety of buildings.

In Area 3, the most obvious thing that we see is the vast expansion of the amount of elastic tissue and its much greater depth off the road (see figure 2.10). The area is surrounded by orderly subdivisions, many of them in rectilinear blocks rather than curving cul-de-sacs. This places them in time at about 1960 to 1970. The commercial, elastic development has changed in character from the closer in Area 2: there are a few remnants of houses-turned-stores, and most of the property development is on much deeper lots.

The deeper lots allow the first instance we see of an interesting layering of retail activity, a trend that becomes deliberate and pronounced in places developed later. Rather than build roads to service deeper lots, developers have come up with a scheme of placing buildings in layers from the road. Here, this seems accidental: the oldest properties are those that occupy the middle layer (these are strip centers); in front of these are the newest buildings, which are fast food restaurants and service stations with logo buildings. Most recently, more strip centers have been added behind the originals, still accessed off the single main road or the intersecting road. It seems that the out parcel, also known as a "pad," may have been created as a strategy in places like this, perhaps as the parking lots were discovered to be oversized. Out-parcel development has several economic advantages: it shares access off the same road of the original street, which doubles the effective "frontage"; it makes use of parking areas that are found to be too large; and it puts some small footprint development in highly visible locations without completely screening the retail areas behind. Unfortunately it creates possibly the most visually confusing environment possible (see figures 2.11A and 2.11B). The very transparency that allows the double frontage destroys the sense of continuous space. The need to advertise the "back row" and the "middle row" leads to a cacophony of signs. The resulting environment even loses the one thing that still holds the elastic area in Area 2 together: the mirroring geometry of the relationship of street and building.

Area 3 is also dominated by a shopping center, which was built on a very large piece of land, adjacent to a (newly opened) freeway. The shopping center is an enormous L-shaped strip maximizing visibility and parking. It has very large

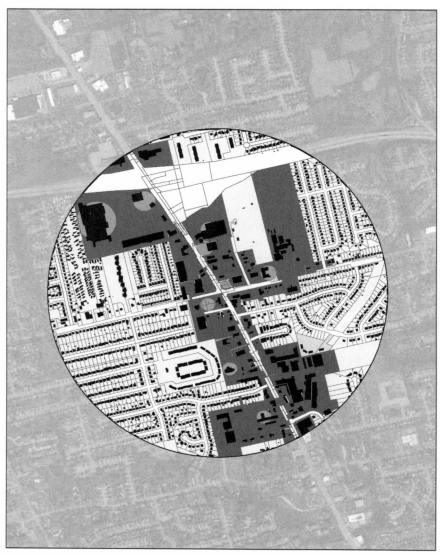

FIGURE 2.10. Area 3, with expansive elastic tissues.
Illustration by author.

FIGURES 2.11A AND 2.11B. Views of the main intersection of Area 3 (Kipling) in 1997 (*A*) and 2013 (*B*).
Author's photos.

stores joined together, a kind of giant-sized version of the smaller strip centers. Smaller retail buildings occupy the parking lot in the foreground.

Area 4 is the latest elastic area in the study (see figure 2.12). It is dominated by much larger lots, the largest of which have been aggregated to make a shopping mall (first built around 1985) surrounded by parking and restaurants on outlots. This area boasts many freestanding chain stores and national franchises such as Jiffy Lube (autos) or KFC (fast food restaurants). Many of these buildings are "logo" buildings—freestanding franchise stores where the architecture has been standardized nationally so as to act as a sign. Unlike the Taco Bell, which is in a more rundown location, logo buildings in newer and more economically demanding zones have very little reuse potential and thus not much longevity. Each new user requires its own logo building, occasioning rapid turnover in the building fabric of this district. This is exacerbated by changing styles in logo buildings, which require even the same franchise to completely rebuild.

Changes since 1994

One hypothesis of the elastic tissue along arterials is that the land uses and development along the road change much more frequently than in static tissues typified by residential neighborhoods. This study bears that out. Since 1994, there have been twenty-six incidences of change in all of the study areas, including the residential neighborhoods. Only three of these involve static tissue: an apartment complex was built and a new residential subdivision and street was platted and built. In only one incident was an established static area changed: nineteen houses were demolished and lots joined to become part of an office park along the circumferential interstate in Area 4. (This is counted as one incident.) In contrast, most of the change incidences are buildings being torn down and replaced or just torn down. In all the study areas, only one additional road was built to intersect Colerain Avenue—a dead-end road that serves the new office park.

The number of incidences rise as you travel out the timeline: 3 in Area 1, 6 in Area 2, and 9 in Area 3. Area 4 had 7 incidences but they involved much more land area and much more dramatic change. As one moves out along Colerain Avenue, change happens more frequently.

Findings

This analysis looks at these four areas as similar in function but corresponding to different time periods in development. It is a way to compare them to see how our standard strip development practices have changed over time. Several key things emerge: changes in scale, underlying disorder, and rates of change.

First, the lots of the elastic tissues are growing in scale compared to the

FIGURE 2.12. Area 4, with the largest elastic area studied.
Illustration by author.

nearby static tissues. Presuburban tissues have many of the same characteristics but are smaller relative to the average size of nearby lots. Research by Moudon and Southworth and Owens has established that house lots are growing larger over time in new (static) subdivisions, and that the form of these subdivisions has changed subtly.[15] The elastic-tissue lots of the arterial have also increased in size, but much faster relative to the subdivision lots, which accounts for the increase in overall land area devoted to the same number of buildings. Buildings have also increased in size.

What is most striking about this change in scale is the possibility that it, in part, can be attributed to pre-urban land ownership patterns. Figure 2.13 is a composite of the lot subdivisions in all four areas in 1956, prior to substantial urban development (except for Area 1). The lot patterns when the areas were basically farmland and small houses are substantially reflected in the subsequent urban form. Although only a few buildings in each place survive from this period (most of which are changed substantially), the pre-urban structure is clearly a formal constraint. Where there were smaller lots (Area 2) (which tended to be closer to town, where a greater level of roadside development is found), the form today is much smaller in scale. Farther out (Area 4), the original land holdings were not subdivided for roadside development to a great extent, because the interstate highway system had already supplanted the highway as an intercity connector by the time of the initial roadside development. Large farm plots remained large, giving an opportunity to create substantial commercial development lots. In fact, the shopping mall was built on an extensive piece of land that had previously been a small country airstrip. Whether the "enlargement" of suburban elastic tissues is a natural consequence of market forces begs the question: Did large commercial types emerge as a market necessity, or did they emerge to take advantage of much larger lots that only became available as new development overtook and surpassed small-scale roadside development?

Other than scale, the elastic tissues show great similarity in their development and origins, beginning with farm plots, roadside houses, or businesses, which quickly converted to larger-scale commercial development. The issue of the disorder in these areas has remained from their earliest urbanization, and it is an issue that is much bemoaned in American life. If we examine these areas in juxtaposition to the much more orderly static tissues that surround them, we can find the following answers to why these places appear so jumbled.

Underlying Disorder

In the static tissues (e.g., subdivisions) that surround each of these elastic districts, there is a strong degree of underlying geometry. Even when streets are curvilinear and lots are pie-shaped, subdivisions usually have relatively small lots that constrain the placement of houses. The houses are all nearly the same

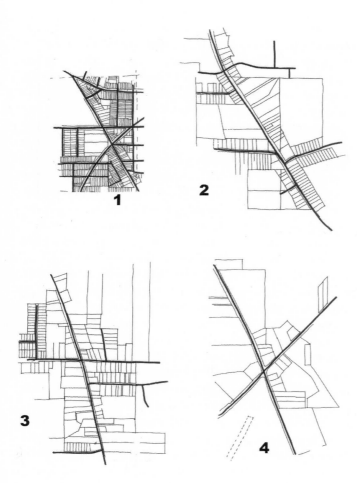

FIGURE 2.13.
Lot subdivisions
in 1956, prior to
most roadside
development.
*Illustrations by
author.*

size and have a constant relationship/orientation to the street. The lots are planned to have a constant size, uniform frontage, and a similarity in shape: conformity is prized.

Contrast this order with the disorder or unclear order of the elastic tissue. In every case studied, the lots of the elastic "district" were highly varied in size (area), length of the frontage, and shape. Visually, it appears that this disorder increases the farther one travels outward along our timeline. In Area 2, frontages are modular and most of the lots are at least perpendicular to Colerain Avenue. Area 3 is similar but the modularity breaks down. In Area 4, there is no modularity and very few lots are perpendicular or rectangular. The trapezoidal shape of parcels in all the areas is related to the radial street's cutting across the Public Land Survey grid—despite the changes in lot configuration, the angle of the street relative to the Land Survey barely changes across the study area.

The underlying disorder of the lots (which also occurs in residential areas prior to their subdivision) is not changed when the property comes under urban development. Unlike a residential subdivision, the commercial lots are rarely subdivided and, in fact, some are aggregated rather than subdivided. One result of this is that, unlike residential subdivisions, there are no additional roads built to access lots—most lots simply remain fronting on the major arterial. Without an "interior" road system or interconnection, the traffic access flow is all forced onto the arterial.

Contrast this condition with the traditional gridded business or village district—which has regular lots, blocks, and cross streets for alternative access, visibility, and traffic.

Another layer of activity consists of buildings on these lots. The residential buildings (houses) are relatively static—many small changes occur over time, but most changes are constrained by the size of the lots and the intrinsic and (little understood) community value of conformity. Neither of these conditions constrains the elastic tissues in this study. A key characteristic of these areas today is the variation in building size—from a shopping mall to a gas station or kiosk. Disorder is manifest as the senses jump from tiny to huge, and thus we cannot get a "sense" of the place in question because there is such a discrepancy in our view from moment to moment.

The orientation and placement of the buildings is also disordered. Although most show at least one "face" to the arterial street, some are deliberately set at angles to maximize visibility in one direction or another. Despite zoning, which has very little physical effect if the lot is large relative to the building, there are no uniform setbacks. The large lots required for parking areas give much freedom for the particular location and orientation of the building, unlike the constraining effects of lot size, setbacks, and orientation in residential areas.

Rapid Change

Compared to static subdivisions, which rarely see significant changes in building type, lot, blocks, and street networks, elastic tissues can change greatly in a relatively short period of time. Building occupancy is one characteristic that can change over and over (remember the Taco Bell building) as the market changes. Service stations become banks, or houses become clinics that become video stores. Beyond that is the severe adaptation of older buildings, or (more often in affluent outlying areas) relatively new buildings that are razed for even more modern ones, sometimes with the same business reinstalled.

The rapid change does not in and of itself signal disorder in the environment; rather, the very disorder of the elastic tissue, which does not demand conformity and which does not constrain physical dimensions, provides an (unprecedented) opportunity for this churning of the environment. Comparing elastic commercial areas with a gridded cityscape, the grid's constraints of size, density, and orientation force modern development to come to grips with the nineteenth century's physical template. As presently constituted in the elastic tissue, the full meaning of twenty-first-century market forces can play out, relatively unencumbered except by the mid-twentieth-century pre-urban fabric of farm fields.

We pay for this level of commercial freedom with disorder and hope (against evidence) that planners can bring some order to this environment in the name of quality of life or sustainability. The disorder and scale of the elastic environment of the strip suggests forces at work that go beyond the traditional planning tools. For one, there are extremely common development formulas that dominate this environment. These could be termed "typologies," but they encompass more than form or even rudimentary function. Shopping malls, for example, have a formulaic form and function, but they also have a formulaic relationship to the street and neighborhood, formulaic parking ratios, the same mix of chain stores inside, and the same kind of signage across the United States. Strip centers and fast food chains have similar formulas, time-tested and safe for developers. Planners have a difficult time addressing this kind of formula except with prescriptions for new, relatively untested formulas. Too, these standard formulas are matched physically and economically to the surrounding subdivisions and apartment complexes.

The underlying land geometry is also discouraging. Unlike a grid system, where land parcels are related geometrically and to the public space of the street, land along the highway strip is like a string of unmatched beads. A landholder with a single piece large enough to build a restaurant, for example, need only think of the market requirements and not have to understand its fit with the remaining pieces. In fact, even if this same landholder were interested in doing something different or better or more community-healing, he would have a difficult time—a single parcel is not large enough to create village-like relationships, and varying from standard formulas is off-putting to both lenders and chain-retail corporations.

Thus the strip represents an interlocking system of underlying lot patterns, rapid development and change, formulaic development types, and symbiotic economic and physical relationships that constrain its solution. Change is possible only if it is done at the level of lot subdivision coupled with changes in development formulas. This requires a consensus on proper planning by planners and by real estate developers, a possibility that might once have seemed elusive but today perhaps is more possible.

1. This article is an update of a previously published study conducted between 1994 and 1997. Brenda Scheer, "The Radial Street as a Timeline: A Study of the Transformation of Elastic Tissues," in *Suburban Form: An International Perspective*, edited by Kiril Stanilov and Brenda Scheer, 102–22 (London and New York: Routledge, 2003).

2. Chester Liebs, *Main Street to Miracle Mile* (New York: Little, Brown, 1985).

3. American Society of Planning Officials, *Highway-Oriented and Urban Arterial Commercial Areas* (Chicago: Planners Advisory Service, Information Report no. 177, September 1963).

4. Robert Venturi, Denise Scott-Brown, and Steven Isenour, *Learning from Las Vegas* (Cambridge, Mass., and London: MIT Press, 1977).

5. See Walter H. Kraft and the Institute of Transportation Engineers (ITE), *Traffic Engineering Handbook*, 6th ed. (Washington D.C.: ITE, 2009); and American Association of State Highway and Transportation Officials, *Policy on the Geometric Design of Highways and Streets*, 6th ed. (Washington, D.C.: AASHTO, 2011).

6. Michael Larice and Brenda Scheer, "A Classification and Analysis of Urban and Suburban Arterial Development: Toward an Understanding of the Strip," paper presented at the Associated Collegiate Schools of Planning, Cincinnati, Ohio, October 2012.

7. Venturi, Scott-Brown, and Isenour, *Learning from Las Vegas*, 20.

8. Grady Clay, *Close-Up: How to Read the American City* (Chicago and London: University of Chicago Press, 1973), 90–92.

9. Brenda Scheer, *The Evolution of Urban Form: Typology for Planners and Architects* (Chicago: Planners Press, 2010).

10. On the livable street movement, see Frederick Dock, William Morrish, and Carol Swenson, *Design Development Principles for Livable Suburban Arterial Roadways* (Minneapolis: Design Center for American Urban Landscape, 2001); and Eric Dumbaugh, "Safe Streets, Livable Streets," *Journal of the American Planning Association* 71, no. 3 (2005): 283–300. On the complete streets movement, see John LaPlante, *Retrofitting Urban Arterials into Complete Streets*, 3rd Urban Street Symposium (Seattle: n.p., 2007); and Barbara McCann, *Complete Streets: Best Policy and Implementation Practices* (Chicago: American Planning Association, 2010). On context-sensitive design, see Timothy A. Bevan, Roger Mason, and John Anthony McKenzie, *Context Sensitive Design Challenges for Major Suburban Arterial Street Projects*, 2nd Urban Street Symposium (Seattle: n.p., 2003); and Institute of Transportation Engineers, *Context Sensitive Solutions for Designing Major Urban Thoroughfares for Walkable Communities*, Institute of Transportation Engineers RP-036, 2006. On the green streets movement, see Cynthia Girling and Ronald Kellett, *Skinny Streets and Green Neighborhoods: Design for Environment and Community* (Washington, D.C.: Island Press, 2005); and Elizabeth Macdonald, Rebecca Sanders, and Alia Anderson, *Performance Measures for Complete, Green Streets: A Proposal for Urban Arterials in California* (Berkeley: University of California Transportation Center, 2010). On traditional streets research, see Allan B. Jacobs, Elizabeth Macdonald, and Yodan Rofe, *The Boulevard Book: History, Evolution, Design of Multiway Boulevards* (Cambridge, Mass.: MIT Press, 2001); and Stephen Marshall, *Streets and Patterns* (London and New York: Routledge, 2004). On various street redesign programs, see Jonathan Reid, *Unconventional Arterial Intersection Design, Management and Operation Strategies* (New York: Parsons Brinckerhoff/William Barclay Parsons Fellowship Monograph, 2004); and Carol H. Tan, "Going on a Road Diet," *Public Roads* 75, no. 2 (2011): 28–33.

11. Michael Southworth and Peter M. Owens, "The Evolving Metropolis: Studies of Com-

munity, Neighborhood, and Street Form at the Urban Edge," *Journal of the American Planning Association* 59, no. 3 (1993): 271–87.

12. Gianfranco Caniggia and Gian Luigi Maffei, *Architectural Composition and Building Typology: Interpreting Basic Building* (Florence: Alinea, 2001).

13. M. R. G. Conzen, "The Plan Analysis of an English City Centre," *Proceedings of the I. G. U. Symposium in Urban Geography*, edited by K. Norburg, 383–414 (N.p.: Lund Studies in Geography, 1961).

14. Brenda Scheer, "The Anatomy of Sprawl," *Places* 14, no. 2 (2001): 28–37.

15. Anne Vernez Moudon, "The Evolution of Twentieth Century Residential Forms: An American Case Study," in *Urban Landscapes: International Perspectives*, edited by J. W. R. Whitehand and P. J. Larkham, 170–206 (London and New York: Routledge, 1991); Southworth and Owens, "The Evolving Metropolis."

CHAPTER 3

Rezoning Montgomery
People, Politics, and Place

GERRIT-JAN KNAAP, AVIVA HOPKINS BROWN,
AND REBECCA LEWIS

Key Points and Practice Takeaways

1. Expect controversy. Zoning is a powerful instrument that makes zoning change unavoidably political and difficult.

2. It is important to clarify whether revisions of zoning ordinances serve only to clean up and modernize existing ordinances or if they are intended to implement policy change. If the latter, it is important to seek consensus before the process begins.

3. Constrain expectations. Those seeking radical change will likely be disappointed.

4. There is no ideal zoning ordinance. The "reformed" zoning ordinance will likely need to blend traditional, form-based, and performance zoning approaches to meet the vagaries and historical roots of local circumstances.

5. Engaging more than the usual suspects will take an unusual effort. Some citizens and constituent groups are always engaged in local government policy issues; engaging people of color, immigrants, and working-class populations will require extra effort.

Politics is the art of looking for trouble, finding it everywhere,
diagnosing it incorrectly and applying the wrong remedies.

—GROUCHO MARX

Few would argue that perceptions and attitudes about development and urban form have changed. Where once there was a near-universal desire for
single-family homes with two-car garages on large lots in suburban settings,
there is now substantial interest in smaller homes or apartments in urban settings with mixed-use buildings and less dependence on automobiles—especially
among the young, the old, and the childless. These preferences for "smarter" or
"more sustainable" development patterns are still not pervasive, but they have
grown significantly in the past two decades. As a result, it has now become
politically viable for local government policies to permit, if not require, newer
forms of compact development. Many suburban jurisdictions across the nation
are thus now in the process of reforming their zoning regulations.

Montgomery County, Maryland, is one such jurisdiction. Well known for its
progressive approaches to land use and development, county leaders in 2008
began the process of revising the county zoning ordinance at least in part to accommodate a more urban, less suburban development pattern. At this writing,
a new draft zoning ordinance is under review by the county council. But while
the last chapter remains to be written, the story is already rich with technical
complexity, political controversy, and hard lessons learned.

In this chapter, we tell the ongoing story of one community's attempts to
reform its zoning ordinance in an era of changing and contested goals for land
use policy change. We begin with an overview of zoning and how zoning has become a nearly ubiquitous—but still evolving—tool for managing urban growth.
We then introduce Montgomery County, its existing zoning ordinance, its varied ambitions, and some technical features of its new draft ordinance. Next, we
explore the politics of zoning reform based on in-depth interviews of fifteen
individuals directly involved in the process of reforming Montgomery County's
zoning ordinance. Finally, we offer lessons for other jurisdictions now or soon
considering a similar effort.

A Brief Overview of Zoning

Zoning remains the most powerful and pervasive regulatory tool used by local
governments to manage growth. The first comprehensive zoning ordinance in
the United States was established in New York City in 1916. The Zoning Resolution contained three sets of restrictions for building within the city: use restrictions, bulk restrictions, and administrative restrictions.[1] In 1920, the resolution

was upheld by New York's Court of Appeals as an appropriate exercise of the state's police power.[2]

The practice of zoning was upheld by the U.S. Supreme Court when in 1926 it heard the case of *Euclid, Ohio v. Ambler Realty*. In the aftermath of the *Euclid* decision, the notion that certain land uses were incompatible and should be separated from one another—and regulated—caught on quickly. Within five years "roughly twenty states had authorized some or all municipalities to pass zoning ordinances"; within ten years that number doubled.[3] Today, almost all large U.S. cities have adopted zoning ordinances as a land use regulation tool.

As zoning became widespread, the scope of zoning grew beyond the separation of uses to include setbacks, height, density, appearance, and other design features. In the late 1960s and early 1970s, some states began to assert control over what local governments could do with land use regulation. States such as Florida, New Jersey, and Oregon began reviewing and approving local plans and zoning regulations, regulating developments of regional significance, and identifying areas they thought required state oversight. State-level authority over land use remains the exception to the rule, however, and zoning remains predominantly a local government affair.

As zoning became the dominant form of land use regulation, it also became the subject of considerable academic research, much of it highly critical.[4] While proponents argued that zoning served the public interest by minimizing land use conflicts, a principle still taught in planning schools today, Euclidean zoning has been widely criticized from both the left and the right. The conservative critique of zoning is that land use can and should be addressed through market transactions, and that zoning tends to be used by the politically powerful to the disadvantage of the powerless. Critics on the left share the latter view, arguing that zoning can raise land and housing prices, exclude the poor, and, by separating land uses, exacerbate urban sprawl. Segregating residential uses from commercial and office uses, for example, typically requires people to drive, sometimes long distances, to work and vital services. The most recent criticism of zoning has come from proponents of New Urbanism and smart growth, who favor compact, mixed-use, pedestrian-oriented development. Such advocates claim that zoning—especially Euclidean zoning—separates uses, constrains development in areas where more development makes sense, and contributes to urban sprawl. As such criticism has become widespread, momentum has grown for alternatives to Euclidean zoning, such as incentive zoning, performance zoning, and form-based zoning.

Incentive zoning is founded in Euclidean zoning principles but provides more flexibility by allowing developers and local government officials to exchange density for community improvements. Essentially, incentive zoning allows developers more density in exchange for public amenities—such as open space, affordable housing, exceptionally well-designed buildings, environmentally sensitive features, or public art—beyond what is already required. This form of zoning is more commonly used in commercial and mixed-use zones than residential zones.

Another alternative to Euclidean zoning is performance zoning. Performance zoning differs the most from Euclidean zoning as it allows multiple uses within the same zone. Development is governed by a scoring system designed to achieve planning goals outlined in the zoning ordinance. Since performance zoning does not directly regulate land use, emphasis is placed on the built structures to create or maintain compatibility with neighborhood structures, transportation, open space, and any other standards specified in the ordinance. Developments are rated on their performance, and those that score sufficient points in the appropriate categories are approved.[5]

Another alternative to Euclidean zoning is form-based zoning, which focuses on the physical form of the structures, addressing the relationship between building facades and the public realm. It is intended to build a sense of place and community cohesiveness by regulating the form, massing, and how buildings relate to one another and the block on which they sit. These forms are often presented in multiple ways: text descriptions, diagrams, models, and other visuals that are tied to regulations and offer guidelines on the form and scale of future development. Unlike urban design guidelines, these guidelines are regulatory, not advisory, and help implement a community plan. Much like Euclidean zoning, form-based zoning is intended to maintain the character of the existing community and the integrity of the new development.

Form-based zoning codes and Euclidean zoning differ on several fundamental levels. The first is their overall approach to zoning: Euclidean zoning is prescriptive and uses zoning to define undesirable development. While form-based zoning also is prescriptive, it uses regulations to outline what development would be desirable in each specified area. Euclidean zoning could be considered reactive whereas form-based zoning is proactive. Thus, form-based zoning ordinances are typically shorter, more concise, and better organized in terms of readability and accessibility compared to Euclidean zoning ordinances. Further, whereas Euclidean zoning focuses on the segregation of incompatible uses, form-based zoning promotes a mix of uses. Form-based codes are more oriented toward design scale and compatibility with the existing neighborhood structure and design. Euclidean zoning tends to deemphasize concern for design and compatibility with the community by focusing on the regulation of use.

In sum, zoning has had a storied but tumultuous past. Although practiced nearly everywhere, it remains the subject of much criticism and debate. Alternatives to Euclidean zoning include performance-, incentive-, and form-based zoning. Whether these new forms of zoning will eventually replace Euclidean zoning will be determined by the decisions made through political processes at the local government level—in places such as Montgomery County, Maryland.

Planning and Zoning in Montgomery County

Montgomery County is well known for its innovative approach to land use planning and regulation. Its 93,000-acre agricultural reserve, inclusionary zoning, affordable housing regulations, and transferable development rights (TDR) programs are just a few of its nationally respected planning tools. Additionally, its "Wedges and Corridors" plan of the 1960s remains a featured example in many planning textbooks.

Located just north of Washington, D.C., Montgomery County is the most populous county in Maryland and among the most prosperous in the nation. With a median household income of close to $93,000, Montgomery County's earnings are almost double the national average and ranked second among U.S. counties with populations over 500,000. Its population is diverse (the county became majority-minority in 2010), well-educated (30 percent hold advanced degrees), and politically progressive (68 percent voted for President Obama in the last election).

Montgomery County's population, which doubled in the 1940s and 1950s, continues to grow at a double-digit rate and now includes over one million residents. The county has a strong and diverse economy, with over eighteen federal governmental agencies and installations and the largest biotechnology cluster in the mid-Atlantic region.[6] Bethesda and Silver Spring are two of Washington, D.C.'s most vibrant and growing edge communities. The I-270 corridor, which runs through Montgomery County from Washington, D.C., in the south to Frederick County in the north, has eclipsed downtown Baltimore as the largest employment center in the state.[7] The Montgomery County landscape is highly diverse and features large areas of undeveloped rural landscapes as well as intensely developed and congested urban corridors.

While Montgomery County is still viewed as a leader in land use planning and regulation, it has struggled to manage its growth. Despite the densification of key urban nodes like Silver Spring (see figure 3.1) and Bethesda, and the extension of the Washington Metro system deep into the county, the county remains predominantly suburban. The multifamily share of its housing stock continues to rise but remains less than 50 percent. Thus, housing in the county is unaffordable to many who work there, especially those employed in the service sector. In early 2013, the county's median sales price for a home was $347,000, compared to $160,500 nationally.[8]

Due to its location in the Washington metropolitan area, traffic congestion in Montgomery County ranks among the highest in the nation. The county has a large agricultural reserve but, as a result, the county is nearly built out.

FIGURE 3.1. Downtown Silver Spring.
The Montgomery County Planning Department.

Due to restrictions imposed by existing zoning regulations, the county has the capacity to accommodate growth on just 4 percent of its land area, creating more pressure on the housing supply and exacerbating the trend in unaffordable housing prices. Its relatively high housing prices also weaken its attractiveness for business investment and economic growth compared to its Northern Virginia competitors.

All of those pressures helped create political support for a comprehensive look at the zoning code, which had been a topic of interest in the county for many years. The seeds of zoning reform were planted in the mid-2000s; planning board chairman Royce Hanson, widely revered for his establishment of the agricultural reserve and back for his second term of office, was a strong advocate for reform. The project did not go far, however, without the energy and commitment of leadership from the Planning Department, which came when Hanson hired Rollin Stanley as planning director in 2008. Stanley, previously a planning director in St. Louis and before that a planner for many years in Toronto, Canada, took the position with the understanding that the county was rapidly transforming from a suburban to an urban county. Further, he understood it was his mission to facilitate that transition—a mission he pursued with considerable zeal. Stanley hired Lois Villemaire, who had led a similar effort as planning director in nearby Anne Arundel County.

Stanley and Villemaire launched the initial phases and got the project off the ground. Before the process was even close to being finished, however, Hanson, Stanley, and Villemaire were all gone. Hanson and Villemaire both retired after distinguished careers and Stanley returned to his native Canada to become the planning director of Calgary, Alberta.

The Process of Zoning Reform

In 2007, the Montgomery County zoning ordinance was complicated, cumbersome, and dated, just about everyone agreed. The ordinance was essentially a traditional Euclidean zoning ordinance, with some overlay and floating zones, which imposed a set of requirements in addition to those of the underlying base zone. However, the zoning ordinance bore the scars of amendments frequently needed to accommodate modern development issues. The county has master plans for more than forty distinct regions, each with its own provisions that ultimately metastasized into the zoning ordinance.

When the reform process began, the zoning ordinance had not been comprehensively rewritten since 1977. Since then, the number of zones had nearly tripled from 41 in 1977 to 120 by 2010. At more than 1,152 pages, the code was widely viewed as hard to use, not concurrent with modern development practices, and lacking in modern principles of sustainable development. With the support of Hanson, who put the project in the Planning Department's annual work program, the Montgomery County Council directed the Planning Department to begin the process of comprehensive zoning reform in 2007.

The process was scheduled to proceed in three phases (see figure 3.2). In phase 1, planners would define the approach and outline what was to come, in what they called the "diagnosis phase"; in phase 2, they would draft the code; and in phase 3, the revised codes would be reviewed by the planning board, the county council's Planning Housing and Economic Development Committee, and then the county council, which holds approving authority over county zoning. Each phase would include extensive public outreach. Phase 3 is ongoing at this writing.

The county hired a consulting firm to help with the revision project. The consultant's first task was to gather input through focus groups, interviews, and online surveys; review the existing code; and make recommendations for what the massive project should cover. County staff took a back seat during the information-gathering stage to avoid the perception of bias. With that input and under the direction of Stanley, staff published a detailed report released in January 2009 titled *Zoning Discovery*. The *Zoning Discovery* was well received, won an award,[9] and set the stage for the project that followed. During the lengthy code-

Project Timeline

Phase 1: Approach & Outline		Phase 2: Code Drafting		Phase 3: Public Review & Implementation	
Fall 2008 – Spring 2010		Summer 2010 – Summer 2012		Fall 2012- 2014	
9/08	Stakeholder sessions Planner analysis	10/10	Districts (Agricultural & Residential)	9/12	Planning Board Review with staff and public
1/09	Zoning Discovery & Technical Appendix	12/10	Uses (Agricultural & Residential)	5/13	Transmit Planning Board Draft to County Council
3/09	Appoint Zoning Advisory Panel	11/11	Districts and Uses (All Zones)	5/13	Council PHED committee review
7/09	Hire Consultant: Code Studio	1/12	General Development Standards	1/14	Full Council Review
9/09	Launch Web site	3/12	Administration & Procedures	3/14	Council Approves ZTA 13-04 (Zoning Code)
1/10	Approach & Annotated Outline	7/12	Consolidated Draft	6/14	PHED Committee Review of G-956 (Zoning Map)
4/10	Open Houses, Planning Board & Council Direction		Collect and review public comments (ongoing)		Full Council Review of G-956 (Zoning Map)

FIGURE 3.2. Project timeline for Montgomery County zoning reform process. *The Montgomery County Planning Department.*

drafting phase, which planners and the consultant tackled chapter by chapter, however, the relationship between the staff and consultant became tense, and animosity arose. The consultant was dismissed halfway through phase 2.

During the drafting phase, the planning board appointed a zoning advisory panel (ZAP). The group of community representatives, architects, developers, and other land use specialists met every month to review, recommend, and provide feedback on new ideas and propose direction for a revised ordinance. The panel met about thirty times as a full group and even more in subcommittees. Many members proved influential throughout the project, both as members of the ZAP but also as liaisons to broader constituencies. The staff also held regular briefings and sought input from county staff, such as the hearing examiner, who used the zoning ordinance in their daily work.

Under state law and the current zoning ordinance, zoning text amendments and district map amendments only require notice via newspaper advertisements. But the county went far beyond that. Over the life of the project, planners organized:

- over eighty public meetings;
- dozens of planning board work sessions;
- numerous council presentations;
- regular email "blasts" to hundreds of parties following the project;
- press releases for project milestones;
- almost weekly website and agenda updates; and
- a direct mailing to about 10,000 property owners of commercial and industrial-zoned properties.

Further discussions on zone consolidation and reorganization were presented at public forums, at open houses, and to the zoning advisory panel throughout 2011 and 2012. In many cases, feedback led to changes in the draft. For example, in response to concerns about the deletion of zoning designations, staff proposed groups or "families" of zones in the consolidated draft published in the summer of 2012.

The project was underway when the county council approved a new Commercial-Residential (CR) Zone in 2010 (see table 3.1). The new mixed-use zone was designed to allow a mix of commercial and residential uses, create interactive streets, provide public space, and foster jobs and services where people could live, work, and access services within a compact area.

The CR zone was established as a family of zones allowing for a range of densities and heights—as low as 0.5 floor area ratio (FAR) near single-family neighborhoods and up to 8.0 FAR for areas near metro stations and within central business districts. Within that range, master plans would use the flexibility of the zones to ensure that development fits within the context of each community.

In the CR zone, developers can earn bonus density in exchange for public amenities beyond the established requirements if they choose the optional, rather than standard, development method. Planners developed a detailed menu of amenities and a scoring system, which were reviewed in lengthy public sessions, and approved by both the planning board and the county council. The benefits were codified in the CR Zone Incentive Density Guidelines document.

The CR zone was used for the first time in the White Flint Sector Plan, which was approved in 2010, and went on to win local accolades and awards, such as the Maryland 2012 Sustainable Growth Award, and garner national media coverage by American Public Media's Marketplace radio program and the American Planning Association magazine. The foundation of the plan rested on its location near a Metro station and within the intensely developed I-270 economic corridor. The plan envisions transforming a car-centric, 1970s-era suburban shopping district with a sea of parking lots into a dynamic urban center featuring housing, shopping, public use spaces, parks, public facilities, and a favorable environment for walking and cycling. It is projected to generate about 19,000 jobs.

The plan notably adds residential development to an area previously vacated after stores closed, placing residents close to a variety of services. Incentive zoning guarantees those services and also achieves environmental goals such as farmland preservation through easement purchases, energy-efficient buildings, increased tree canopy and vegetative plantings, green roofs, and recycling.

As the White Flint Sector Plan draft advanced through the layers of review under the new CR zone, some suggested adding the new zone to the rewrite process. Those who worried about too much change thought it would be a strategy to halt the White Flint plan. The White Flint plan, however, was adopted and was held up as a national model for smart growth. Since then, the planning board has approved three development applications for mixed-use areas on former strip shopping centers and a transformative plan to remake the White Flint Mall into a more complete community.

The New Draft Zoning Ordinance

From the beginning, the zoning reform process in Montgomery County was burdened by the tension between those who supported the status quo and those who wanted the landscape to change to adapt to twenty-first-century realities. While opposing views can be healthy, in Montgomery County those forces were intensely polarized. As a result, the zoning code revision project became a pitched battle, almost meeting by meeting and paragraph by paragraph.

The *Zoning Discovery*, the sixty-page document intended to garner buy-in from the planning board and county council, set out the goals of the zoning reform effort:

- simplify and streamline the standards and process;
- match land use to development patterns;
- rationalize development standards;
- accommodate change and recognize consistency; and
- update technology.

The Drive to Simplify

The *Zoning Discovery* listed simplification of the massive code as a priority. Indeed, the draft ordinance goes a long way toward simplifying the document:

TABLE 3.1. Public benefits in the commercial residential (CR) zone that can be exchanged for increases in density

- Mixed uses
- Public facilities (public plazas, tree-lined promenades, movie theatres, schools)
- Transit proximity
- Connectivity and mobility (pedestrian- and bicyclist-oriented streets and networks)
- Quality building and site design
- Protection and enhancement of the environment
- Agricultural protection (mandated purchases of building-lot termination easements)
- Affordable housing

creating one table of uses rather than specifying what is allowed to occur in each zone throughout the document; adding easy-to-follow diagrams and tables; and separating sections on Euclidean zones, floating zones, and standard and optional methods. Simplification also was achieved by adding new use categories: agricultural, residential, civic, commercial, and industry. These seemingly uncontroversial tasks created much consternation among proponents of the status quo, who voiced suspicions that planners were changing zoning policy.

Under the current code, some nonresidential uses were allowed in residential zones (see table 3.1). Dentists' offices required property owners to seek a special exception, but uses like small daycare centers with less than eight children were allowed by right. In the revision, planners kept some of those uses, consolidated some with other uses, and phased out others. A use other than residential was defined as a "general building."

Among the issues that became the subject of debate was the regulation of accessory apartments. Accessory apartments had been permitted throughout Montgomery County for decades by special exception. In the 1980s, county policymakers established accessory apartment provisions to provide more affordable housing options for county residents. For homeowners, the units provided a source of income and/or allowed family members, such as seniors, to stay in their homes with caregivers. For renters, the apartments provided a low-cost option to live in single-family neighborhoods or fill a transitional housing need.

Planners proposed allowing accessory apartments by right in residential zones in the zoning revision, but the idea brought vocal opposition from a number of groups, particularly neighborhood organizations that were concerned about parking and the changing face of Montgomery County neighborhoods. As the controversy grew, the planning board directed staff to take up the accessory apartment issue separately from the zoning rewrite project and propose it as a stand-alone zoning text amendment (ZTA) to be considered by the county council.

Planners held two public meetings that packed the room with close to 100 people in each meeting. Following staff's recommendation, the planning board, in its advisory role to the county council, voted in favor of the ZTA to allow by-right accessory apartments, although members said they needed to be more strictly regulated and limited to a maximum number based on the location of existing units in the neighborhood. The county council followed suit.

The zoning revision reflects the accessory apartment ZTA by allowing small, attached accessory apartments to be licensed and approved by right, without the time or expense required by the special exception process. Small apartments would be up to 800 square feet; large units would range from 801 to 1,200 square feet. They were subject to regulation by the Department of Housing and Community Affairs and a new rule requiring a maximum number per block.

Building Typologies

A major change in the draft code establishes building typologies, which are listed in appropriate zones. For example, uses such as a medical office are permitted in appropriate building types, rather than being specified in zones. The building types are as follows:

detached house	townhouse	multiuse building
duplex	apartment/condo	general building

Planners believe that attaching the use table to the building typologies provides a helpful visual image for the code user (see figures 3.3A and 3.3B).

Rationalizing Development Standards

The application of building typologies made it easier to review and alter development standards, as rules governing heights, setbacks, and so on were tied to each building type. Over the last few decades, recent changes to address the changing market and increasing applications for infill housing had added complexity to the code. During the rewrite, planners worked to replace those standards and to address issues such as the size of buildings on sloped lots.

When those development standards were presented as part of the rewrite team's outreach to communities, they were received favorably, largely because they were more restrictive when applied to large infill houses. Some of the existing standards were changed, most notably side-yard setbacks. Staff spent a lot of time working on the procedures and processes associated with zoning, such as subdivision regulations, with the intent to make the application and approval process clearer.

In 2008, the Montgomery County Office of Legislative Oversight (OLO) published a report recommending that the county's parking policies and practices should be revised to promote alternative travel modes rather than encourage single-occupancy vehicle use.[10] Previously, minimum parking requirements had been used to protect nearby streets from spillover parking if uses could not accommodate the need on site. The OLO report said that policy had resulted

Section 4.1.3. Building Types in the Agricultural, Rural Residential, and Residential Zones

Building types regulate the form of development allowed within each zone. Uses allowed within any building type are determined by the uses allowed within the zone under Section 3.1.6; the building type does not determine use. The building type only determines the applicable development standards. All graphic depictions of building types are for illustrative purposes only and are not meant to limit or exclude other designs.

A. Detached House or a Building for a Cultural Institution, Religious Assembly, Public Use, or Conditional Use allowed in the zone

A detached house is a building containing one dwelling unit that may contain ancillary nonresidential uses, such as a Home Occupation or Family Day Care. A Building for a Cultural Institution, Religious Assembly, Public Use, or a Conditional Use allowed in the zone is a building that accommodates only a Cultural Institution, Religious Assembly, Public Use, or an approved conditional use allowed in the applicable zone under Article 59-3, Uses and Use Standards. This building type includes buildings used for agriculture associated with Farming.

B. Duplex

A duplex is a building containing 2 principal dwelling units that may contain ancillary nonresidential uses, such as a Home Occupation or Family Day Care.

C. Townhouse

A townhouse is a building containing 3 or more dwelling units where each dwelling unit is separated vertically by a party wall. A townhouse may contain ancillary nonresidential uses, such as a Home Occupation or Family Day Care.

D. Apartment Building

An apartment building is a building containing 3 or more dwelling units vertically and horizontally arranged. An apartment may contain up to 10% of the gross floor area as Retail/Service Establishment uses, otherwise it is a multi use building.

Section 4.1.5. Building Types in the Commercial/Residential, Employment, and Industrial Zones

Building types regulate the form of development allowed within each zone. Uses allowed within any building type are determined by the uses allowed within the zone under Section 3.1.6; the building type does not determine use. The building type only determines the applicable development standards. All graphic depictions of building types are for illustrative purposes only and are not meant to limit or exclude other designs.

A. Detached House

A detached house is a building containing one dwelling unit that may contain ancillary nonresidential uses, such as a Home Occupation or Family Day Care.

B. Duplex

A duplex is a building containing 2 principal dwelling units that may contain ancillary nonresidential uses, such as a Home Occupation or Family Day Care.

C. Townhouse

A townhouse is a building containing 3 or more dwelling units where each dwelling unit is separated vertically by a party wall. A townhouse may contain ancillary nonresidential uses, such as a Home Occupation or Family Day Care.

D. Apartment Building

An apartment building is a building containing 3 or more dwelling units vertically and horizontally arranged. An apartment may contain up to 10% of the gross floor area as Retail/Service Establishment uses, otherwise it is a multi use building.

E. Multi Use Building

A multi use building is a building with Retail/Service Establishments along the majority of the ground floor facing any street or open space and other nonresidential uses or residential uses above.

F. General Building

A general building is a building typically containing nonresidential uses including office, commercial, industrial, civic and institutional, or public uses.

FIGURES 3.3A AND 3.3B. Building typologies established in the draft code. *The Montgomery County Planning Department.*

in an oversupply of parking. It also found that applicants and planners were overestimating the amount of parking required for some projects.

In 2009, the Montgomery County Department of Transportation and the Planning Department contracted with a transportation consultant to complete a study that would review current parking requirements for urban mixed-use districts. The results were to be folded into the zoning revision project. Among the report's recommendations were that county policies should, in urban, mixed-use districts, reduce parking requirements, promote shared parking, increase flexibility in parking standards, and codify standards in a way that was clear and predictable.

The parking standards suggested in the zoning revision drew on the study's recommendations. Parking would be regulated by use; each use was then assigned a targeted range for parking that would fall between a minimum and maximum based on square footage. Mixed-use zones were treated differently because their location near transit indicated they would generate fewer car trips. The draft zoning ordinance requires parking requirements to be calculated for each project, using a target range set between a baseline minimum and maximum rather than a specific number.

The draft zoning revision also adopted the study's recommendation for shared parking between property owners. Shared parking was incentivized by allowing developers to significantly reduce minimum parking requirements below the previously required 1.2 spaces per unit.

Consistency and Change

The new code includes a large chart of uses that eliminates pages of repetitive uses. The focus of much scrutiny, the use chart achieves several advancements, including the deletion of obsolete uses like haberdasheries. New industrial classifications also updated many antiquated terms.

A major change was to update single-use commercial areas that had led to car-centric, low-rise strip shopping centers. Under the leadership of Stanley, planners focused on commercial areas to create a tool that would help provide more attractive amenities to a changing population, expected to grow by 30 percent by 2030. Not only was the county expected to grow, it also was expected to change. New demographic groups—those 65 and older and the Millennial Generation of 24- to 35-year-olds—were going to predominate. Those groups, it was predicted, would seek smaller, more compact lifestyles, forgoing large homes and personal automobiles.

Planners believed that the zoning rewrite would create a tool for more compact, sustainable living. To achieve this, county staff sought to consolidate uses and zones and update single-use commercial areas with mixed-use zones. Those changes would better utilize large surface parking lots and start the transition away from obsolete office parks. Permitted densities and heights would remain mostly the same but become more flexible in their application. Many of the changes are reflected in the updated parking, open space, and landscaping requirements.

The zoning revision project also addressed industrial zones, which in the old ordinance had few limits on density but large setbacks regardless of the intensity of use. Even light industrial uses that may have had smaller impacts than more noxious commercial uses were similarly regulated. The proposed ordinance limits uses and standards and adds buffering requirements. Most industrial uses in the Washington, D.C., region include computer hardware and software development, research, science, and education, not heavy manufacturing. For heavy industrial uses, planners retained the Heavy Industrial Zone.

The planning board transmitted the document to the Montgomery county council in May 2013. Since transmission, further changes in the document have been made, but the draft zoning ordinance remains significantly different from the zoning ordinance currently in place.

As in most public processes, the final product reflects the input of many, leaving no one fully satisfied. That seems to be the case here. While there were many changes in the code that apply throughout the county, the specific land-use designations on individual properties changed little. In the end, the percentage of land in the county for which the specific zoning designation changed is miniscule—probably less than 5 percent.

The Politics of Zoning Reform

Like any public document, the substance of the draft zoning ordinance reflects both the process and the people involved in its production. As described, staff went to great lengths to post information on the web, host community meetings, and engage the general public. But it's probably safe to say a relatively small group of less than fifty people participated in the regular meetings and public dialogue through which the draft ordinance was created.

In what follows, we present the results of the fifteen structured interviews conducted with individuals involved in the Montgomery County zoning revision process. We classify interviewees into four groups:

- county planning staff and elected officials;
- land use lawyers and developers;
- neighborhood/community activists; and
- special-purpose activists (such as historic preservationists or affordable housing activists).

We use these labels to characterize the perspectives of individuals, while protecting their identities.

To gain insights into the politics of the zoning rewrite we asked the following questions:

- Do you think the zoning ordinance needs revision or rewriting? If so, what are the most important reasons for doing so?
- Are you pleased with the process through which the zoning rewrite has been undertaken? If not, why?
- Which parts of the new draft zoning ordinance represent the most important improvements? Which parts of the new draft zoning ordinance are no better or worse than before?
- What parts of the new draft zoning ordinance have been and are likely to be the most controversial? Why are these controversial? Who are the stakeholders in the controversy? And what are their concerns?
- Do you think the new zoning ordinance will be adopted?
- What do you think are the most important lessons you have learned from the Montgomery County zoning revision process?

Our sample was not randomly selected; neither were the quotes we offer below. Further, we edited several of the quotes for context and clarity. For these reasons we make no claims about the ability to generalize our findings. But the interviews can be used to explore the complexities involved, help formulate hypotheses for future research, and structure a more in-depth understanding of the politics of zoning reform.

Do you think the zoning ordinance needs revision or rewriting? If so, what are the most important reasons for doing so?

All fifteen respondents said they believed the zoning ordinance needed revision, even though there was disagreement as to why. The reasons given were essentially twofold: (1) because the ordinance itself needed to be simplified and improved, and (2) because change in the zoning ordinance was needed to foster an improved development pattern. Most community activists felt it was the zoning ordinance, not development patterns, that needed to be improved. One community activist stated:

> Oh yeah. Absolutely. It's outrageous, it's disorganized, it's redundant, it's full of special cases, it's too complicated for a citizen to use. It's a lawyer's dream.

Many of the land use lawyers held this view as well. Perhaps because most represent landowners and developers, they were often supportive of changing the code to be more flexible. One land use lawyer put it this way:

> Yes. I think it needs it [revision] because it's been close to 40 years since it was last comprehensively written and the world has changed many times in that 40 years. And while some provisions of the code are enduring, and need

relatively little revision in the conceptual sense, there are other portions of the code that are increasingly anachronistic—and I think lead to inefficiencies in how we use land. And so I think it needs revision both to modernize and to reflect different realities that underpin the structure of the ordinance.

On the other side were most of the special interest activists and most of the county staff. They saw revision of the zoning ordinance as an opportunity to change development patterns in the county. According to one staffer:

> I think we need zoning that allows for more flexible uses, that is targeted to the right areas, that allows the building of the kind of places that reflects the shifts in priorities and desires of the creative class.

Not all staff, however, expressed the same point of view. While some clearly viewed the zoning revision as an opportunity to transform the county from a typical suburb to a modern urban community, others viewed the task as merely a chance to clean up the zoning ordinance.

Are you pleased with the process through which the zoning rewrite has been undertaken? If not, why? If so, what have been the most important parts?

Nobody interviewed found the process pleasurable. All agreed the process was long, tedious, and at times painful. But the majority view was that the staff handled the process well and that a task as complicated as a complete code revision is unavoidably difficult and painstaking.

> "Pleased" is too strong a word. It is an enormous undertaking . . . I think it could be better, but I certainly don't fault . . . the staff who have tried to do it well. They have given it their all and it is an imperfect process inherently. I'm relatively satisfied, but pleased would be too strong a phrase.

Some, however, expressed a more cynical view. More than one community activist believed the process was intentionally structured to further the interest of those who favored transformation. One stated it this way:

> This ought to be a case study in how not to do it . . . this thing was mishandled from day one because the staff and the planning director at Park and Planning had no political judgment and that's why it's a total mess.

Which parts of the new draft zoning ordinance represent the most important improvements? Which parts of the new draft zoning ordinance are no better or worse than before?

Opinions on which parts of the new draft zoning ordinance were most improved varied but generally not by constituent group. Many sang the praises of the CR zone, noting that the zone would allow more flexibility and higher densities. Others praised the removal of the countless footnotes and simplification of restrictions in the residential zones. A few others noted the new parking requirements. Said a member of the county planning staff:

> If the CR zone can get through to apply to most of the commercial areas, then it is completely worthwhile. And to whittle down the number of zones is huge. It makes our organization more sustainable because it makes it less costly to keep this document going.

Even a community activist conceded:

> I think that the streamlining is advantageous. The extent to which they had advertised this as a goal it has been accomplished and I think that is very good. I really like the fact that it is written as an online document so that you with hyperlinks get to things so that when you are reading something you can link to the definition and back. And I think that a lot of the redundant zones and getting rid of that are fine.

Some, especially those who seek to change development patterns, were disappointed at the lack of change in the residential zones. Others were comforted in the lack of changes to the agricultural reserve. A special interest advocate remarked:

> I mean 95 percent of it I think is pretty much the same as it was.

What parts of the new draft zoning ordinance have been and are likely to be the most controversial? Why are these controversial? Who are the stakeholders in the controversy? And what are their concerns?

No one failed to recognize the controversial nature of the process in which they were engaged. Interviewees mentioned both substantive and interpersonal issues. Many mentioned Rollin Stanley by name. Staff and representatives of special interest groups lamented his departure. Community activists readily expressed their delight. Stanley himself expressed the view that his departure would have little influence on the outcome of the process. One community activist stated:

> The planning director here had no political judgment. He thought he did, but I'm telling you he didn't and that is why he's no longer there . . . the proof of the pudding is that the civic community and the development community have never agreed on anything in the many years I have been there except this.

Not surprisingly, the CR zone, the provision that allowed accessory apartment units, and the overall changes in the development pattern of the county were most often identified as the most controversial. On these issues, the division among interest groups was clear and well understood. A select set of community activists were readily identified as the opposition while most others were viewed as neutral or in favor of change. By others, the community activists were viewed as defenders of the status quo, though often in less favorable terms. Further, most believed that these activists were disproportionately influential, did not represent a broad constituency, but had direct and longstanding links to people of power in the county. Said one community activist:

> The big problem, the big mistake that they made was to go off and try to basically reinvent an ordinance for a very established community . . . and come up with new terminology, new phrases, new concepts. They're going to redo everything and it caused a firestorm both in the civic community and the development community and it took them the longest time to back away from that.

Do you think the new zoning ordinance will be adopted?

Despite the well-understood and widely recognized controversy, most still believed the revised zoning ordinance would be adopted. But staff remained concerned. Noting that the next countywide election was only eighteen months away, staff worried about getting the new zoning ordinance through the planning board, county council's committee, and the county council before election politics stymied the entire process. Trying to get the new ordinance passed after the election of a new slate of council members was something nearly every one wanted to avoid. But not everyone. While no one expressed intent to slow the process as a means to kill the whole effort, several expressed suspicions that others intended to do so. Said one staffer:

> We have backtracked on so many accounts to try and make this palatable to the huge majority of people . . . I don't think they should still be opposed to it. But the fact that there's still so much flexibility in it. I mean they're just saying things that we totally disagree with them on. But they run a lot of ground. The internet is an amazing tool. They can reach a lot of people with it. And we're up against such a tight time deadline and that's what really has me scared.

What do you think are the most important lessons you have learned from the Montgomery County zoning code revision process?

Opinions on the lessons to be drawn from the Montgomery County experience varied widely but a few issues came up many times. All agreed that the process was arduous and demanding; some felt that was an important lesson. Said one lawyer/developer:

> You shouldn't shy away from a comprehensive revisiting of . . . institutions like the zoning ordinance. . . . But when you do them you should understand that they are multiyear, multieffort undertakings hence therefore can only be done sort of once in a generation . . . . You know it's easy to suggest a monumental undertaking until you have endured one and realized how monumental in fact that it is.

No one expressed major disappointment with the administration of the process. Most felt the staff performed admirably; no one thought there weren't enough public meetings or that the county did not skillfully use both conventional and social media. Most felt the Zoning Advisory Panel served a useful purpose, though some complained about not getting materials in time to read before meetings.

More than a few focused on politics and the chasm that grew between some community activists and planning leadership. Said one community activist:

> The answer is you've got to have people in charge that have political antenna. If you're going to let arrogance and hubris get in the way, you're going to have nothing but trouble in river city.

There is no disputing that in zoning reform, politics matters. And it would be hard to dispute that it therefore should be handled delicately or that it is probably better not to change the planning board chair, planning department director, and the project leader in the middle of the process. But the process survived, and there are those who would argue that the change in leadership—from a team of protagonists to a team of executioners—has served the county well.

Finally, there was this lament from a member of the staff:

> It probably would have been more helpful if we talked to a few more jurisdictions that had done a zoning code rewrite to find out the lessons they learned because I don't think there was kind of an argument when we first started whether we were really going to wrap this code and write just a brand new code that bore very little resemblance to the current code or whether we were mainly trying to make this one easier to use, easier to read, easier to understand.

As with any important change in public policy, the process of zoning reform in Montgomery County has engaged individuals with a variety of perspectives, bringing to the surface some strongly held views and eliciting conflict. Despite the conflicts and other changes in personnel, the reform process in Montgomery County appears on track, though still some distance from complete. As the process moves from what has largely involved a relatively small number of stakeholders and staff to the broader political arena, it is certain to engage a broader constituency and encounter new political challenges. This could change the dynamic and significantly alter the narrative. From our perspective, and from what we have observed from a variety of sources, the story goes something like this.

The impetus for zoning reform in Montgomery County came from the chair of the planning board and accelerated with the arrival of a new and aggressive planning director. The county council approved the allocation of resources to move the process forward—including substantial dedication of staff time, the hiring of a consultant, the engagement of students from the University of Maryland, and the formation of a Zoning Advisory Panel to provide stakeholder input. But it is fair to say that the impetus for reform came from within, not from the public at large.

The process of developing the draft ordinance was long, tedious, and contentious. It survived extensive turnover in the membership of the Zoning Advisory Panel, the lead staff member, the planning director, the planning board chair, the dismissal of a consultant, and some ugly interpersonal exchanges in the press. Even before the process was complete, an innovative new Commercial-Residential zone was adopted to accommodate a major new and nationally acclaimed edge city. Provisions to allow accessory units were also adopted in advance of the complete zoning revision. As a result, important changes in the zoning ordinance already took place long before the new draft zoning ordinance went to the planning board or county council.

As with most documents produced through a public process, the final product satisfies none of the stakeholders completely. The new draft ordinance retains much of its Euclidean character, but with fewer zones, a digital representation, and far fewer footnotes, and with aspects of incentive, form-based, and performance zoning woven in. Most significant is the fact that, while the new zoning code will have been significantly simplified, planning staff estimate it will have little impact on 95 percent of property in the county. There are those who will view this lack of more sweeping change as a measure of success, but many—including most of those who championed the effort—will view it as disappointing and a missed opportunity. Why—in a county with a national reputation as an innovator in land use policy—was it not possible to achieve more extensive policy change?

The answer is not simple. Change is hard—especially in communities with active and informed citizens with long-held beliefs. That's certainly the case in Montgomery County. Consistent with its national reputation, Montgomery County is a place where active citizens show up at every public meeting, well informed, and primed for debate. But these participants are often not representative of the general public. More than half of the residents of Montgomery County are now nonwhite and 65 percent are less than forty-four years old. The Zoning Advisory Panel, in contrast, was almost exclusively white, wealthy, and over forty. What's more, many of the innovative policies for which Montgomery County is widely known focus more on conservation than on development: specifically, Wedges and Corridors, the rural reserve, the transferable development rights program, and the adequate public facilities ordinance, all of which are generally designed to prevent development and preserve the status quo—not to encourage dense development, facilitate infill, or stimulate the transformation of low-density suburbs into mixed-use town centers. Given the political forces at work in Montgomery County it is perhaps not surprising that the agricultural reserve was preserved, that residential regulations were largely unchanged, and that overall densities remained largely intact. Only in commercial districts, where few residents live, was there political will for significant change.

We offer a few "lessons learned" from this case study of zoning reform. First, it seems as though it would have been helpful to clarify the objectives and build consensus early on in the process. In the Montgomery County case, it was clear that the proponents of zoning reform had a twofold objective: to improve the zoning ordinance and to change development patterns in the county. There was clear consensus on the former, but a clear lack of consensus on the latter. Stanley himself lamented that the county had not gone through some sort of visioning exercise that might have led to more of a consensus on the need for a change in the development pattern. Without such a clear consensus, many of the documents produced by staff had to place far greater emphasis on fixing the zoning ordinance and not fixing development patterns. This ambiguity in intent seemed to be the elephant in the room at every public meeting.

Second, it may be advantageous to separate the critique of zoning regulation from the critique of development patterns. Montgomery County seems to have done this by default. The major substantive changes in the zoning ordinance are the introduction of the new family of CR zones, the loosening of restrictions in accessory units, and the reformation of parking standards. To a large degree these improvements were made outside of the formal zoning reformation process and adopted ahead of schedule. With those achievements largely complete, the remainder of the process can focus on fixing and simplifying the zoning ordinance.

Third, expectations should be constrained. Significant policy change is often incremental; land use policy change perhaps especially so. It is not surprising that residents would resist change in the character of their neighborhoods. Zoning is, by design, a tool created to prevent change. Even in what is often considered one of the most progressive jurisdictions in the nation, changes in plans and zoning regulations often focus on key nodes, corridors, and other activity centers, leaving low-density single-family neighborhoods largely untouched.

NOTES

1. New York City Department of City Planning, *About Zoning*, 2011, http://www.nyc.gov/html/D.C.:p/html/zone/zonehis.shtml. See also Stanislaw J. Makielski Jr., *The Politics of Zoning: The New York Experience* (New York: Columbia University Press, 1966), 7 ("New York City's Zoning Resolution of 1916 was a major innovation in municipal public policy. It was the product of municipal reform, a set of responses to complex economic and social problems, and the claims of local and special interests").

2. *Lincoln Trust Co. v. Williams Building Corporation*, 128 N.E. 209 (N.Y. 1920).

3. Michael Allan Wolf, *The Zoning of America: Euclid v. Ambler 29* (Lawrence: University Press of Kansas, 2008).

4. See, e.g., W. A. Fischel, *The Economics of Zoning Laws: A Property Rights Approach to American Land Use Controls* (Baltimore: Johns Hopkins University Press, 1985); K. Ih-

lanfeldt, "Exclusionary Land Use Regulations within Suburban Communities: A Review of the Evidence and Policy Prescriptions," *Urban Studies* 41, no. 2 (2004): 461–83; G. Knaap, S. Meck, T. Moore, and R. Parker, *Zoning as a Barrier to Multifamily Housing Development* (Chicago: American Planning Association, 2007).

5. See http://www.psrc.org/growth/hip/alltools/perf-zoning/.

6. See http://www.choosemontgomerymd.com/business-community/federal-government.

7. See Eli Knaap, Chengri Ding, and Yi Niu, "Polycentrism as a Sustainable Development Strategy: Empirical Analysis from the State of Maryland," University of Maryland.

8. See Montgomery County Trendsheet: Housing Monitor, 2013, http://www.montgomery planning.org/research/data_library/trendsheets/documents/housing-monitor-apr-2013 .pdf.

9. Winner of the Maryland chapter of the American Planning Association's Outstanding Project or Program award (November 2009).

10. Report available at http://www.montgomeryplanning.org/development/zoning /documents/ParkingStudyPacket.pdf.

CHAPTER 4

The Personal Decisions That Govern Sprawl

MATTHEW SALENGER

Key Points and Practice Takeaways

1. A survey of 101 residents in Phoenix, one of the most sprawling cities in the United States, asked residents about living preferences, lifestyle choices, and how they "connect" to the city.

2. People living close to urban centers tend to support local cultural and social communities; those residing on the outskirts tend to maintain a connection to the surrounding natural landscape; and those living in between tend not to connect to either cultural or natural features, producing a vast "middle zone" of disengaged communities.

3. The middle-zone communities tend to shop, dine, and entertain themselves in shopping malls and national chain establishments. They are more content with where they live, but also much more likely to move away.

4. Mobility creates a need for familiarity at every destination, thus creating a market for national chains and regularized architecture.

5. People living disconnected from the cultural and/or natural landscape still shape the politics, economics, cultures, and aesthetics of a city through their actions (and/or inactions). We must recognize the causes of

disengagement and find a way to reengage the mobile middle class. By doing so, we can positively affect all aspects of urban life.

Sprawl has been blamed for all kinds of social, economic, and environmental problems. High levels of poor air quality, low physical fitness, social isolationism, heat-island effects, urban decay, and widespread apathy have all been attributed to sprawl.

So why do so many people choose to live in sprawl? We sought to answer that question by interviewing 101 residents of Phoenix, Arizona—one of the most sprawling metropolitan areas in the United States—about their individual choices as they relate to suburban sprawl.[1] Our project is based on the idea that we each control our environment through separate, individual choices concerning where and how we live. In a variety of ways, these individual decisions combine to create the culture, politics, economy, and aesthetics of sprawl.

This was not a stratified, random-sample survey to be used to generalize about the living preferences of all residents in sprawling places. Our purpose, rather, was to use the survey results to formulate hypotheses and dig deeper into the possible associations between living preference, individual decision-making, and the perpetuation of sprawl. We wanted to find ways to express the impact of those individual decisions, which, taken together, have been damaging.

Mobile suburban inhabitants often do not act in the best interests of the natural and urban environment. Their decisions have an effect that reaches beyond personal domains, as diagrammed in figure 4.1. Our hope is that this research will help planners, developers, and policy makers, as well as anyone living in sprawl, to better understand the ways in which resident choices, everyday decisions, and lifestyle preferences reflect the broader implications of sprawl. We also hope our results reach people in a much more personal way, ultimately helping them make better decisions about where and how to live in order to create a more sustainable city.

This project was undertaken by a design firm, Colab Studio, working with students and faculty at Arizona State University.[2] The research covered all of Metropolitan Phoenix and included participants from Buckeye, Wittman, Anthem, Apache Junction, Gilbert, Laveen, and everywhere in between. We broke the city into three different zones (see figure 4.2):

Zone 1 (z1): Downtown cores of Phoenix, Glendale, Scottsdale, Mesa, and Tempe, and areas between these cores. We considered these areas to be centrally located and containing higher densities of housing, entertainment venues, commercial centers, cultural venues, and major sports facilities.

Zone 2 (z2): Outside of Zone 1 and within the 101 and 202 loop freeways. We considered these areas outside the urban core but not at the outer edge.

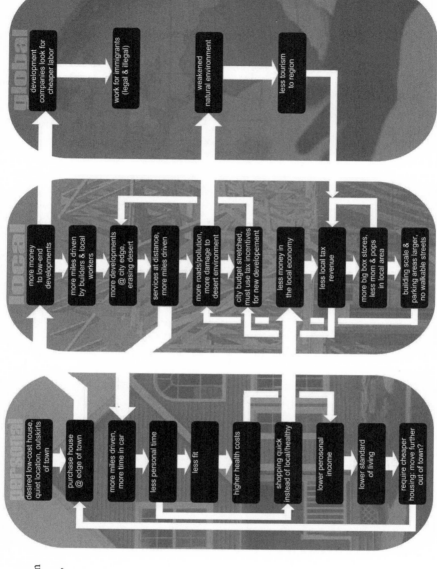

FIGURE 4.1.
This flow chart, which is based on an amalgam of Zone 3 participants' decisions may affect their lives, the region, and the world.
Author's graphic.

personal

desired low-cost house, quiet location, outskirts of town → purchase house @ edge of town → more miles driven, more time in car → less personal time → less fit → higher health costs → shopping quick instead of local/healthy → lower personal income → lower standard of living → require cheaper housing: move further out of town?

local

more money to low-end developments → more miles driven by builders & local workers → more developments @ city edge, erasing desert → services at distance, more miles driven → more roads/pollution, more damage to desert environment → city budget stretched, must use tax incentives for new developement → less money in the local economy → less local tax revenue → more big box stores, less mom & pops in local area → building scale & parking areas larger, no walkable streets

global

development companies look for cheaper labor → work for immigrants (legal & illegal)

weakened natural environment → less tourism to region

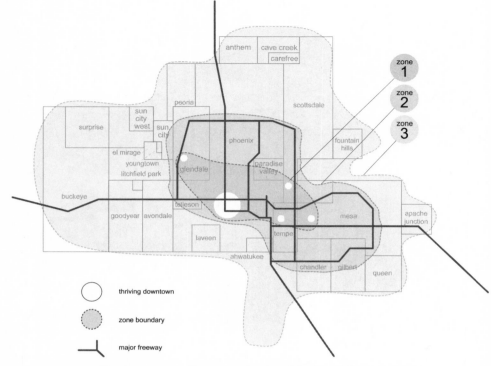

FIGURE 4.2. The three metropolitan zones developed for this study of metropolitan Phoenix.
Author's graphic.

Zone 3 (z3): Suburban areas of Metropolitan Phoenix outside of Zone 1 and Zone 2 including "bedroom community" developments such as Anthem, Wittman, Queen Creek, and Laveen.

The survey contained sixteen questions:

1. Where do you live?
2. How long have you lived at your current location?
3. What factor(s) contributed to your decision to live where you reside? (Consider not just the city in which you live, but the particular location within that city.)
4. Where do you mostly shop for: groceries, clothes, necessities, etc.?
5. Where do you mostly dine out?
6. What are the entertainment/commercial events that are most important to you (sporting, cultural, concerts, lectures, museums, libraries, etc.)?

7. How would you describe your level of contentment with your current living location?
8. Would you rather live somewhere else (locally or nationally), and what is keeping you from moving there?
9. How often do you speak to your neighbors (people within a five-minute walking distance from your home)?
10. How do you feel about your relative fitness, and how does your living location help or hinder your fitness?
11. Approximately how many miles per year do you put on your vehicle?
12. Where do you mostly vacation (in state, out of state)?
13. How do you feel about the aesthetics of your neighborhood?
14. Do you see your neighborhood improving or declining (speaking long-term, irrespective of the economic downturn)?
15. Do you see Metropolitan Phoenix improving or declining (speaking long-term, irrespective of the economic downturn)?
16. Do you see suburban growth on the outskirts of town as a positive or negative?

We collected a total of 101 surveys ($z1 = 44$, $z2 = 37$, $z3 = 20$; total $= 101$), across nearly every municipality within the Valley of the Sun. The interviews were completed in May and June 2011. We also asked for participants' range of age, sex, and economic level to ensure a wide spectrum of types of participants. We collected two interviews from nondocumented immigrants and three homeless residents of Phoenix. We attempted to be as diverse as possible, utilizing racially diverse and multilingual research team members.

All participants' names were coded within the analyzed data to protect anonymity with a number chosen at random between 1 and 110. Thus, research notes are provided by interview number and question numbers 1 through 16 (e.g., 58.16 indicates interview participant #58, answer to question #16). Research is also cited via percentages of participants organized by the three zones (e.g., $z1 = 50$ percent indicates 50 percent of the participants in Zone 1 provided a particular answer).

Hypothesis #1: The Separated Middle

The most surprising finding our research uncovered is how people in Zone 2 tend to be much less connected to a sense of community, culture, and environment than those living in other areas of the city, even those on the outskirts. We expected people living downtown to have a raised sense of connection to culture and community, which would diminish as one moved toward the perimeter. However, we found that those living in Zone 2, the middle area between downtown and the outskirts, have a significantly lower sense of place than those in Zone 3.

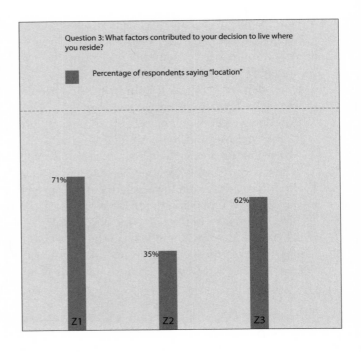

Question 3: What factors contributed to your decision to live where you reside?

Percentage of respondents saying "location"

71%

62%

35%

Z1   Z2   Z3

For instance, when asked what aspects led to a participant's decision on where to buy or rent their home, we found people in Zone 2 were far less likely to answer that "location" was a determining factor than people close to downtown or outskirt areas (see figure 4.3; $z_1 = 71$ percent, $z_2 = 35$ percent, $z_3 = 62$ percent). To people in the middle zone, it seems less important where they live, or what is around them, but rather it is just that the home fits their needs. Also interestingly, people in Zone 2 were most likely to be content about where they are living at a surprising 91 percent (see figure 4.4; $z_1 = 79$ percent, $z_2 = 91$ percent, $z_3 = 76$ percent), yet also far more likely to want to live somewhere else ($z_1 = 50$ percent, $z_2 = 73$ percent, $z_3 = 19$ percent). What this suggests is Zone 2 residents are uncommitted to a particular place or community, and seem content to live that way. They appear to be flexible about staying or leaving.

Zone 2 residents also tend to prefer stores and restaurants that are national chains over locally owned businesses (see figure 4.5). When we asked participants to tell us where they shopped for food, clothes, and necessities, the highest percentage of nationally franchised (chain) stores occurred in answers from Zone 2 respondents at 97 percent ($z_1 = 88$ percent, $z_2 = 97$ percent, $z_3 = 76$ percent). Conversely, the lowest amount of nonchain locations occurred in the answers of Zone 2 participants as well, at 17 percent ($z_1 = 23$ percent, $z_2 = 17$ percent, $z_3 = 24$ percent).

Similarly, Zone 2 participants are 50 percent more likely to dine at a chain

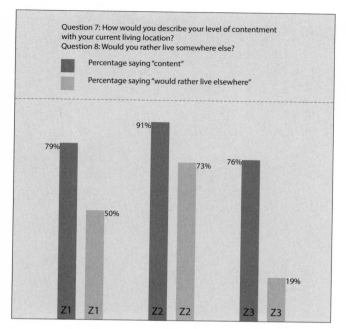

FIGURE 4.4.
Zone 2 respondents seem to contradict themselves in being content and yet wanting to move elsewhere.
Author's graphic.

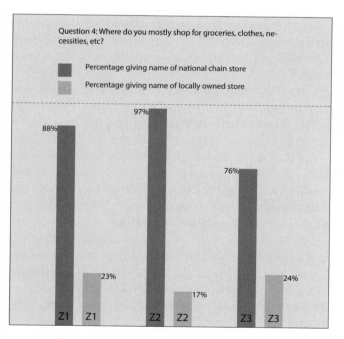

FIGURE 4.5.
Zone 2 respondents overwhelmingly favor shopping at national chains over locally owned shops.
Author's graphic.

FIGURE 4.6.
Dining locally is
preferred toward
the core.
Author's graphic.

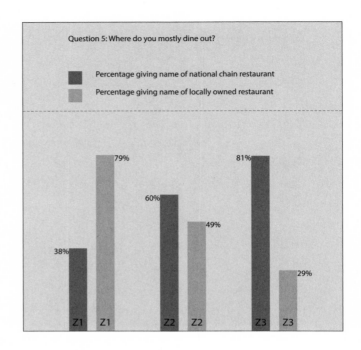

Question 5: Where do you mostly dine out?

■ Percentage giving name of national chain restaurant
▨ Percentage giving name of locally owned restaurant

79% 60% 81% 49% 38% 29%

Z1 Z1 Z2 Z2 Z3 Z3

restaurant than people living in downtown areas (see figure 4.6; $z_1 = 38$ percent, $z_2 = 60$ percent, $z_3 = 81$ percent). And, unlike Zone 3 dwellers, most Zone 2 residents often have a conveniently located locally owned option and still seem to gravitate toward chains.

When asked to name where they shop for their groceries and necessities, one z_2 resident said, "medications and things at Walgreen's, which is a about a mile from our house. And other things, what—Walmart? (Husband responds from other room with 'Walmart and Costco'), which is about two miles. And, then, yeah, we go to Costco." Another spoke about big box chain stores as an attractor: "Where I lived prior to this was kind of Central Phoenix, which was kind of near the Biltmore, but the reason I was okay with leaving there was because the area where I'm at now has developed a lot more. I mean they put in a Target within the last 4 years. There's a bunch of new restaurants to eat at."

While big box stores are frequented everywhere, Zone 2 residents show the most skepticism toward locally owned businesses, including one respondent stating, "you cannot just wander into a mom and pop and think it's going to be awesome, because you might get horrible, horrible food poisoning."

In addition to the lack of shopping at locally owned businesses, Zone 2 residents appear far less likely to visit local cultural organizations, such as museums, performance venues, libraries, and community events (see figure 4.7). They even appear less likely to visit such venues than those living in z_3 ($z_1 =$

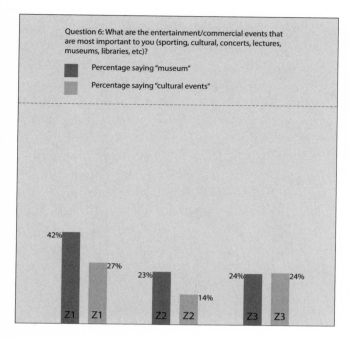

FIGURE 4.7.
Respondents in
Zone 2 indicated
less interest in
local culture than
respondents in
Zone 3 and Zone 1,
which are nearly
equal.
Author's graphic.

Within the figure:

Question 6: What are the entertainment/commercial events that are most important to you (sporting, cultural, concerts, lectures, museums, libraries, etc)?

■ Percentage saying "museum"

▨ Percentage saying "cultural events"

42% Z1 27% Z1 23% Z2 14% Z2 24% Z3 24% Z3

27 percent, z_2 = 14 percent, z_3 = 24 percent). People in Zone 3 support cultural institutions of Phoenix more than those in Zone 2, and show this commitment by driving an hour each way to participate.

Zone 2 residents also appear to be less likely to know their neighbors than people living in downtown areas. When asked how often they speak to people within a five-minute walking distance of their home, the highest percentage of people saying "never" were in this middle zone (z_1 = 19 percent, z_2 = 26 percent, z_3 = 14 percent). One Zone 2 respondent, who has lived in their home for fifteen years, answered, "Seldom to never. I seriously don't even know my neighbors."

Zone 2 residents also hold a slightly worse opinion about the future of the city. When asked whether Metropolitan Phoenix is improving or declining, Zone 2 participants were less likely to say "improving" (see figure 4.8; z_1 = 67 percent, z_2 = 57 percent, z_3 = 62 percent) and more likely to say "declining" (z_1 = 27 percent, z_2 = 34 percent, z_3 = 24 percent).

What the interviews reveal is that, in our survey, most people in the middle zone have a greater disconnection with the people and places of Phoenix, a less favorable outlook for Phoenix, and are far more likely to move away than those living in the other two zones.

A recent study published in the *Journal of Personality and Social Psychology* provides a possible explanation. The study found that "residential mobility breeds familiarity-seeking" in people,[3] whereby more mobile people prefer to

FIGURE 4.8.
Zone 2 respondents
hold less positive
and more negative
views of the city.
Author's graphic.

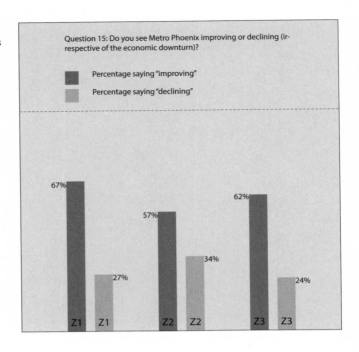

Question 15: Do you see Metro Phoenix improving or declining (irrespective of the economic downturn)?

■ Percentage saying "improving"
■ Percentage saying "declining"

67% | 27% | Z1 Z1
57% | 34% | Z2 Z2
62% | 24% | Z3 Z3

live in cities and areas containing national chains they are acquainted with out of a desire to balance the unknown appearance of their new town. This suggests that mobile people tend to move in and out of locations within multiple cities that have less connection to a sense of place. Large areas of sprawl, between culturally accented downtowns and suburban outskirts, might be likely to have populations living disconnected from the social cohesion of the communities in which they live.

While it may seem possible that some of the disconnection with the city may relate to life-cycle position and/or immediate availability of options (for culture, shopping, dining, etc.), the wide range of ages and income levels of our participants suggests otherwise. It appears people who desire connection to the city in which they live actively seek it out, whereas others who don't value such links do not, thereby isolating themselves. Because respondents in Zone 2 have weaker connections to key aspects of Phoenix, and are less involved with the community, their answers suggest they are less likely to be active participants in the effort to remedy suburban sprawl.

Hypothesis #2: People Who Need People

Our findings produced some familiar results about the preferences of people living around downtown cores, where respondents expressed typical sentiments about the benefits of living close to the center.

One clear benefit of living centrally is the greater number of choices that exist for cultural and social engagement. As stated above, people in Zone 1 are more likely to support local businesses. When asked where people dine out, for instance, Zone 1 participants were far more likely to frequent a nonchain business (z_1 = 79 percent, z_2 = 49 percent, z_3 = 39 percent). As one Zone 1 participant stated, "It's just been important for us to identify those businesses that are part of our local community . . . we are proponents of supporting local businesses." Many seemed aware that supporting local business is critical to a local economy (indeed Local First Arizona has shown that for every $100 spent at a locally owned business $43 remains local, versus $13 spent at a non–locally owned business).[4]

People in Zone 1 are also more likely to be involved with local social and cultural venues and amenities. When asked what factors contributed to the decision of where to live, one Zone 1 participant stated, "I lived down here (downtown) for ten years before this new home, so I've lived down here for a while and I wanted to stay down here. I work downtown. And, well, central Phoenix as well. Just the amenities, the culture. There's First Fridays, the bars and restaurants and all that stuff. Also the homes are all different, so I liked that." This sentiment reflected a recurring theme of people wanting to stay close to downtown once they live there. Another Zone 1 participant echoed these remarks, saying they chose to live downtown "because it's more diverse. It's where the action is. Because of the art, and a lot of the entrepreneurs, a lot of the creative class have come to downtown Phoenix."

The number of participants seeking museums is also much higher in Zone 1 (z_1 = 42 percent, z_2 = 23 percent, z_3 = 24 percent). Perhaps consistent with this, people living in Zone 1 also seem to utilize movie theaters less than other zones as a source of entertainment (z_1 = 15 percent, z_2 = 34 percent, z_3 = 33 percent). And while shopping malls are used as a form of entertainment for Zones 2 and 3, not a single one of our Zone 1 respondents said they visit a mall for this reason. This suggests Zone 1 residents are more engaged and connected to the social and cultural fabric of the city.

Hypothesis #3: Connected to the Landscape

As opposed to the social and cultural connections prevalent in Zone 1, many people living on the outskirts trade social engagement for awareness of the desert environment. The pristine Sonoran landscape around Phoenix is still a huge draw for people moving from other parts of the country. We encountered many people living at the edge of the city who moved there for the purpose of "escaping" the city and being close to the Sonoran environment.

Most of the people interested in living close to the desert were more affluent than average, with household incomes above $100,000 per year. Nearly all work within Zones 1 or 2 and have very long commute times. As one Zone 3 person stated, they moved just outside the built edge of town for "the land, the openness, the quietness, just all around the valley I guess. And getting out of the city—nice and calm, quiet out there. Because I live on 2 acres of land out in the middle of the desert. I like my space." Later on, the same person spoke about their distance to amenities, saying, "[it's] a 15-mile drive to the nearest town."

Another person provided several reasons for moving to North Scottsdale, saying, "The lot we found is in the desert. It's very private and it's just a perfect location, gated community . . . the area sits high, so it's cooler up here in summer time . . . and the views and scenery." A resident in New River told us he moved there because they are "out in the desert. It's nice. I get a lot of exercise because I'm out in the desert and have a chance to run and mountain bike." A person living in the northeast corner of Mesa moved there "because I'm still up north, so it's far enough out to where I still get stars at night. My kids go to a good school. And I'm close to the lake. I have a boat, so we go to the lake all the time. Canyon Lake's right there."

Hypothesis #4: On the Outskirts of Town

Not everyone has the ability to appreciate the landscape. Our research uncovered many people who moved to Zone 3 for financial reasons. There are new communities on the outskirts in areas with dense lots and little connection to the natural desert. Such developments are built on relatively cheap land, with inexpensive materials and labor, cost efficiencies resulting from minimal impact fees and ease of development approval, all providing lower costs to consumers. Over twice the percentage of Zone 3 over Zone 1 respondents said they chose their home for financial reasons (z_1 = 17 percent, z_2 = 28 percent, z_3 = 38 percent).

In many ways, the outskirts isolate residents from the larger metropolitan area. New developments are sometimes isolating because neighborhoods have not yet matured and contain few, if any, authentic public attractions. In addition, many typical contemporary developments are not planned to provide for social interaction, lacking walkable community spaces and social or community "cores." Also, most of the houses are patio homes, meaning they have almost no exterior yard space. Thus there is little incentive to spend time outside the home.

Our research suggests people living in Zone 3 are highly isolated from the communities they live in. Of the respondents we spoke to, Zone 3 individuals

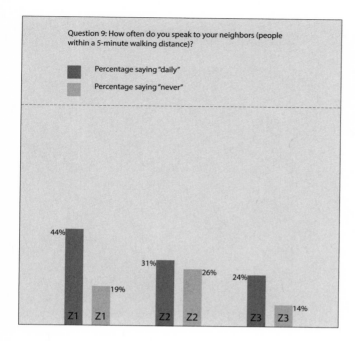

Question 9: How often do you speak to your neighbors (people within a 5-minute walking distance)?

■ Percentage saying "daily"
■ Percentage saying "never"

44% Z1
19% Z1
31% Z2
26% Z2
24% Z3
14% Z3

FIGURE 4.9. Respondents in Zone 2 experience greater isolation than those in Zone 1 or Zone 3. *Author's graphic.*

had the lowest percentage of daily connection with their neighbors (see figure 4.9; $z1 = 44$ percent, $z2 = 31$ percent, $z3 = 24$ percent). We have observed several developments, particularly in areas such as Laveen and Buckeye, where homes are densely arranged, with no part of the house opening to the street except a large garage door and a small, recessed front entry door with no front-facing windows. People often drive into their garage, close the overhead door, and enter their homes through an interior door, completely bypassing any connection to the neighborhood. In such developments, long streets filled with identical impervious front facades are often completely devoid of street life. Privacy and the desire for personal vehicles in a secure location seem paramount.

When asked how often they speak with their neighbors, one Zone 3 resident in Buckeye said, "Oh man. I would say once a year. . . . We hardly know any of our neighbors at all. Yeah, it's sad." Another respondent said, "People just generally aren't outdoors. Like, you could walk around outside right now and it's just dead. There's nothing. There's nobody walking around outside." A person living in Laveen told us, "Everyone just pulls into the garage and the garage closes. Some people we don't ever see because they just go in their house and they don't really go outside or socialize. In three years, that is intense."

When we asked people to name where they go for entertainment and/or culture, we were surprised to hear shopping malls as an answer. Not a single Zone 1 person provided this answer, and twice as many Zone 3 people gave

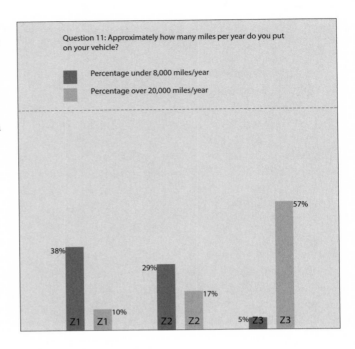

FIGURE 4.10.
Zone 3 respondents drive far more miles and create much more pollution than those who live closer to downtown areas.
Author's graphic.

this response as those in Zone 2 areas (z_1 = 0 percent, z_2 = 11 percent, z_3 = 20 percent). Perhaps the lack of cultural amenities in these areas stimulates a need to satisfy social connection via shopping. To the degree that shopping is an individual act, this may in turn result in a weakened sense of community for those living in the metropolitan edge.

Living on the outskirts also seems to create costly expense in the form of added fuel costs for residents driving greater distances for work, shopping, amenities, schools, and socializing. According to our estimates, the number of miles driven by Zone 3 residents is much higher than the national average of 13,500 miles per year (source: U.S. Department of Transportation website).[5] Respondents in Zone 1 were more than seven times more likely than people in Zone 3 to drive under 8,000 miles per year (see figure 4.10; z_1 = 38 percent, z_2 = 29 percent, z_3 = 5 percent). Conversely, Zone 3 people were overwhelmingly more likely to drive more than 20,000 miles each year (z_1 = 10 percent, z_2 = 17 percent, z_3 = 57 percent). And, as we found, many Zone 3 respondents drive larger than average cars, often trucks or sports utility vehicles (SUVs).

As an example, one respondent living in Zone 3 owns a house on the far northwest corner of the metropolitan area, north of Verrado in Buckeye. This person works fairly centrally, close to Zone 1. Because this participant and her spouse often travel with an RV camper, they own a large diesel SUV to pull it. This person drives over 70 miles each way to go to work in their SUV. They estimated their average annual mileage was over 30,000. At an estimated 12 miles per gallon for fuel efficiency of their vehicle, this equates to 2,500 gallons of fuel at an annual cost of $8,750 (at $3.50/gallon).

Many of the respondents from Zone 3 drove much more than 20,000 miles each year. One respondent in Buckeye said they drive more than 25,000 miles; one in Anthem said they also drive over 25,000 miles; and a respondent in Peoria said they drive over 35,000 miles. In an interview a person from New River said they drive over 40,000 miles each year. These reports amount to an estimated combined carbon dioxide output of over 132,000 pounds from just these five vehicles annually, based on an average fuel efficiency of 18 MPG.

People living on the outskirts, however, are very willing to handle large commutes. When asked why they chose their area to live, one person in the extremely distant suburb of Anthem with an annual household income over $100,000 said, "Well, my husband works in Scottsdale, right at the bend of the 101, right when it goes from eastbound to southbound, and we couldn't afford to live in Scottsdale, but we wanted him to be able to be home for dinner. And so we thought, okay, 30 minutes is the longest commute." She continued, "My commute on the days that I go into the office is about 40 miles round trip. And then his is about 60 miles round trip," making their daily commute as long as 100 miles per day combined. Even if they get an average of 20 miles per gallon in their vehicles, this would cost about $17.50 per day, or approximately $365 per month, for the commuting fuel alone.

Those costs, along with time spent driving, seem worth it because of what they gain in home amenities. They told us, "it would be hard for us to afford the size of house that we need for our family close to town." Another Zone 3 participant said of their home, "I guess you would call it a cookie-cutter home, and there's probably five houses that I could throw a baseball to that look exactly like my house. . . . So [it] just loses a little personality, but that doesn't mean I'm any less comfortable." Another person living on the outskirts explained why they moved further out of town by saying, "When I looked out here, I got a lot more. I get a nice place with a little . . . better amenities. There's a nice clubhouse. There's a nice pool. . . . There's a trail right around here [for] biking."

When asked how content they are with their home, another outer Zone 2 participant said, "a 7 or 8 right now. Some of that [negative score] is due to most of my friends [living] in Central Phoenix. I work in Tempe. So it's purely location. It's a little bit further than I would like. . . . Working down here it's doubled my trip, but like I said, the house is worth it. Just to have your own everything— there's a pool, a yard, stuff like that, outweighs a couple restaurants." Owning a larger house with individualized amenities seems to be a higher priority than most other considerations.

There seems to be a connection between the desire for a larger house, escaping from the city, and personal isolation. A Zone 3 respondent from the edge of

Mesa said, "I can drive into the city, [and] come back out so I can get away from everything." This separation then permeates the entire family, including children. The participant added, "we really don't do much, you know. We download a lot of movies. We don't really go out too much. If my kids want to go out to the movies, I take them out to the movies." The respondent also believed they were different from most people, even those around them. When asked whether they speak to their neighbors, the respondent said, "I don't know, because people, they're not really into what we do. You know?" The desire for the perceived benefits of an isolated lifestyle seems to be a worthwhile draw for some people, even when it means separation from the larger community.

Hypothesis #5: Mixed Feelings

We asked everyone we interviewed to give us their general impression of sprawl. People from every zone provided negative answers, though these feelings were less common among those living toward the city's edge. Sometimes people were aware of a certain inner conflict over sprawl, yet still choose to live within it. As one person in Zone 3 explained, "I shouldn't be the one talking—I think it's bad. But here I am living on the outskirts anyway. So it's like do as I say, not as I do sort of thing. . . . I feel like normally I would have said everything needs to be denser, toward the center." People in Zone 1 tended to think of sprawl in negative terms (although not uniformly), with sentiments like "it's not environmentally responsible" and "[the way we build] has got to sometime change. There has to be a shift."

Counter to this sentiment, most people living on the outskirts of town overwhelmingly saw this type of development as positive. One Zone 3 person felt "it's positive overall because it's going to bring more business into this state . . . if you don't have the suburban [development] then you can't fund all the work and jobs that are here." Another Zone 3 participant felt that sprawl is positive because "it definitely allows for more people to want to come here, and move here . . . in a comfortable warm environment. So, yeah. I would say it's positive. Not everybody wants to live in the city." Another Zone 3 resident suggested the growth is positive because "we would never run out of land, you know. You could just go on forever." Consistent with this view, the expansion of freeways was seen positively, as with a respondent from Apache Junction who felt "the freeway systems [are] improving, which is going to bring in more industry hopefully, which can only be good." A person from Laveen remarked, "When the highway comes in and the real estate people come in and start building, it will be very positive."

A few people in Zone 1 also had positive things to say about outward growth. Multiple respondents felt growth was important for economic stability. One Zone 1 participant said, "I think it's positive because it is development that's going to allow Metropolitan Phoenix to continue to be a highly competitive economic place. . . . If we didn't have that, if we stopped it, a million prices would go up and we would lose some of our competitive advantages. So I think it's important it continues, it just has to continue maybe in more responsible ways." Another Zone 1 person equated development with improvement, saying simply that "growth is improvement." And another Zone 1 native of Phoenix told us, "I see Metro Phoenix continuing to grow. Continuing to rejuvenate itself. . . . I just hope that in that progression we can still keep that small town feel where people can still raise their kids, have a sense of community, have a great sense of celebrating the diversity that is here, and being . . . just being a great place to live." One resident in Zone 2 explained how growth on the outskirts is a positive alternative to an eroding downtown, saying, "I think it is a good thing if you have growth. When I go into the center of Phoenix or the center of places and see it kind of becoming desolate, or a lot of empty things, it makes me sad because I know there are a lot of problems with that. And you see people losing hope in an area like that where there is no work."

Some residents of Zones 2 and 3 had negative views of the downtown areas. A respondent from Zone 3 remarked: "The central areas are definitely declining . . . when I grew up in Chandler, in Hartford and Shannon Street, that was a really nice neighborhood. And I know now it's definitely not as desirable . . . there's more crime and that kind of thing." Another person, from Zone 2, said there was more crime and less safety in the downtown area, stating, "I see so many drug addicts walking the streets . . . that's why I want to go to the north and get into a community where you know, or at least it's hidden."

Overall, perceptions of sprawl varied widely. Opinions varied based on what criteria residents used. If a respondent chose to view outward growth as a symbol of freedom, of living in "open space," the impression of sprawl was positive—an extension of manifest destiny. If a respondent chose to examine sprawl from an environmental or traffic-congestion point of view, the impression was negative.

The variety and duality of these views is summed up well in a response we received from a 20-year resident of Laveen, in Zone 3. When asked if sprawl is a positive or a negative, they answered, "Both. I think it is positive because it shows growth. It shows people are moving out here and doing well and creating more community elsewhere in Arizona—rather than . . . congesting one particular area. At the same time, spreading out is not the best because it keeps us all separated." And when asked whether Metropolitan Phoenix is improving or declining, the respondent seemed to sum up the complexity of respondents' views:

I kind of see it as both. I see it as improving in many ways where the city is spreading further out and I think there are some other suburbs that have emerged that did not exist when I first moved here that are really nice. I think it is declining in the fact that they wanted to build up the whole downtown area and it never really happened. . . . So it is good that we are spread out, but it is also bad that we are spread out because you have to travel from one place to another and there is no sense of [the city's] heart. . . . But I still don't see that walking traffic, true downtown area, that they wanted to have. I think they need [that]. I think they really desperately need it to understand what Phoenix is.

Phoenix is a sprawling metropolis, spread out over nearly 17,000 square miles. At the height of construction before the economic downturn, it was said that an acre of desert was lost every hour to development. The environmental consequences of this, including rising pollution levels, reports of asthma in children, and loss of agricultural land, are well known.[6] Currently, there is something of a paradigm shift happening that emphasizes the need to increase density and walkability in downtown areas in an attempt to counteract the spread of sprawl and promote greater central-area vitality. But as our survey showed, both the expansion of suburban development and the creation of walkable urban areas are issues that affect individual choices and preferences in complex, sometimes contradictory ways.

Particularly pressing is the need to reach the mobile, often disconnected residents living in Zone 2. This zone not only has little connection to the natural desert environment that defines the region but also appears to be far less connected to social and cultural organizations and communities that help give Phoenix its identity and cohesion. Zone 2, in other words, generally contains less quality of place—less desert environment and less walkable urban area. In addition, as the outer Zone 3 continues to sprawl outward, distance and separation from the desert landscape also increases, further separating residents of Zone 2.

Developing a greater sense of place takes time to develop. One approach to advancing this imperative is to increase awareness within the general public of the consequences of their living preferences—to reorient the smaller decisions residents make about where to shop, dine, and seek entertainment toward decisions that support community building and place making. An obvious way this could be significantly advanced is by focusing on the promotion of small-grain, locally owned businesses. Policymakers can promote this change by providing incentives for landowners to offer easier access for local small businesses, changing financing criteria toward locally focused lending, and supporting co-operatives of smaller businesses that create "locals-only" areas within neighborhoods.

Changing behavior, however, will require an inclusive language that promotes a "yes/and" rather than a "no/or" response. Will it be possible for people to achieve what they view as the American Dream, yet also live sustainably? Perhaps a first step toward the resolution of this perplexing task will be to ensure that residents are aware of how their everyday decisions affect and ultimately create the environments we live in.

NOTES

1. See, for example, data on Phoenix growth, Arizona Department of Economic Security, "AZDES," 2012, retrieved December 10, 2012, https://www.azdes.gov/.

2. Colab Studio is Matthew Salenger, Karl Eicher, and Maria Salenger; members of the ASU School of Art and Pyracantha Press are Dan Mayer, Prof. John Risseeuw, Prof. Mark Klett, and Patrick Vincent; research assistants from thirteen ASU students hired through a research grant from the ASU Phoenix Urban Research Laboratory are John Armendariz, Raymond Banker, Amie Dabu, Alexandra Fuentes, Kylie Huffman, Camarie Kroeger, Heather Liddle, Alison Magley, Molly Morgan, Sarah Rowland, Sharee Tavilla, Harold Thomas, Kristi Utter, and incalculably important guidance from our research guru, PhD student Angela Hines.

3. S. Oishi, F. Miao, M. Koo, J. Kisling, and K. A. Ratliff, "Residential Mobility Breeds Familiarity-Seeking," *Journal of Personality and Social Psychology* 102, no. 1 (2012): 149–62.

4. Local First AZ., "Local First AZ," 2012, retrieved December 10, 2012, http://www.localfirstaz.com/local/index.php.

5. U.S. Department of Transportation, Federal Highway Administration, accessed October 8, 2014, http://www.fhwa.dot.gov/ohim/onhoo/bar8.htm.

6. See, for example, the facts presented in Andrew Ross's book *Bird on Fire: Lessons from the World's Least Sustainable City* (New York: Oxford University Press, 2011).

Case Studies

CHAPTER 5

Urban Design Tactics for Suburban Retrofitting

JUNE WILLIAMSON

Key Points and Practice Takeaways

1. A primary lesson of the early-twenty-first-century financial crisis is that new types of economic landscapes—and attendant urban design tactics—are required to expand the economic potential of suburbanized space.

2. Practitioners and policymakers must work together to build a resilient future suburbia that is compact, climate-sensitive, pedestrian- and bike-friendly, accessible to all, and responsive to changed demographics and contemporary lifestyles and values.

3. Suburban retrofitting is not a monolithic practice. Reinhabitation, redevelopment, and regreening are three major urban design strategies to pursue, alone or in combination, depending on context, opportunities, and available resources.

4. Ten urban design tactics in support of these strategies are introduced and illustrated with built and proposed examples, many drawn from innovative ideas submitted to the 2010 Build a Better Burb competition for suburban Long Island.

5. Pursuit of these tactics supports the policy goal of "incremental metropolitanism," the gradual emergence of a robust and efficient multicentered network of retrofitted centers and corridors within an existing metropolitan region.

Historically, America's economic growth has hinged on its ability to create new development patterns, new economic landscapes that simultaneously expand space and intensify our use of it.

—RICHARD FLORIDA, foreword to
Retrofitting Suburbia: Urban Design Solutions for Redesigning Suburbs, updated ed. (2011)[1]

How might languishing areas in North American suburbs be creatively retrofitted—that is, reinhabited, redeveloped, and/or regreened—in ways that are economically productive, environmentally sensitive, socially sustainable, and aesthetically appealing? This question was at the heart of the Build a Better Burb urban design competition brief I drafted in 2010 for the nonprofit Rauch Foundation.[2] The competition sought bold new ideas for reinvigorating thousands of acres of vacant land and surface parking lots in Nassau and Suffolk counties on New York's Long Island, within suburban downtowns and adjacent to commuter rail stations.

The Long Island region, self-styled as America's "first suburb," takes pride in an identity as the birthplace of postwar suburbanization. Long Island is home to iconic Levittown and hundreds of other subdivisions of detached houses, spread across the flat plains landscape, at one time part of the most productive agricultural region in the United States.[3] The expansion of North American urban areas into their hinterlands, through land annexation by cities and the growth of suburbs, led to the emergence of vast metropolitan regions. This urbanization process, which developed hand in hand with the intensification of land use from agriculture and a suburbanized settlement pattern of residential subdivisions, office and industrial parks, and shopping centers, undoubtedly contributed to America's post–World War II economic growth. In the early twenty-first century, however, the game seems to have changed. A primary lesson of the financial crisis of 2007–8 and the consequent Great Recession is that new types of economic landscapes—and attendant urban design tactics—are required to expand the economic potential of suburbanized space, as Richard Florida suggests.

The formation of the central question in the Build a Better Burb competition, about creatively retrofitting languishing areas, stemmed from the findings of a decade of urban design research I conducted in collaboration with Ellen Dunham-Jones. We wondered what was being done across North America with its vacant big box stores, dead malls, dying commercial strips, traffic-choked edge cities, outdated office parks, and aging garden apartment complexes. For our book *Retrofitting Suburbia: Urban Design Solutions for Redesigning Suburbs*, first published in 2009 and updated in 2011, we traveled around the country to find some answers, and what we found was eye-opening. We documented and analyzed over eighty trenchant examples of suburban retrofitting that, taken together, demonstrate the significant potential for profound transformation, over time, of the unsustainable sprawling patterns of late-twentieth-century suburbanization. Since the book's publication we have collected hundreds of additional retrofit examples. North Americans spent half a century building and, in ever larger numbers, living in these suburban landscapes. The next generations will retrofit them for the new needs of this century to help build a resilient future suburbia that is compact, climate-sensitive, pedestrian- and bike-friendly, accessible to all, and responsive to changed demographics and contemporary lifestyles and values.[4]

Some might say that the answers to resiliency must be sought primarily in building up center cities, glossing over the fact that suburbs now comprise the majority of our urbanized areas—in land area, population, and economic activity. This line of thinking overlooks the potential that more gain could be achieved by focusing on adapting our least sustainable landscapes, in suburbia, to transform them into more resilient, equitable, adaptable, walkable, transit-oriented, and more public-oriented places. In a stagnant economy it is imperative that the built landscape be as self-sustaining and energy efficient as possible. Retrofitting and planning for retrofitting are more important than ever, a point emphasized in the book *Designing Suburban Futures: New Models from Build a Better Burb*, which reports on the winning and most noteworthy schemes from the competition. *Designing Suburban Futures* places the search for a more resilient future for suburban areas in North America, and across the globe, in historical and discursive contexts to bolster the argument that change is not only possible but necessary.[5]

The three main urban design and planning strategies that Dunham-Jones and I identified in *Retrofitting Suburbia* are:

- reinhabitation, or various forms of adaptive reuse of existing buildings, structures, and landscapes;
- redevelopment, or urbanization by increasing built density, walkability, and use mix; and
- regreening, from small parks and public plazas to restoring regional wetlands ecologies and wildlife corridors.

Taken together, these strategies and the various tactics used to pursue them support our ideal of "incremental metropolitanism"—that is, the gradual emergence of a robust, efficient, multicentered network of infilled centers and corridors within existing and already urbanized North American metropolitan regions to replace the past pattern of ever-outward sprawl. Often, these approaches are used in combination, with reinhabitation and regreening the most popular strategies due to their lower cost in the face of difficult-to-finance redevelopment strategies. However, changing the underlying urban morphological structure rather than current building uses and densities—which are more easily changed—constitutes, in our view, the primary task of suburban retrofitting.[6]

How are these strategies implemented? Following are several suburban retrofitting tactics, illustrated with exemplary projects that demonstrate a range of opportunities for retrofitting suburbia toward sustainable urbanism and a more resilient suburban future. These tactics are drawn from lessons learned through extensive case study research as well as insights derived from recent design competitions. These are lessons that might fruitfully guide innovation in the next generations of suburban retrofits.

Tactic #1: Reuse the Box

Adaptive reuse of vacant large-footprint commercial buildings for new, often community-serving uses, such as libraries or medical clinics, is both socially desirable and reduces waste.

In the Denver, Colorado, metropolitan area, two multilevel anchor department stores were retained at shopping malls that were otherwise demolished. Both stores were built in the 1980s to exactly the same prototype design. The concrete boxes, with distinctive chamfered corners, were not a wonder to behold, but the buildings were of comparatively sound, relatively recent construction. One, extant in the notable regional shopping mall retrofit Belmar in Lakewood, was reinhabited as a LEED-certified office building, with retail use retained only on the ground floor (see figures 5.1 and 5.2). The remainder of the approximately 100-acre mall site was cut through with new public streets, resulting in a retrofitted urban morphology of almost two dozen separate urban blocks, with a public realm of sidewalks, street trees and lighting, benches, bike parking, and so forth, rather than one large superblock. The reused "box" is embedded in this new street-and-block town center with a relatively shallow "liner" building of new construction that, together, create a more continuous streetscape. The other, nearby at CityCenter Englewood, was transformed from a mall anchor department store into Englewood Civic Center, housing the city offices of the suburban municipality of Englewood. Daylight filters in from a new public-art-filled central atrium cut through the prototype building's floor slabs.[7]

Architecturally interesting examples of reusing the box include FABG Architects' conversion of a 1966 prototype Standard Oil gas station designed by Ludwig Mies van der Rohe on Nuns' Island, southwest of Montreal, to a youth and senior activity center. Elegant stainless-steel air intake and exhaust vents replaced the gasoline pumps. In Woodburn, Oregon, Clark Kjos Architects reinhabited a dead K-Mart into WellSpring, a health and wellness center featuring curved walls, cut-in garden courtyards for daylight, and planted drainage swales

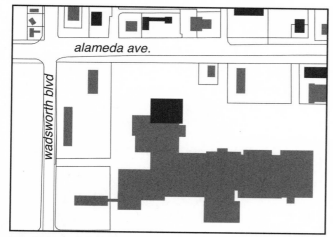

FIGURE 5.1.
Belmar figure-
fields, before and
after the retrofit.
Author's graphic.

before retrofit

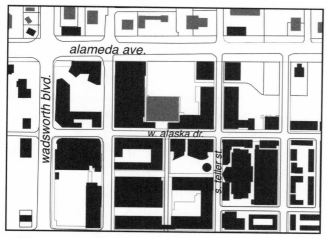

after retrofit

in the parking lot. The Vanderbilt University Medical Center now occupies the entire upper level (300,000 square feet) of the One Hundred Oaks Mall in Nashville, Tennessee.

Other examples include numerous churches, public and charter schools, government offices, performance spaces, and other nonretail, community-serving uses that have emerged in empty big-box stores, strip centers, and regional malls.[8]

There is much potential in vigorously pursuing this tactic. The advantage is axiomatic: square footage reused equates to the avoidance of an equivalent

FIGURE 5.2. Photo of Dick's (formerly Foleys) in Belmar, a retrofitted shopping mall. *Photo by author.*

amount of new construction. This tactic generally equates to savings in embodied energy, reductions in the urbanization of greenfields, and, sometimes, the preservation of historically and/or architecturally significant buildings.

Tactic #2: Provide Environmental Repair: Restore Wetlands, Creeks, and Wildlife Corridors; Sequester Carbon

Retrofits sometimes provide the opportunity to reconstruct wetlands, creeks, and wildlife corridors, components in the metropolitan watershed that were erased or diminished by suburban development patterns. Planted areas, both public and private, have great capacity to sequester carbon dioxide emissions, a significant contributor to global warming.

Many malls and strip centers that predate wetlands protection legislation were built on wetlands, areas where large contiguous parcels of land could more readily be assembled, preferably near highway interchanges. Some of the properties have continuously suffered from poor drainage and occasional flooding.

In the Northgate neighborhood of Seattle, Washington, a little-used overflow parking lot for a busy regional shopping mall was prone to flooding. The headwaters of Thornton Creek were buried in a large culvert beneath the parking lot's surface asphalt, and local environmentalists lobbied hard for "day lighting" the creek. Developers were also interested in the property, and planners hoped to see more density because the terminus of a new light-rail line to downtown was planned for the adjacent quadrant of overflow mall parking. The win-win solution? It includes a combination of new "soft" stormwater infrastructure in the form of a very sophisticated vegetative bioswale—the Thornton Creek Water Quality Channel—plus mixed-use development with hundreds of attractive new housing units in Thornton Place.[9]

In the town of Meriden, Connecticut, a two-story, 230,000-square-foot enclosed mall, built in 1970 over a filled brook in an ill-conceived economic revitalization scheme, suffered frequent flooding. It has been demolished for a project called Meriden Hub; Harbor Brook and its floodplain are to be restored to a fourteen-acre downtown park that will be a reservoir for future flood control. New mixed-use transit-oriented development will be built in and around the park in infill sites adjacent to an existing Amtrak station that is slated for expansion into an intermodal, high-speed hub.[10]

In addition to stormwater management, suburban green spaces have underused capacity to sequester carbon dioxide emissions. "Building C-Burbia" was a winning scheme in the Build a Better Burb competition by a landscape architecture team led by Denise Hoffman Brandt (see figure 5.3). The scheme proposes systems of soft infrastructure that co-opt suburban "open" spaces—

FIGURE 5.3. Detail from the Building C-Burbia competition.
Courtesy of Denise Hoffman Brandt, Alexa Helsell, and Bronwyn Gropp, 2010.

highway verges, tree lawns, vacant lots—for plantings selected for their high capacity to sequester carbon in living organic material and thereby reduce greenhouse gases in the atmosphere.[11]

Tactic #3: Revise Zoning Codes and Public Works Standards (Redevelopment)

Make it easier to build compact, mixed-use developments with walkable, complete streets, and make it harder to build single-use, auto-dependent places. Plan and participate in events that demonstrate the benefits of revised codes, standards, and incentives.

This tactic primarily operates at the level of local government where land-use decisions are made. A promising trend is the reexamination of outdated zoning codes that require separated uses, deep setbacks, and wide streets that practically guarantee automobile dependency. Instead, form-based codes are being drafted and calibrated to guide new development and protect desirable places, and new infrastructure standards are being adopted that consider more than the needs of automobiles. This is not to say that cars are going away anytime soon, although technological advances may soon render next-generation automobiles unrecognizable to us; instead, it is a matter of articulating shifts in emphasis and priority in codes and standards.

A 3.5-mile stretch of Columbia Pike, in Arlington County, Virginia, is one noteworthy example of the successful implementation of a form-based code. The overlay code, adopted in 2003, provides incentives to redevelop and densify in clearly demarcated districts or nodes along the strip while exerting significant controls on form, such as implementing build-to lines for buildings and setbacks for parking lots. A regulating plan indicates what type of building can be built in any location and its frontage type to the pike, as well as the aforementioned built-to lines. Streetscape standards provide recommendations for sidewalks, planting strips, open space, and civic squares.[12]

Citizen-activists can also apply this tactic by staging temporary events, for example by participating in PARK(ing) Day, "an annual worldwide event where artists, designers and citizens transform metered parking spots into temporary public parks," held every September.[13] The simple concept: on-street parking spaces are reclaimed for non-auto use by feeding the meter and occupying the space with a temporary public park—perhaps 150 square feet of sod and a few folding chairs. Begun as a small ad-hoc urbanism project in 2005 by REBAR, a San Francisco design collaborative, it had grown significantly by 2011 to 162 cities in 35 countries.

A similar but more involved program is Better Block, a planning initiative based in Dallas begun by Jason Roberts and Andrew Howard (see figure 5.4). Better Block provides a template for community members to temporarily trans-

FIGURE 5.4. Better Block example, Square 67, Dallas.
Courtesy of Andrew Howard and Jason Roberts of Team Better Block.

form streetscapes with street trees in tubs, sod curbs, pop-up sidewalk cafes, and so on as a way to permit people to engage in a visioning process that is visualized—albeit temporarily—at full scale. Their first project was on a faded shopping street in the Dallas neighborhood of Oak Cliff, a place that over the years had lost out to malls and big box stores. In 2011 they paired with architect Wanda Dye and a group of students to design and build a mini Main Street in the parking lot of Square 67, an aging strip mall in South Oak Cliff, using converted shipping containers, temporary shade structures, and the pièce de résistance—a portable fishing pond, stocked with catfish.[14] These projects can help lead the way to more permanent retrofits.

Tactic #4: Keep Block Size Walkable

Without careful modulation, the hybridization of suburban building types and parking into urban blocks and streets can lead to oversized blocks and monotonous building fronts. The rule of thumb for a walkable block is a perimeter dimension of less than 1,700 linear feet.

The main thrust of this tactic is to design the smaller block sizes that support walking. The general rule for a block conducive to walking is a perimeter dimension of no more than 1,700 linear feet.[15] A typical Portland, Oregon, block is a compact square of 200 by 200 feet, yielding an 800-linear-foot perimeter, whereas a typical Manhattan block of 200 feet by 600 feet yields 1,600 linear

FIGURE 5.5. Plano's Legacy Town Center, showing the Texas Donut. *Photos by author.*

feet. Adding midblock pedestrian passages or paseos to supersized blocks can also increase walkability.

The successful apartment building prototype known as a "Texas Donut," such as at Legacy Town Center in the large Dallas suburb of Plano, Texas, consists of embedding unadorned parking decks in the center of a four-story residential apartment block, resulting in an inviting streetscape with no surface parking lots, blank walls, unsightly gates, or excessive setbacks (see figure 5.5). However, the resultant blocks can be somewhat large, just barely walkable in dimension. Mixed-use buildings with below-grade parking can also yield walkable blocks, though below-grade parking is more expensive than parking decks, which are, in turn, more expensive than surface parking.[16]

Paseo Verde in North Philadelphia is an infill project of affordable and workforce housing that revives a "high-density low-rise" building type, built at three to four stories, while featuring the latest green building technologies and materials. The project is designed to support walkability and transit use and is compatible with an existing built morphology of row houses and detached dwellings.[17]

There is much room for further architectural and urban design innovations in devising new housing and block types that reduce energy use and support walkability. Smaller unit types—"microloft units," for example—could meet the needs of one- and two-person households and might result in a greater range of standardized dimensions for the design of new residential buildings. Building dimensions for commercial uses can also be more varied than the usual developer standards. The dominant variable in setting building footprint dimensions is often parking, so reducing the proportion of building area used for parking can significantly reduce overall building dimensions (and also unit cost). Reductions in parking ratios in transit-served areas (Paseo Verde has 0.5 spaces per unit and is directly adjacent to a commuter rail station), or the use of automated stack parking systems, could also yield improvements in walkability by allowing more compact residential and mixed-use building forms and blocks. Locating residential parking remotely, that is, decoupling parking areas from the buildings they serve, would also contribute to increasing the base affordability of housing (by making the added cost of a parking spot an optional add-on) and could allow the supply of parking spaces in any given location to be much more efficiently managed. Car-free "communities of choice," such as Vauban on the outskirts of Freiburg in southwestern Germany, might be built in some North American suburbs if bike transit networks become sufficiently robust.[18]

Tactic #5: Establish a More Continuous Streetscape with Shallow Liner Buildings

New additions of "wrappers" can be employed around reused box buildings, and shallow liner buildings can screen surface parking lots to provide a more continuous streetscape.

Due credit must be given to Mashpee Commons, a retrofit of a strip shopping center on Cape Cod in Massachusetts, developed incrementally since the mid-1980s, for pioneering many tactics that challenge conventional suburban development and zoning and have become increasingly routine.[19] For example, there are twenty-foot-deep "liner" buildings, typically leased to non-chain stores, sited around the perimeter of surface parking lots to provide two-sided streets throughout the Commons.

Shallow liners can also be incorporated into larger buildings. A structured parking deck, for example, might have a liner on the ground floor of small retail shops or artists' studios. These shops could be as shallow in depth measuring back from the sidewalk as twenty feet (the same depth as one row of parking spaces). Or, a new liner building can be built around existing big-box commercial and light industrial buildings, to create a more continuous street wall, as proposed by the comprehensive "HIP Retrofit" entry to the Build a Better Burb competition, proposing transformation of a light industrial area in Hauppauge, Long Island (see figure 5.6).[20]

Tactic #6: Use Appropriate Street Types and Real Sidewalks

Many suburban streets are overly wide, and lack sufficient sidewalks and crosswalks. The 2010 recommended practice manual of the Institute of Transportation Engineers (ITE), *Designing Walkable Urban Thoroughfares*, provides recommended design guidelines for a broad range of context-sensitive street types.[21]

Santana Row in San Jose, California, is the upscale mixed-use retrofit of a

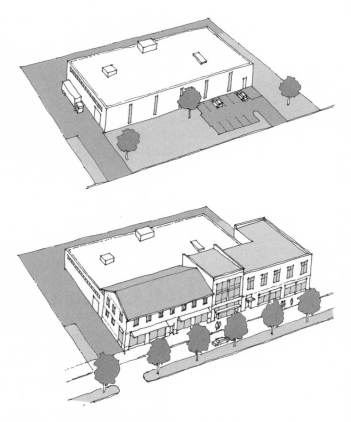

shopping center that boasts a very well proportioned Main Street, with appropriately scaled on-street parking and small, landscaped gathering areas in the median.[22] Santana Row is not particularly well connected to adjacent streets, but its internal streetscapes are a good model, soon to be expanded in a new phase of midrise office buildings catering to tech companies. Silicon Valley seems to be beginning to move away, in baby steps, from the completely car-dependent business park model.[23]

Getting the design details of this tactic right is crucial: aligned building setbacks, continuous and properly graded sidewalks and bike paths, safe and accessible crossings, well-proportioned street widths and building heights, and climatically appropriate plantings all contribute. Sidewalks are important, though often undervalued, public spaces. Maintaining their publicness—and avoiding privatization—while providing comfortably scaled dimensions for sidewalks should not be overlooked in the retrofitting of sprawling spaces in suburbs.[24]

Many suburban streets seem overly wide and lack comfortable sidewalks and crosswalks. In residential areas within an interconnected street system, an overall right-of-way of 60 feet, with 16-foot sidewalk and treeplanting strips on either side of a 28-foot roadway, should be sufficient.[25]

Tactic #7: Improve Connectivity for Drivers, Bicyclists, and Pedestrians

Build interconnected, complete street networks to increase walkability and public safety, while distributing traffic and reducing overall vehicle miles traveled (VMT).

For the full gains of retrofitting to be realized, any redeveloped node should make connections to the adjacent built fabric, so that people can walk, bike, or drive shorter distances to get from any given point A to point B. Every retrofit of a "campus-type" suburban property—a shopping mall, strip mall, office park, or garden apartment complex, or any large property with one or multiple buildings but only one or fewer points of road or path connection to surrounding fabric—is an opportunity to drastically improve connectivity to surrounding streets. The urban design of Belmar in Lakewood, Colorado, was based on extending the adjacent street network through the 100-plus-acre site, creating multiple points of connection and a multitude of streets and sidewalks to drive, bike, or walk along to navigate to and through the district. These tactics create lots of on-street parking spaces (metered, so that there is sufficient turnover of the spaces for those on quick errands). It also keeps traffic speeds slow, and drivers more attentive to the presence of pedestrians and those on bikes.

At a larger scale, the 1,700-acre edge city of Tysons Corner, in Fairfax County, Virginia, is poised for dramatic transformation as large parcels are redeveloped into smaller blocks with higher-density, mixed-use buildings. The new zoning code was drafted to redress the dramatic jobs/housing imbalance in Tysons (120,000 jobs but only 17,000 residents) not only by facilitating the construction of thousands of residential units but also by encouraging, with the cooperation of the major landowners, the emergence of a new, more finely grained network of streets and pedestrian paths, leading to and from four new Metrorail stops on the line to Dulles Airport.

As of January 2012, more than 350 U.S. communities—including half of all states as well as numerous metropolitan planning organizations, counties, cities, suburbs, and rural towns—had passed "Complete Streets" legislation, requiring state and local transportation agencies to factor non-car uses of streets and sidewalks into all projects. Complete streets is "a movement that encourages and provides for safe access to destinations for everyone, regardless of age, ability, income, ethnicity, or mode of travel."[26] Some exemplary policies adopted by suburban municipalities include those of Baldwin Park, California; Winter Park, Florida; Babylon, New York (on Long Island); and Rockville, Maryland, which also boasts a high number of suburban retrofits.[27]

Tactic #8: Consider Future Connectivity and Adaptability

If desired street connections cannot be achieved when the retrofit is initially designed and constructed, because of NIMBY concerns or other barriers, one strategy is to "design in" easements for future linkages. If desired densities and parking decks cannot be justified yet, parking lots can be designed as future building sites, with utilities placed in the future streets at the outset.

The exemplary retrofits of Mashpee Commons and Belmar illustrate one dimension of this tactic, which hinges on the advantages of high-quality, well-informed urban design with a longer-than-typical time horizon (see figure 5.7). At Mashpee Commons the owners of a neighboring apartment complex were wary of forming a direct street connection, so the master plan includes a stub out location. At Belmar, a strip of land to the east wasn't part of the retrofitted property, but the new streets align with the grid of the subdivision beyond and could be connected some time in the future.

Another dimension of the tactic is to design parking lots in lower-density commercial developments for anticipatory or planned retrofitting. The process is to preplan for tomorrow's retrofits today in the cases where walkable place-based projects may not be immediately implementable for reasons of financing, market potential, or regulatory barriers. As explained by Lee Sobel of RCLCO, an advocate of this idea, "Planned Retrofit embeds many of the techniques of place-making into an auto-oriented development: putting roads in the right place, the infrastructure aligned with the roads, the easements and rights of way, and a few strategic legal considerations. Whatever project gets built today, all of the legal and physical infrastructure is in place for retrofitting in the future when the time is right."[28]

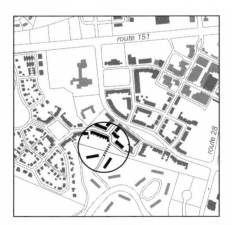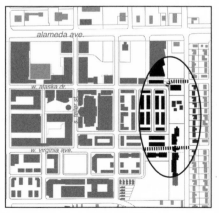

FIGURE 5.7. Potential future connections at Mashpee Commons (*A*) and Belmar (*B*). *Illustrations by author.*

Tactic #9: Diversify Housing Choice and Price

The future success of suburbs will hinge on their ability to respond to changing demographics by providing more housing choices.

One of the main characteristics of suburban housing is the preponderance of single-family houses and the attendant lack of racial, age, and income diversity within neighborhoods (although there may be quite a bit of difference between neighborhoods, contributing to persistent conditions of de facto segregation). The future success of suburbs will hinge on the ability of housing markets to be nimble in response to changing demographics. Demographic trends in the United States include a shrinking percentage of households with children, with an associated increase in the percentage of one- and two-person households, and increases—albeit unevenly distributed—in foreign-born residents and residents from minority groups in suburbs. The diversification of housing choice and price—realized through introducing a variety of types of housing, protecting affordability with policies and programs, and providing accessibility to all—is essential to development of adequate responses to these trends. Housing for empty nesters and older adults can form part of retrofitting plans in order to allow people to age in place or to be near their families.[29] A key part of this tactic is to introduce and integrate housing choice into existing neighborhoods that are homogeneous in dwelling type.

An innovative housing type that might appeal in many suburbs is comprised of residential suites, with three or more bedrooms, each with a private bathroom, designed for unrelated adults to share. An example is The Towers at University Town Center, a 910-bed apartment building in an office park retrofit in Hyattsville, Maryland. The building is close to transit (bus and D.C. Metrorail) and part-time service jobs. This building caters to college students and recent graduates, but a similar building type could appeal to single older adults of more limited means who might be interested in living in a shared suite. In North American center cities with tight housing markets such as New York and San Francisco, researchers have begun to document how the apartment types available (and supported by codes and standards that date back to the post–World War II housing shortage crisis) no longer fit well with current housing demand. Single people looking to affordably share with others or live alone outnumber families seeking the more traditional apartment layouts that the codes are oriented toward. The "Making Room" initiative in New York City in 2011 invited design explorations of a microloft housing type, consisting of 300-square-foot or smaller units.[30] The issue of increases in one-person households, and the lack of appropriate legal housing to suit, is just as pressing in suburbs as in center cities and promises to become more so in the future.

In edge cities, there is often an imbalance of jobs and housing, as discussed above for Tysons, providing opportunity to apply this tactic. In economically depressed suburbs, retrofits can add some higher-priced units to increase the tax base and potentially improve the value of existing housing stock. In suburban municipalities with high housing prices due to limited supply or other factors (discriminatory "exclusionary" zoning effected through minimum lot sizes and prohibitions on second units, for example), add smaller, lower-priced units, with public subsidy if necessary.

Tactic #10: Add Units to Existing Subdivisions

Infilling residential neighborhoods of detached dwellings with second units or accessory dwelling units (ADUs) can provide affordable housing choices for singles and seniors, and increase residential density without dramatically altering the morphological pattern.

A change in zoning can allow the legalization and addition of accessory dwellings, attached or detached in backyard cottages, to existing homes. The benefits, beyond affordability and density, include more housing choice, the opportunity to accommodate immediate or extended family, and increased flexibility in living arrangements.

Several municipalities in the Pacific Northwest have recently passed widespread zoning revisions permitting detached accessory units. In the early stages of the process in the late 1990s, in order to gain public support, the City of Seattle launched a design competition and built three attractive demonstration units. More recently, Seattle's Planning Commission and Department of Planning and Development issued a comprehensive "Guide to Building a Backyard Cottage."[31]

Meri Tepper's scheme "Site in the Setback" illustrates this tactic applied, in a systemic way, to backyards in the iconic Nassau County suburb of Levittown, New York. Second-unit permits are already available in the town, restricted to homeowners who meet an age threshold and can demonstrate need. The permit is voided if ownership of the home is transferred.

Tactic #11: Invest in Durable, High-Performance Architecture and Landscape

The most successful and sustainable retrofits will be beautiful, durable, culturally significant, and built to meet high standards of environmental performance in the public spaces, the landscape, and the buildings.

Solidly built buildings in retrofits should be designed with the capacity to accommodate innovative architectural additions and infill over time, complemented with attractive, high-performance landscapes that can function as "soft" stormwater infrastructure. The road ahead will require design professionals to become more knowledgeable than they already are about real estate financing and pro forma financial statements so as to find the most effective ways to argue for the market value and potential returns—both economic and ecological—of good design and durable, high-quality materials and methods.

LEED standards for green buildings and interiors and for neighborhood design set a high bar for energy performance and provide clear metrics—continually reviewed and revised by membership committees—for calculating results. Other guidelines for environmentally friendly design and construction, such as the Living Building Challenge standards of the International Living Future Institute, set the bar even higher, aiming for energy- and carbon-neutral buildings that capture rainwater for supply, treat all grey and black water, and apply the highest standards for the sourcing and performance of specified building materials and construction systems. At a time when most buildings and building materials are designed and tested for lifespans that range from 10 to 40 years, buildings designed to this new standard seek durability in excess of 200 years.

Consistent application of "long life, loose fit" approaches to building design, combined with the widespread implementation of new urban morphologies of walkable blocks and interconnected streets in redevelopment retrofits, would radically transform the suburban landscape as we know it. These transformations could break the cycle of obsolescence in suburbs, perhaps even leading to a dramatically decreased need for suburban retrofitting in the future. Strategic deployment of the tactics outlined above, along with new ones sure to be innovated as the next generations of suburban retrofits are designed and implemented, can help get us there.

How great would that be?

NOTES

1. Richard Florida, Foreword to Ellen Dunham-Jones and June Williamson, *Retrofitting Suburbia: Urban Design Solutions for Redesigning Suburbs*, updated ed. (Hoboken, N.J.: Wiley, 2011). See also Florida, *The Great Reset: How New Ways of Living and Working Drive Post-Crash Prosperity* (New York: Harper, 2010).

2. Build a Better Burb, a project of the Long Island Index, sponsored by the Rauch Foundation: http://buildabetterburb.org/; http://www.longislandindex.org/, accessed March 17, 2013. For a more extensive treatment of the competition and the lessons learned from it, see June Williamson, *Designing Suburban Futures: New Models from Build a Better Burb* (Washington, D.C.: Island Press, 2013). The general outline of the tactics explained here were first described and illustrated in June Williamson, "11 Urban Design Tactics for Suburban Retrofitting," written in 2011 for the Build a Better Burb website: http://buildabetterburb.org/article.php?aid=145, accessed March 17, 2013.

3. Especially if one includes Queens and Kings Counties, consolidated since 1898 into the City of New York but co-located with Nassau and Suffolk on Long Island. See, for example, Marc Linder and Laurence S. Zacharias, *Of Cabbages and Kings County: Agriculture and the Formation of Modern Brooklyn* (Iowa City: University of Iowa Press, 1999).

4. For more on changed and changing demographics and the transformative impacts they will have on the market for new development, especially for housing, see Arthur C.

Nelson, *Reshaping Metropolitan America: Development Trends and Opportunities to 2030* (Washington, D.C.: Island Press, 2013).

5. See, especially, the chapters "Context for Change" and "Design Culture Responds to Sprawl: 1960s to 2010s," in Williamson, *Designing Suburban Futures*, 2–34.

6. For a similar argument, see Galina Tachieva, *Sprawl Repair Manual* (Washington, D.C.: Island Press, 2010).

7. On Belmar and CityCenter Englewood, see Dunham-Jones and Williamson, *Retrofitting Suburbia*, 129–34, 154–71. See also: http://www.denver.org/metro/neighborhoods /belmar-lakewood, accessed March 17, 2013.

8. An early source on big box reuse is Julia Christensen, *Big Box Reuse* (Cambridge, Mass.: MIT Press, 2008). See also Dunham-Jones and Williamson, *Retrofitting Suburbia*, 67–72.

9. Dunham-Jones and Williamson, *Retrofitting Suburbia*, xviii–xx. See also SvR Design, "Thornton Creek Quality Water Channel Final Report," October 28, 2009, http://www .seattle.gov/util/groups/public/documents/webcontent/spu01_006146.pdf, accessed March 17, 2013.

10. The Meriden TOD Plan design team was led by Parsons Brinckerhoff with park design by Milone and MacBroom. The City of Meriden, partnered with the Connecticut Department of Economic and Community Development, received a HUD Sustainable Communities Challenge Grant to develop TOD Zoning. See http://meridentod.com, accessed March 17, 2013.

11. Williamson, *Designing Suburban Futures*, 80–85.

12. For more on the revitalization of Columbia Pike, including links to the form-based code, see http://www.columbiapikeva.us/.

13. See Street Plans Collaborative, Mike Lydon, ed., *Tactical Urbanism Handbook* 2, 2012, available for download at http://issuu.com/streetplanscollaborative/docs/tactical_ urbanism_vol_2_final, accessed March 17, 2013. For more on PARK(ing) Day see http:// parkingday.org, accessed March 17, 2013.

14. For more on Better Block see http://betterblock.org. For the Square 67 project in South Oak Cliff, see http://teambetterblock.com/blog/2011/08/23/deconstructing-a-big -box-in-south-oak-cliff/, accessed March 17, 2013. Eran Ben-Joseph, *ReThinking a Lot: the Design and Culture of Parking* (Cambridge, Mass.: MIT Press, 2012), thoughtfully considers parking lots.

15. Michael Mehaffy et al., "Urban Nuclei and the Geometry of Streets: The 'Emergent Neighborhoods' Model," *Urban Design International* 15 (2010): 22–46.

16. For a good primer on the relationship between parking and common current residential building types, see Neal Payton and Brian O'Looney, "Seeking Urbane Parking Solutions," *Places* 18, no. 1 (Spring 2006), http://escholarship.org/uc/item/0897x236.

17. Paseo Verde was designed by WRT for Jonathan Rose Companies, developer of the highly regarded Via Verde project in the Bronx. See http://www.wrtdesign.com/projects /detail/paseo-verde/251, accessed March 17, 2013.

18. Elisabeth Rosenthal, "In German Suburb, Life Goes On Without Cars," *New York Times*, May 11, 2009.

19. Dunham-Jones and Williamson, *Retrofitting Suburbia*, 95–107.

20. Williamson, *Designing Suburban Futures*, 115.

21. Institute of Transportation Engineers and the Congress for the New Urbanism, *Designing Walkable Urban Thoroughfares: A Context Sensitive Approach: An ITE Recommended*

Practice (Washington, D.C.: ITE and CNU, 2010); see http://www.ite.org/css/, accessed March 17, 2013.

22. Dunham-Jones and Williamson, *Retrofitting Suburbia*, 78–80.

23. George Avalos, "San Jose's Santana Row Plans Three Office Buildings to Cater to Tech Companies," *Oakland Tribune*, March 12, 2013.

24. A point made by Anastasia Loukaitou-Sideris and Renia Ehrenfeucht in *Sidewalks: Conflict and Negotiation over Public Space* (Cambridge, Mass.: MIT Press, 2009). See also June Williamson, "Protest on the Astroturf, July 4, 2007," in Christopher Niedt, *Social Justice and the Diverse Suburb: History, Politics, and Prospects* (Philadelphia: Temple University Press, 2013).

25. Patrick M. Condon, *Seven Rules for Sustainable Communities: Design Strategies for the Post-Carbon World* (Washington, D.C.: Island Press, 2010), 54–59.

26. For more on complete streets see Smart Growth America's National Complete Streets Coalition website: http://www.smartgrowthamerica.org/complete-streets, accessed March 17, 2013.

27. Smart Growth America and National Complete Streets Coalition, "Complete Streets: Policy Analysis 2011" (August 2012). The policy adopted by the New Jersey Department of Transportation, a prototypically suburbanized state, scored highest in its category in the policy analysis. See http://www.smartgrowthamerica.org/documents/cs/resources/cs-policyanalysis.pdf, accessed March 17, 2013.

28. Emailed comments to author from Lee S. Sobel, then with the U.S. EPA's Office of Policy, Economics and Innovation, February 29, 2012.

29. See Henry Cisneros, Margaret Dyer-Chamberlain, and Jane Hickie, eds., *Independent for Life: Homes and Neighborhoods for an Aging America* (Austin: University of Texas Press, 2012).

30. Making Room was sponsored by the Citizens Housing and Planning Council and the Architectural League of New York. See http://makingroomnyc.com. Subsequently, the New York City Department of Housing Preservation and Development invited developers to submit proposals for a prototype project of microloft units to be built on a parking lot owned by the New York City Housing Authority in Kips Bay, Manhattan. The project will receive regulatory waivers. See http://www.nyc.gov/html/om/html/2012b/pr257–12.html, accessed March 17, 2013.

31. The City of Seattle's webpage on backyard cottages provides a good overview: http://www.seattle.gov/dpd/Codes/Backyar D.C.:ottages/Overview/, accessed March 17, 2013.

CHAPTER 6

Suburban Downtowns

DAVID DIXON

Key Points and Practice Takeaways

1. Today, roughly three-fifths of all households consist of singles and couples, such that demand for multifamily housing far outstrips demand for single-family houses.

2. Suburban "downtowns" are not large lifestyle centers. They evidence a strong civic mission that reflects growing suburban aspirations for community-rich environments. They are generally sponsored by local government, have an unmistakably public character, and are denser and more socially diverse.

3. The qualities that define a successful suburban downtown are essentially similar to those that traditionally defined Main Streets and downtowns in smaller cities: walkability, direct connections to adjacent neighborhoods, civic spaces, public streets that define typical city blocks, and diverse ownership.

4. These characteristics require a critical mass of people, disposable income, and active uses. Rough rules of thumb suggest two to four thousand households within a ten-minute walk to retail activities, civic uses, and jobs.

5. Three case studies illustrate one consistent quality: a robust community engagement process.

The story of American suburban development starts logically enough. America's earliest suburbs, spawned in the 1850s, made it possible for the wealthy to work in crowded, noisy commercial centers like Philadelphia, New York, Boston, and Chicago and yet escape to a calm, refreshing semirural setting in the evening. Lively "downtowns" developed around suburban train stations and became the focus of community life from Wellesley (outside Boston) to Evanston (outside Chicago). As cars entered mainstream American life in the 1910s and 1920s, car-focused suburban schemes began to appear—often inspired by utopian ideals, such as those of England's Garden City movement—drawn on the assumption that suburbs would remain discrete, identifiable communities. The freedom that cars offered meant that, for the first time, suburban communities did not need a nearby commercial district, and thus the concept of a suburban downtown disappeared for almost fifty years. In the decades after World War II, suburbs took on many of the qualities we recognize today. Prompted by newfound prosperity, universal auto ownership, and racial fears, rapidly growing middle-class households pursued a new American Dream of mass-produced single-family houses on quarter-acre lots that offered an escape from work and the city.

The American Dream not only separated home and family from work but also eliminated—to borrow sociologist Ray Oldenburg's phrase—"third places" that were not about home or work but instead about connecting to, and enjoying the benefits of, being part of a community.[1] In the 1960s and 1970s, as people, jobs, and wealth flowed to the suburbs, developers followed. They created what author Joel Garreau labeled "edge cities"—suburban centers dominated by office buildings that became alternatives to traditional downtowns in places such as Clayton (outside St. Louis), Buckhead (outside downtown Atlanta, although still within the city limits), and Rosslyn (outside Washington, D.C.).[2] Beginning in the 1980s major developers built de novo downtowns for suburbs styled as "new communities" like Reston (outside Washington, D.C.) and The Woodlands (outside Houston). However, these latter-day suburban downtowns shared little more than a name with their pre-1920s forebears; they were car-oriented, often characterized by lifeless streets; they served entire regions; and they focused on commerce, not community.

But today an emerging generation of suburban downtowns shows a remarkable shift in this narrative. In critical ways these new downtowns represent a reaction to the privatized nature and anonymity of their more immediate predecessors. They are consciously planned; they are typically sponsored by a local government; they pursue a mission of public benefit rather than private profit; and, most intriguingly, they function in a way similar to the early railroad suburbs, with walkable centers, a mix of uses, and a distinctive character. They suc-

FIGURE 6.1. More than a decade after community activists in Somerville (outside Boston) blocked development of a big-box mall as the wrong model for new development in their dense community, Federal Realty Investment Trust has completed the first phase of Assembly Row—a mixed-use development that includes a dedicated transit station and will grow to nearly 5.7 million square feet. *Courtesy of Federal Realty Investment Trust.*

ceed in the marketplace by satisfying a growing demand for places that offer the benefits of being part of a community. Put another way, they increase economic value by creating social value.

This link between social value and economic value that is central to the emergence of new suburban downtowns began to reshape development in some urban neighborhoods fifteen to twenty years ago. An example is Assembly Square in Somerville, once a streetcar suburb and about three miles from downtown Boston. In 1980 a new mall introduced retail onto a seventy-acre site in Somerville that had previously housed a Ford Motor factory. In the early 1990s a developer applied to redevelop the mid-market mall as a suburban-style "power center" of big-box stores. To the developer's surprise, adjacent neighborhoods rebelled and initiated a ten-year battle for a development that would not "offer all of the problems of a downtown, but none of the benefits." In other words, the "power center" version of the American Dream had not captured the imagination of neighborhood residents. Their vision instead was rooted in memories of Somerville's lively mixed-use—and walkable—"squares" before they were drained of vitality by suburban competition. These squares had functioned as commercial centers and the heart of social, cultural, and civic life. They drew people from many walks of life, for many reasons, at all times of the day. The squares were not designed for cars, and everyone walked, making it common to run into friends, neighbors, and family members. The squares offered a strong sense of connection to the larger community.

The developer responded that the residents' goals either cost too much or ignored market realities—arguing, in effect, that social and economic values were in conflict. A new mayor invited more developers to evaluate the site. Federal Realty Investment Trust (FRT) had already completed projects in other cities that matched the residents' vision—a mix of uses, concentrated density, and lively streets that created a community setting. It ultimately won the right to develop Assembly Row using this model. FRT had noted growing market demand for the same qualities the residents wanted and knew such development could generate the significant economic premiums needed to support the higher costs of mixing uses and building structured parking to accommodate greater density. Assembly Row's first phase opened in 2014, and a second phase began. The development will ultimately reach 5.7 million square feet and embody the live/work/shop/play qualities of a traditional downtown.

The New Suburban Downtowns

Assembly Square's tortuous history demonstrates a remarkable evolution. "Location, location, location" still determines real estate value, but today that means proximity to mixed-use, walkable areas that offer possibilities for community connection rather than a highway interchange. Housing analyst Laurie Volk sheds light on factors contributing to this transition.[3] In contrast to the top priorities Americans listed when describing where they wanted to live during the fifty years after World War II (golf courses, individual yards, escape from work, and privacy), Americans today list very different priorities, including walkable Main Streets, opportunities to enjoy the benefits of diversity, live/work/play environments, and nearby opportunities for social interaction. The types of housing people prefer has shifted along with priorities for where they want to live. Households without children already represent half to two-thirds of all households in most regions.

The dominance of the single-family house has been undone by these changing demographics. As a preponderance of households with children gives way to singles and couples, University of Utah professor Chris Nelson reports that lofts, apartments, and townhouses have supplanted single-family houses as the default preference for a majority of Americans—and he projects that this preference will extend at least until 2030.[4] Nelson also notes that many suburbs will face new market pressures as America ages and growing numbers of seniors sell their suburban single-family houses in favor of apartments in walkable environments where they do not have to depend on a car.

These changes are stirring a number of suburbs out of years of complacency into an awareness that, like cities, they too will need to change with the times. Singles and couples will soon represent a majority in suburbia. Traditional racial, religious, and even economic homogeneity is giving way to diversity. These changes are awakening the same aspirations in many suburban neighborhoods that Somerville's residents expressed more than a decade ago when they called for convenient access to lively, walkable places that foster community.

These trends are particularly true for college-educated millennials (ages 25–34), a demographic that many suburbs, concerned about an aging population and dwindling school enrollments, would like to capture. The 2010 census demonstrated that the number of college-educated 25- to 34-year-olds increased by 25–40 percent or more in many large and midsized city downtowns and close-in neighborhoods. Observers like the Brookings Institution and CEOs for Cities report that over the last decade housing values have begun for the first time to correlate with increased walkability—in suburbs as well as cities.

The appearance of "lifestyle centers" in the early 2000s—redevelopment of failed suburban malls offering a taste of the walkability and community of urban life—demonstrated that these qualities can succeed in a suburban marketplace. While lifestyle centers themselves are too limited by their private development model to meet growing suburban aspirations for public, community-rich environments, they have helped a number of suburbs gain confidence to take a much more ambitious step—to create an entirely new "downtown" in their midst that relies on a more urban type of development that is denser, socially diverse, and mixed-use. This choice is driven by a desire both to meet emerging aspirations within their community and to ensure that their suburb will remain competitive with a nearby city as values are shaped more by walkable community than convenient automobile access.

No specific formula exists for these emerging suburban downtowns, but certain characteristics appear repeatedly:

- Walkable. They offer substantial variety in food, culture, entertainment, or other amenity uses within a five-minute walk of one another (roughly 1,200 feet—about the distance most Americans are willing to walk to a nonessential destination). The mix and range of uses invites walking, which fosters the informal interactions that can make a place the social heart of a community.
- Accessible. Residents of every neighborhood can reach a new downtown in a variety of ways: by car, of course (these are suburbs, after all), but also by bike, on foot, or on a bus.
- Civic space. The new downtowns often feature a "town green" or other public space. Unlike traditional New England greens, these spaces are designed and programmed to invite sharing by the full spectrum of people, ages, and income levels in the larger community.

- Civic place. A city hall or other public facility that "belongs" to the entire community often anchors a new downtown and functions as the default location for community-wide activities, from picnics to protests.
- Built around public streets. Downtown streets form a full network; are always accessible (at least to pedestrians), even when they cross private property; and define typical city blocks.
- Controlled by many owners. They are neither dominated by a single developer or landlord nor confined by a single land ownership, but instead reflect the contributions of a variety of developers, architects, landscape architects, and others who shape a community and can grow and change with their community.
- Full of choices. New downtowns offer a variety of options for living, working, shopping, entertainment, and similar elements of livability that enhance quality of life for people of diverse ages, incomes, and backgrounds.

Each of these characteristics requires a critical mass of people, disposable income, and activity to succeed. For example, two blocks of Main Street shops, restaurants, and entertainment represent a reasonable minimum to function as a destination for a larger community. Two to four thousand households within walking distance (preferably five but up to ten minutes) can play a significant role in attracting these businesses—and, more important, provide sufficient market support to encourage unique, independent enterprises geared to the community rather than a franchise that depends on regional traffic. This same concentration of households represents a reasonable threshold for supporting a bus and possibly a rail transit stop and to activate a small park or town green. Add a city hall or similar civic use (50,000–100,000 SF), and preferably enough office or research space to contribute at least 200–300 jobs to the mix (50,000–100,000 SF), and a variety of other activities and 3,000,000–5,000,000 SF becomes a reasonable threshold for creating a successful suburban downtown. The densities required to ensure that this development is walkable requires primarily structured parking. Parking costs are often reduced by sharing parking between uses with different peak period requirements (e.g., housing and office) and taking advantage of reduced auto-dependence to reduce parking requirements.

Because most suburban markets will only support frame construction, which under most building codes limits buildings to five or fewer stories, suburban downtowns remain predominantly low-rise (which often lines up with community aesthetic preferences). Given the limits that lower buildings place on density, and the need for sufficient area to accommodate streets and a town green while concentrating activity to promote walkability, suburban downtowns usually require at least 50–100 acres. A site that surpasses 200 acres will likely require more than 3,000,000 SF of development to maintain walkability.

Case Studies
Sandy Springs, Georgia: From Auto-Oriented Strip to Walkable Downtown

Sandy Springs illustrates opportunities and constraints that would likely confront many suburbs seeking to create a new downtown. One of metro Atlanta's most affluent communities, Sandy Springs grew rapidly in the mid-1960s following the construction of the Georgia 400 and I-285. The *New York Times* (June 24, 2012) described the city's conservative politics in a 2012 article on the decision to privatize most municipal services. Sandy Springs' main artery, Roswell Road, evolved from a country road in the early twentieth century to an eight-lane arterial. Today the closest claim that Sandy Springs could make to a "center" is a roughly one-mile stretch of Roswell Road lined with shopping centers and drive-through businesses.

In the initial phases of redevelopment, a new urban neighborhood of lofts together with retail, arts, cafés, and similar street-level activities extends one to two blocks on either side of Main Street (see figure 6.2). Over time, as the value of higher density, mixed-use development supports redevelopment of additional, higher-value shopping centers facing Roswell Road, the Main Street will extend and remain the downtown's central focus (see figure 6.3).

In 2011 the mayor floated a trial balloon: Should Sandy Springs invest in creating a new civic center together with a town green, perhaps enhanced by a small Main Street that provided a better alternative to the strip centers along Roswell Road as a new "city center"? Neighborhood leaders responded with enthusiasm and urged the city to be more ambitious—why not several blocks of Main Street so that people could stroll, enjoy cafés, and have a place to meet friends?

The city hired consultants to identify a potential site and to analyze housing and commercial real estate markets and test the feasibility of the plan. The results were positive, but not in ways city officials had anticipated. They had assumed the city might redevelop a shopping center on Roswell Road as a lifestyle center that included a city hall. Roswell Road did in fact make a great deal of sense as a location, but market studies pointed toward a different path. An analysis of retail and office demand found little interest from the national businesses that fill lifestyle centers. Instead it found strong unmet demand for several hundred thousand square feet of development devoted to unique shops and restaurants and "cool" office space geared to start-ups. Even more surprising, an analysis of housing markets uncovered strong demand for lofts and other high-quality multifamily housing in a walkable, mixed-use setting—more than a thousand units over five to seven years. This redevelopment strategy, however, would only work on side streets, not Roswell Road itself. Traffic counts of 50,000-plus cars per day made its highway-oriented retail too valuable to redevelop. The new downtown would occupy roughly a hundred acres one block away.

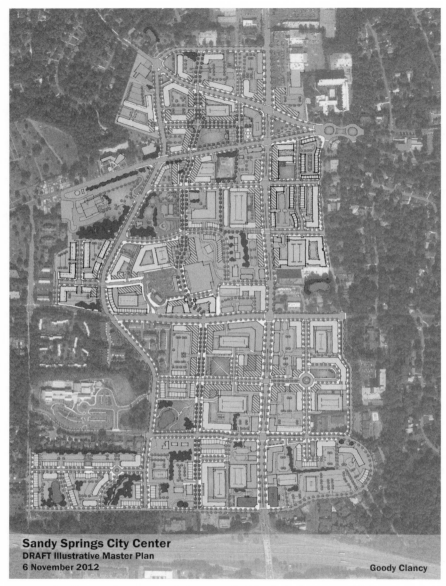

Sandy Springs City Center
DRAFT Illustrative Master Plan
6 November 2012

Goody Clancy

FIGURE 6.2. In 2011 the mayor and city council of Sandy Springs, one of Atlanta's most affluent suburbs, announced that the time had come to create a new "village green" and city hall.
Plan courtesy of Goody Clancy.

FIGURE 6.3. Sketch of redevelopment potential for City Center in Sandy Springs, Georgia. *Courtesy of Goody Clancy.*

The market studies upended assumptions about the redevelopment plan. They showed that surging demand for high-quality, multifamily housing in settings with such "urban" amenities as a mix of uses, walkable streets, a town green, and structured parking would provide the real engine for redevelopment, rather than commercial uses. As in many comparable communities, the feasibility of creating a new downtown turned out to rest on a housing market that would barely have registered five years earlier—and had certainly never figured in anyone's vision of Sandy Springs or suburbs in general.

Breaking a stereotype of politically conservative suburbs, the mayor won widespread support from the city council and neighborhood leaders for a new downtown. From the start, residents voiced two concerns. They did not want the city to divert dollars from their neighborhoods to pay for a new grid of streets or a town green—and they expressed even stronger opposition to raising taxes to help fund the project. The mayor offered a convincing response: the new downtown's higher-density, higher-quality development would increase property-tax revenues by five to ten times. Neighborhood leaders held firm on another point: They wanted urban amenities and could accept the necessary urban densities needed to make them happen, but urban scale in the form of high-rise development was off the table, no matter what amenities or public benefits it might bring.

Dublin, Ohio: Downtown as an Alternative to Sprawl

Dublin also calls itself a city but is, in fact, a quintessential suburb. The second-wealthiest community in Ohio and host to the largest concentration of high-quality jobs in the Columbus region, Dublin ranks at or near the top of national community-satisfaction surveys and has been named as a top place to live by *Forbes* (July 2009), MONEY (April 2011), and similar mainstream media. Because Ohio has an employment tax, Dublin's well-paid workforce supports top-notch public services, parks, and schools that would be the envy of virtually any other suburb or major city. The city had earned the right to be complacent.

Dublin didn't earn its laurels by chance. The credit goes to a tradition of planning and development policies that have anticipated market shifts. From the 1970s to the 1990s, Jack Nicklaus–designed golf courses and beautifully land-scaped class-A office parks positioned Dublin as the region's premier housing and office market. A farming village of 2,500 in 1960, it has grown into a suburb with more than 40,000 residents and 50,000 workers. In 2008, however, the city's leadership began to question the viability of a sprawl-form growth model from both an environmental and a market perspective. The time had come again to innovate.

Figures 6.4–6.5 show new mixed-use squares, each with a specific mission— entertainment, civic and cultural activities, and technology. Mixed-use neigh-borhoods of lofts and row houses are concentrated within a five-minute walk of each square. Rubber-tire transit connects the neighborhoods. The plan pre-serves the historic village center and adds a new central park spanning both sides of the Scioto River.

Two trends in particular worried Dublin's leaders. An aging population meant that (largely older) sellers in the housing market would soon outnumber

FIGURE 6.4. Bridge Park, Dublin, Ohio. The plan focuses on transforming Dublin's Bridge Street Corridor into a high-density, mixed-use, walkable downtown. It is currently dominated by underperforming shopping centers and office buildings. *Courtesy of Crawford Hoying Development.*

FIGURE 6.5. Aerial rendering of Bridge Park, Dublin, Ohio. *Courtesy of Crawford Hoying Development.*

(largely younger) buyers. Because older households gravitated toward more urban settings, this imbalance represented a particular threat to a suburb that essentially comprised almost solely single-family-housing subdivisions. At the same time Dublin's high-tech and research-based businesses faced increasing challenges—even at the height of the recession—in attracting educated, creative workers who preferred urban settings.

On a scale that far exceeded Sandy Springs' ambitions, Dublin launched a community-based planning process to create a new downtown that would offer the urban qualities that both residents and employees sought at a scale that would reposition Dublin as a suburb known for urban amenities and committed to smart growth. The first task was to identity a location for a future downtown—in this case a mile-long stretch of Bridge Street that encompassed the historic but tiny village center dating to Dublin's earliest days, together with roughly a thousand acres of outmoded shopping centers and office parks on either side. Market studies indicated that demand existed for 10 to 15 million square feet of mixed-use development over twenty to twenty-five years—with half to two-thirds of that in the form of lofts and similar high-quality multifamily housing. This housing represents roughly one-third of all housing demand for Dublin—a dramatic shift from previous decades, when demand for single-family houses defined the market. Increased interest in walkable environments will enable the new downtown to compete for roughly half of Dublin's office and retail development, significantly slowing the pace of sprawl.

The concept of a "lively, walkable, higher-density" downtown that offered a rich sense of community won wide support. People readily endorsed the downtown's dual mission of enhancing residents' quality of life and attracting the talent required to sustain the city's employment and tax bases. However, residents expressed skepticism about a vision so different from the way real estate markets had worked for sixty years. The city invited a series of nationally recognized figures to speak at public meetings about changes in real estate and job markets. The speakers also briefed the city council and met with property owners and developers. These meetings introduced a series of workshops and design charrettes that emphasized market realities and implementation strategies. In 2011, Dublin's community (and ultimately its city council) embraced a plan that few had believed possible a few years earlier.

Rosslyn, Virginia: Humanizing an Edge City

Connected to Washington, D.C., by two highway bridges and a heavily used Metro line, Rosslyn (one of twelve communities that together constitute Arlington County) at first glance represents a sharp contrast to Sandy Springs and Dublin. Yet from a different perspective it represents another version of the

FIGURE 6.6. The existing view along Nash Street in Rosslyn, Virginia, an edge city in suburban Arlington County, Virginia. Rosslyn is being retrofitted into a high-density, walkable, mixed-use downtown. Shown is the existing view along Nash Street. *Courtesy of Goody Clancy.*

same story. Arlington is intent on transforming Rosslyn from a suburban environment designed around the car into a walkable, community-rich downtown. However, today Rosslyn's eight million square feet—largely housed in roughly twenty office towers—continues to belie its edge-city heritage (see figure 6.6). Arterial highways built to move traffic quickly between Washington and Virginia suburbs still dominate its streets. Skywalks still pull pedestrians off these wide, often traffic-clogged streets. Neither the skywalks nor the streets below as of yet support much retail, and pedestrians intrepid enough to use public sidewalks still encounter the blank walls of parking garages.

Redevelopment of more than half of Rosslyn's existing buildings over the next decade—a direct response to the growing premium that real estate markets place on the ability to create mixed-use, walkable environments—unlocks the ability to transform this iconic suburban edge city. A mix of incentives and requirements ensures that each new development also represents an investment in uses that animate the streets and create great public spaces, a growing role for the arts, and similar qualities of a vibrant downtown.

Rosslyn's early success as an edge city was based on its ability to attract large corporate tenants from downtown Washington, D.C., to its modern office buildings with good access to the District. As the 1990s progressed, newer suburban office developments offering lively streets began to compete with Rosslyn for this market. Nearby neighborhoods increasingly complained about Rosslyn's antiseptic character. Meanwhile Arlington's planners found success in shaping development around other Metro stations that produced lively, walkable, mixed-use environments and enjoyed strong public support. In the mid-1990s the county launched the first of a series of community-based plans intended to achieve these same qualities in Rosslyn. However, despite some victories these plans were largely thwarted by the reality that potential development lacked sufficient value to induce redevelopment of the seventies and eighties office towers and ever-present parking structures that characterize the area.

As the Washington, D.C., region emerged from the Recession in 2009, this real estate equation began to shift. Over the next three years developers approached the county with proposals for a new generation of 25- to 30-story office and residential towers whose value made it possible to replace increasingly outmoded seventies- and eighties-era buildings. Property owners, developers, and local businesses banded together to establish a Business Improvement District, which invited the larger community to participate in festivals and a full calendar of arts and performance events. In 2012 the county's planners engaged the community in yet another planning process, but in this case one tied directly to implementation strategies that leveraged increased real estate value to achieve longstanding goals. As the process drew to a close in 2013, the county's commitment to planning began to pay off.

Armed with an agenda that commanded wide support from neighborhood leaders and developers alike, Arlington went to work. The plan identified priority "walking streets," and the county required that all new development line these streets with shops, restaurants, and other uses that engaged passersby (see figure 6.7). The two most egregious traffic arteries that cut through the center of Rosslyn were put on a "road diet"—traffic lanes were converted into wider sidewalks with more room for cafés and an ambitious public art initiative. Through-traffic was diverted around Rosslyn and developers and property owners agreed to remove the skywalks. The county offered height bonuses in return for public benefits, which ranged from a Whole Foods supermarket in the base of one office building to creation of three new public squares lined with cafés and including amenities like play fountains or farmers' markets. Another development is funding reconstruction of an air-rights park located over a highway into an outdoor performance venue. By mid-2013 roughly three million square feet of mixed-use development was moving through the county's approvals process. Several residents who for years had opposed another round of development in Rosslyn reversed position and cited Manhattan's vitality as an aspirational model for Rosslyn's future.

FIGURE 6.7. Proposed mix of housing, office, retail, and lively street life for Rosslyn, Virginia.
Courtesy of Stantec's Urban Group.

The Future of Suburban Downtowns

City officials in Sandy Springs and Dublin were initially concerned that their community's reaction to a new downtown would literally be "not in our back-yard." Instead, while some residents did express these views, they were outnum-bered by residents who asked: How soon can it happen? Can I walk or ride my bike to get there? This change in attitude does not imply blind acceptance of urban densities and mixed-use development, but it does indicate a willingness to balance the costs and benefits in terms of quality of life, the environment, and fiscal impacts. More and more often, these benefits are seen to outweigh the costs. Increasingly, suburban communities that may oppose a new shopping mall in their midst will embrace a new walkable downtown.

However, other challenges are more intractable. A new downtown is only feasible in a relatively small number of affluent suburbs that can leverage surging real estate markets for high-quality multifamily housing (Sandy Springs and Dublin) or transit-oriented development (Rosslyn). While this state represents progress compared to even five years ago, without significant investment—such as a new transit connection—most suburbs have a long way to go in terms of building market support. In addition, supporters of suburban downtowns often advocate the benefits of diversity, but such diversity is much more likely to involve ethnic, age, or racial—but not economic—diversity. The economics of suburban downtown development are often sufficient to invest in new streets and the public realm, but they do not yet stretch far enough to support affordable housing. As this new age of suburban downtowns is about building community, the next task will involve making this vision of community fully inclusive.

NOTES

1. Ray Oldenburg, *The Great Good Place: Cafes, Coffee Shops, Community Centers, Beauty Parlors, General Stores, Bars, Hangouts, and How They Get You through the Day* (New York: Paragon House, 1989).

2. Joel Garreau, *Edge Cities: Life on the New Frontier* (New York: Anchor Books, 1991).

3. Research available on the Zimmerman/Volk Associates webpage, http://www.zva.cc.

4. Arthur C. Nelson, *Reshaping Metropolitan America: Trends and Opportunities to 2030* (Washington, D.C.: Island Press, 2012).

CHAPTER 7

The Public Sector Steps Up— And Retrofits a Zombie Subdivision

ELLEN DUNHAM-JONES AND WESLEY BROWN

Key Points and Practice Takeaways

1. The public sector is taking an increasingly proactive role in the second generation of suburban retrofits by rezoning corridors for mixed-use—often with form-based codes, public land, complex public-private partnerships, and, in a few cases, taking on the role of master developer for failed projects.

2. The small town of Covington, Georgia, took on the role of master developer of a failed subdivision, Walker's Bend, and not only profited on its investment but also increased affordable housing and protected overall property values.

3. Creative partnerships were key to the successful integration of affordable housing into Walker's Bend.

4. Small towns pressured by surrounding sprawl can be as successful at retrofitting as larger municipalities—but it helps to have a history of good planning and support from a local foundation.

5. Great retrofits are led by great champions.

The Great Recession that began in 2007 has significantly altered the suburban retrofit landscape—but it has done so very unevenly. To better understand the new patterns, we find it useful to differentiate between three distinctive generations of retrofits. We focus on the expanded role of the public sector in second-generation retrofits, with particular attention to the case of Walker's Bend where the city of Covington, Georgia, has taken on the role of master developer to rescue a zombie subdivision and provide a diverse range of affordable housing.[1]

Some of the larger questions that the story of Walker's Bend helps illuminate include: How is the practice of retrofitting suburbia evolving and what does it tell us about the prospects of "fixing sprawl"? Is retrofitting limited to the redevelopment of defunct retail properties in first-ring suburbs? Has the public sector's role increased or diminished as a result of the Great Recession, stimulus spending, and budget cuts (including elimination of California's redevelopment authorities)? Is the gentrification resulting from redevelopment exacerbating the problems of the increasing number of suburbanites in poverty or contributing to increased affordability?

First-, Second-, and Third-Generation Retrofits

As described in *Retrofitting Suburbia: Urban Design Solutions for Redesigning Suburbs*, retrofitting is not simply a matter of upgrading existing suburban buildings and uses.[2] Rather, it involves changes to properties with a suburban form (regardless of location) that help them become healthier, more sustainable places. This might mean improving social sustainability by reinhabiting a dead big-box store or strip mall with more community-serving uses such as a school, library, medical clinic, place of worship, or major jobs center. Our database documents over eighty-five such reinhabitations in the United States, and there are doubtless many more. In other cases, declining use of a property allows for it to be regreened either by reconstructing the wetlands or introducing parks or agriculture.

Both reinhabitation and regreening are important strategies. But, meeting sustainability's triple bottom line requires more extensive redevelopment of auto-oriented sites into mixed-use, walkable, urban formats.[3] For example, over fifty enclosed shopping malls have broken ground for such redevelopment, often providing their suburbs with the downtowns they never had. This more sustainably accommodates population growth in existing communities with existing infrastructure instead of directing it to costly greenfield expansion at the exurban edge. It also provides the choice of an urban lifestyle in a suburban location for the rapidly growing market of one-person and no-children households.[4]

In fact, this continues to be the majority of the market for all generations of suburban retrofits: downsizing empty-nester baby boomers, divorced dads looking to remain in their children's community, and unmarried young professionals working in suburbia but looking for nightlife and social activities that don't revolve around schools. They are increasingly complemented by those who rent office space, hoping to recruit the "creative class" with a more urban setting; and by retailers and restaurateurs, chasing the discretionary spending of baby boomers and Generation Y with street life and cafés rather than landscaped berms and food courts. But this is not the only market benefiting from retrofits. A growing number of projects are addressing the needs of lower-income families and seniors.

As shown in table 7.1, if the first generation of suburban retrofits are predominantly developer-led projects in first-ring suburbs, the second generation of retrofits are predominantly public-sector-led and as likely to occur in downtowns (mostly as retrofits of urban renewal–era downtown malls), exurbs (mostly in the form of zombie or stalled subdivisions), and the corridors in between (either as conversions to transit boulevards or pedestrian-oriented streetscaping paired with mixed-use rezoning).

Born out of the contractions of the Great Recession, the second-generation retrofits set up the conditions for ambitious and expansive third-generation retrofits at the metro scale. Mostly limited so far to a few hot markets (e.g., Washington, D.C., Vancouver, and Austin), third-generation retrofits integrate combinations of reinhabitation, redevelopment, and regreening into transfor-

TABLE 7.1. Three generations of suburban retrofits

FIRST-GENERATION SUBURBAN RETROFITS

- First-ring suburbs
- Developer-led
- Redevelopments, wherever a deal can be made
- Pockets of walkability
- Modeled on the architecture and urbanism of the past

SECOND-GENERATION SUBURBAN RETROFITS

- Downtowns, corridors, and exurbs
- Public sector–led
- More reinhabitation and regreening
- More attention to affordability

THIRD-GENERATION SUBURBAN RETROFITS

- Integration of large private redevelopments with public infrastructure improvements along transit lines
- Maturing retrofits with expansions, civic uses, and diversification of uses
- More integrated public-private partnering
- More high-rises and forward-looking design
- Greater integration of sustainability features (transit, biking, renewable or district energy, affordability, etc.)
- Greater integration of reinhabitation, redevelopment, and regreening in combination

mations of large swaths of both public infrastructure and private development. In other words, the third generation of retrofits do indeed hold tremendous promise to "fix sprawl." However, they can only do so through the expanded role of the public sector, and that is best understood by examining the second generation of retrofits more closely.

The Public Sector Steps Up

In the boom years leading up to the Great Recession, municipal planners in active markets were bombarded with rezoning requests as developers sought to retrofit greyfield "underperforming asphalt" into denser, mixed-use New Urbanist communities. Escalating prices and the frenzied pace of construction left little time for planners to catch up, let alone lead.

The recession changed all that. It provided many planners with a chance to catch their breath and shift from a reactive to a proactive position, cognizant of the "new normal" and the "lean economy." The recession laid bare the high costs of sprawl—both in terms of transportation costs to households and of infrastructure costs to municipalities.[5] At the same time, studies showed that walkable New Urbanist neighborhoods closer to downtown were holding value far better than drivable suburban neighborhoods further out.[6] As the recession lingered, more and more communities began planning processes that asked critical questions about what kind of place they wanted to become and what kind of development they hoped to attract when—and if—the economy recovered. To assist this kind of planning, during 2009–2012, the Obama administration's Partnership for Sustainable Communities funded $240 million in planning grants and over $3.5 billion in overall assistance and implementation to over 700 communities.[7]

Many of those funds have gone toward plans to retrofit suburban arterials. The twenty-some case studies of corridors that June Williamson and Ellen Dunham-Jones were monitoring in 2008 have been joined by an additional 160 proposed projects in 2013—and that's still only a partial list.

Why so much attention to commercial strip corridors? Despite the obvious challenges of implementation, in many respects they are low-hanging fruit. Often lined with aging, unloved properties, many are prime for redevelopment with little NIMBY resistance. They also provide great opportunities to link much-needed affordable housing to affordable transportation as commercial strip corridors are retrofitted into safe and attractive transit boulevards.

Whether it's regreening a downtown mall (as at Columbus Commons in Ohio), coordinating the redevelopment of large suburban parcels along a new transit corridor (as at Airport Boulevard in Austin, Texas, and the Silver Line in Tysons Corner, Virginia), or directing the reinhabitation and redevelopment of a stalled exurban subdivision (as at Walker's Bend in Covington, Georgia), the public sector has indeed stepped up. In the process, it has expanded the suburban retrofit toolkit—from negotiating complex and innovative public-private partnerships to acquiring and leveraging publicly owned land. These are perhaps best illustrated in the case of Walker's Bend, one of the more extreme examples of the public sector taking the lead.

Case Study: Walker's Bend, Covington, Georgia

Like many other small towns on the outskirts of metropolitan American cities, Covington, Georgia, saw expanded development throughout the 1990s and early 2000s. Also similar to other towns, Covington's growth retracted with the Great Recession. Unlike most other municipalities, however, the City of Covington intervened as master developer to retrofit Walker's Bend, a foreclosed subdivision. As a result, Walker's Bend today has a more diverse mix of uses, public spaces, housing types, and housing tenure options, while meeting the environmentally friendly criteria of an Earth Craft Community (see figure 7.1). In addition, the Covington Redevelopment Authority (CRA) stands to make a profit from its land acquisitions.

How did a city council reach this decision and what did it require of the chief planning officer? Could/should more cities take on the role of master developer, or is Walker's Bend a unique case because of its rather unique planning history?

Located 35 miles east of Atlanta, Covington is the county seat for Newton County and is graced with a historic downtown and central green courthouse square. Its 13.9 square miles house approximately 13,000 citizens. This intact southern small town has served as the setting for numerous films and television shows, such as *In the Heat of the Night* and *The Dukes of Hazzard*. However, as Atlanta sprawled, Newton County became one of the fastest-growing counties in the nation, prompting local and metro-wide concern about how to preserve both its small towns and its predominantly rural landscape.

In 1997, the Georgia Conservancy inaugurated its Blueprints for Successful Communities program by sponsoring a workshop on the City of Covington. The Blueprints program was a very early example of environmentalists and members of the business community coming together around the ideas of new urbanism and smart growth as a means to combat sprawl and boost existing local economies. Professor Randal Roark of the Georgia Institute of Technology led five teams of architecture and city planning students, working with professionals on five sites, to demonstrate how the city could absorb twenty years' worth of higher-density growth while improving the quality of life and protecting the environment. The Walker's Bend site, called at the time "the Southern Site," is essentially a 100-acre peninsula surrounded by the winding tributaries of Indian Creek. The team proposed a village center bordering SR 81, backed by a gridded residential neighborhood of walkable blocks with

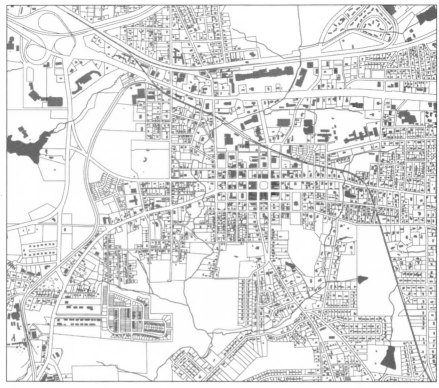

FIGURE 7.1. Figure-field of Covington, Georgia, 2007.
Courtesy of Wesley Brown.

modest-sized lots of declining density toward the site's extensive eastern border with Indian Creek. Opposite the creek, they also proposed extensions to existing subdivisions to flank the creek and provide possible future bridged connections.[8]

Excited by the potential of the ideas and sketch plans proposed by the Blueprints study, in 2000 one of the sponsors, a local charitable foundation named the Arnold Fund, collaborated with the city to bring in leading New Urbanist firm Duany Plater-Zyberk & Company (DPZ) to do a more detailed master plan and form-based code for the downtown, a Transit-Oriented Development (TOD), two Traditional Neighborhood Developments (TNDs), and a hamlet on four of the original sites (see figure 7.2).[9] The plan proposed that accommodating 1,000 new residents within a mile or two of downtown would provide the base of additional support for downtown businesses to help them compete against the growing number of big box stores out on the highways.

The eight-day charrette led by Galina Tachieva produced a revised and more

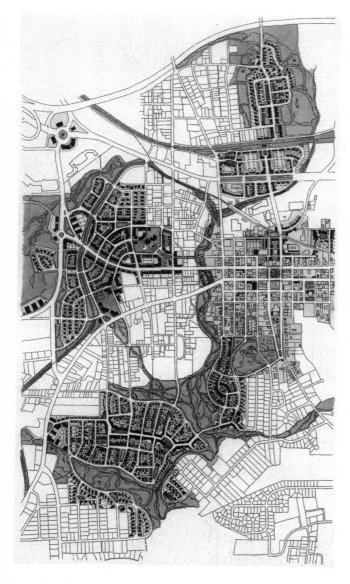

FIGURE 7.2.
DPZ master plan for
Covington, 2000.
*Courtesy of
DPZ & Co.*

detailed plan for Walker's Bend, now a TND called "Parker Pasture" (see figure 7.3). In the DPZ plan the walkable blocks are now in a more "relaxed" street grid that warps to create a sense of place through intimate deflected vistas and elongated small parks. Again, it concentrates density along SR 81 and allows larger single-family homes on larger lots facing the slopes to Indian Creek. It introduces a central spine flanked by higher-density townhomes and anchored by two urban squares with sites for small civic buildings.

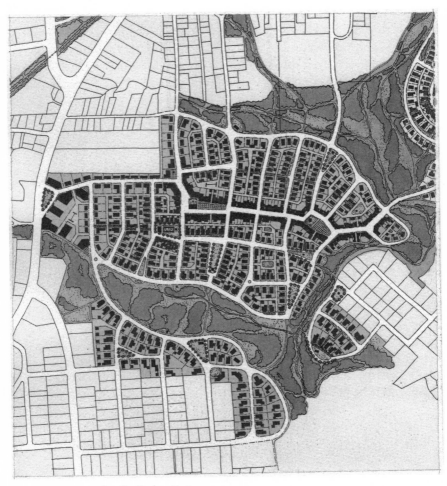

FIGURE 7.3. DPZ plan for Parker Pasture.
Courtesy of DPZ & Co.

To shepherd the vision into reality, the city made zoning changes that encourage, but do not require, mixed-use and smaller lots.[10] As is often the case
in such situations, the results are mixed. One of the TND sites was developed
as a very attractive demonstration project by Clark's Grove, LLC, a for-profit
company established by the Arnold Fund. They gathered a team both knowledgeable in and committed to the New Urbanist plan.[11] Clark's Grove's neotra-
ditional Earth Craft–rated apartments, live-works, and houses feature a range
of price points ($157,000–$500,000 for Phase I) and front onto a green square
designed as an outdoor room. The walkable infill neighborhood incorporates
a Montessori School, a few restaurants and shops, and a studio and dorms for

the University of Georgia Metropolitan Design Studio. The first homes became available in 2003.[12]

In the same year, as metro Atlanta was charging into the housing boom, Timber South Inc. and Mitchell Builders created their own plan for 249 owner-occupied dwellings on the central fifty acres of the second TND site and called it Walker's Bend. Although the plan included narrow lots (from 35' × 110' to 55' × 110') and a mix of attached dwellings, fee-simple townhouses, and single-family detached residences, DPZ's quirky street grid, organization of buildings fronting onto public spaces, and the village center site on SR 81 were gone. Instead, the village center site was developed with light industrial buildings flanking the now inauspicious and unwalkable entry into Walker's Bend.

Construction for the project kicked off in 2004, and by 2007 seventy-two single-family detached homes and eight attached townhouses of the 249 lots had been built. With sale prices from $115,000 to $160,000, they were comparable to the median range of housing stock in the Covington/Newton County area at the time. By early 2007, fifty homes had sold to their occupants. But then, the housing bubble burst and sales stopped.

The Great Recession ended seventy-three consecutive months of economic expansion in the United States—much of it fed by subprime mortgages and the seemingly inexhaustible demand for new housing. Timber South Inc. and Mitchell Builders were early casualties. They along with eight different banks—with assets exceeding $5,000,000 in the development—soon filed for bankruptcy. Between 2008 and 2011, three of the banks themselves were shuttered by the FDIC, further complicating the task of reassembling land ownership.

The banks began auctioning the twenty-two unoccupied finished homes in 2008. The average sale price had declined to $57,000, and most were purchased by remote investors as rental properties. Fully half of the community's finished homes were now rentals.

Fearful of the impact of such declines on property values throughout the small town and eager to implement the city's long-term master plan (which had been further updated with a corridor study in 2005, adoption of a new zoning code in 2008, and economic development plans with the county in 2009), the Covington City Council decided to intervene. Relying upon the state's Urban Redevelopment Act, enabling legislation dating back to 1955 for urban renewal, in 2009 the city established an Urban Redevelopment Plan and the Covington Redevelopment Authority (CRA). By designating the "Redevelopment Area" as meeting the definitions of a "slum area," the city expanded its implementation tools and ability to qualify for state and federal financing. Walker's Bend was included as part of the Washington Street Corridor, one of thirteen subareas in the Redevelopment Area.

To reverse the cycle of disinvestment and gain control of enough of Walker's Bend to redirect its future, the city council loaned the CRA about $570,000 and allocated to it the entire $428,070 received in federal Neighborhood Stabilization Program (NSP) dollars, for a total of $1,000,000 for purchasing vacant lots and unoccupied homes.[13] The goal was to refine the original design and finish the development as a mixed-use, mixed-income, Earth Craft Community.[14]

This task fell to just the right person, Randy Vinson, a landscape architect and Covington's director of planning and zoning. Having previously served as town planner and project manager for Clark's Grove, LLC and as one of the professional leaders on the Blueprints' team, Vinson had both experience as a New Urbanist developer and familiarity with the site to bring to the city's new role as master developer.

What neither Vinson nor many other developers had experience with prior to 2008 was trolling online auction foreclosure websites in order to find and procure the now highly disaggregated lots. The properties were spread among multiple lending institutions, most of them flooded with foreclosed properties that they disposed of through online auctions—but without a central clearinghouse to make it possible to find specific properties. Rigorous title searches to find owners were further hindered because so many of the foreclosed properties were routed through the FDIC. "Once the FDIC owns the property, it [becomes] increasingly more difficult to identify an owner's representative who can [legally] authorize a sale," said Vinson.[15] His goal was to purchase key clusters of lots to allow strategic replatting and repositioning of the failed subdivision. The only way to do so was through the auctions, a process with a learning curve steeper than he expected.

A state of urgency was created when a sign announcing an FDIC auction for a key parcel at the entrance to the neighborhood was posted in October 2009. At this time no funding had been approved for the newly created CRA, let alone a checking account. In order to prevent the project from getting derailed before it even started, Vinson elected to use his personal funds to secure the $6,900 parcel. At the time, the CRA was deliberately not publicizing the city's procurement intentions. They hoped to avoid a price hike during the seminal stage of assembling parcels. However, Vinson admits to being coaxed at a real estate auction to disclose the city's interest to another auction attendee and subsequently fell victim to shill bidding. Eventually, news of the city's plans made headlines in the local paper when a resident insinuated that Vinson's secretive activities were unethical.[16] The stir the news created prompted an inspection of the city's finances, which led to the discovery that the city had actually shorted Vinson 10 cents on his reimbursement.

Once public, a small contingency objected to the city's position as the "master developer." The CRA received a considerable amount of negative comments posted to articles regarding the project. Nevertheless, the mayor and council—sometimes by narrow margins—continued to support both the revitalization of Walker's Bend and the long-term commitment to the larger plan for revitalizing the city. Initially drawn to the city because of Covington's legacy of planning, Vinson said, "The citizens expect [this city] to continue to achieve this plan."[17]

With the majority of the community in favor of the project, the city forged on. From its initial purchase in 2009 of 18 lots for approximately $5,500 each, by 2011 it had assembled 92 lots from six different banks and the FDIC.

While assembling lots, the CRA also assembled partnerships with key allies:

- Habitat for Humanity: After the CRA purchased eight overgrown and never-occupied townhomes with NSP funds, Habitat for Humanity found qualified customers to purchase them with sweat equity and move in (see figures 7.4A and 7.4B).
- Covington Housing Authority: CHA agreed to serve as the civic anchor for the mixed-use New Leaf Center at the entry to Walker's Bend,

FIGURES 7.4A AND 7.4B. Habitat for Humanity townhomes before and after redevelopment. *Courtesy of* Covington News.

where it offers various counseling and training programs and owns and manages twenty-eight transitional housing units and a workforce development/business incubation space. Construction began in 2012 with move-in scheduled for fall 2013.[18]

- Viewpoint Health Services: The local Health Services Board will own and operate twenty-six supportive housing units for the developmentally disabled in a building adjacent to the New Leaf Center. Construction is expected to begin in late 2013.

- Affordable Equity Partners: AEP is a for-profit, tax-credit housing developer who replatted a block with 28 lots into 32 lots with a common green and clubhouse. Called "The Village at Walker's Bend," the homes are on fifteen-year lease-to-purchase payment plans with income restrictions of 50–60 percent of AMI and were fully occupied by early 2013 at gross rents of $811–$926 for units of 1,400–1,525 square feet. AEP expects to follow up with a $9 million senior housing complex shortly.

- University of Georgia Metropolitan Design Studio: Established in 2006, the studio brings a dozen landscape architecture students to live in the Clark's Grove TND for a semester each year while working on real projects in the city. In 2009, with Vinson as their instructor, the students revised the master plan. They reestablished a minimal mixed-use cluster at the entry, established a neighborhood park, and shortened some of the excessively deep lots to produce shared green spaces.[19] Some of the students went on to produce a pattern book in collaboration with local homebuilders of small, market-rate, owner-occupied, 800–1,400-square-foot, well-insulated, affordable homes called "Covington Cottages."[20] These come with downpayment assistance through Georgia Department of Community Affairs CHIP grants and are priced at $75,000–$95,000. As of mid-2013 none have been constructed. Continued 50–70 percent discount prices on foreclosures have resulted in prohibitive appraisals for new for-sale construction, but Vinson hopes to wait it out.[21]

- Walker's Bend residents: One of the homeowners was appointed to the CRA board of directors, and all were consulted on the drafting of an overlay ordinance in 2010 to address issues of property maintenance and architectural design guidelines. Instead of belabored legal descriptions, the ordinance requires that all applications for construction be reviewed by the planning and zoning director and "must comply with the standards set forth in Marianne Cusato et al., *Get Your House Right* (2007)."[22]

As master developer coordinating all of these partnerships, the CRA was helped enormously by having a strong vision based on the planning work that had already been completed for the site. Targeted replatting restored many of the

TND features of the DPZ plan including inclusion of multifamily housing, albeit now for a much leaner economy, and more diverse, affordable housing types. The revised master plan allowed the CRA to direct different partners to focus their efforts and different housing needs on targeted clusters of lots. At the same time it linked them together around a sequence of distinct public spaces: the mixed-use entry with an incubator kitchen, community meeting rooms, and other social spaces at the ground floor; the Village's town green to the north; the new community park and playground to the south (assembled out of ten undeveloped house lots); and the parallel greenswards to the east (see figures 7.5A, 7.5B, and 7.5C). The master plan is complemented by the controls of the new overlay zoning ordinance. Once adopted in 2010, the CRA no longer needed to continue to acquire the remaining lots. Vinson said that at that point they were happy to get out of the way and let the market take over.[23]

So what did the city receive in return for its $570,000 loan to the CRA? Over $30 million in capital investment is in new, green, affordable housing, most of it from private sources according to the chair of the CRA, Nita Thompson.[24] In addition, the CRA has collected $63,000 in income from lot sales and expects to gain $8,000–$900,000 more. Those funds, according to Thompson, will go "to expand the neighborhood redevelopment initiative to other neighborhoods in Covington."[25] This means that in addition to rescuing Walker's Bend from an indeterminate fallow future, retrofitting it back into a mixed-use and mixed-income TND, and improving the quality of affordable housing options in the city, the CRA's intervention is expected to support continued urbanization of other underperforming properties to realize the city's long-term plans to accommodate growth in ways that boost the downtown instead of sprawl.

Did the retrofit of Walker's Bend stem the bleeding when Atlanta-area housing prices began to hemorrhage in 2008? Precise comparisons are difficult to make. Covington's price points did not have as far to fall as several other parts of the Atlanta market. Metro Atlanta's freefall in housing prices lasted five years, hitting a fourteen-year low in March 2012 before trending upward. The 30014 zip code that includes Walker's Bend and downtown Covington saw the median price of home sales drop significantly in 2008 before stabilizing with a more gentle decline during 2009–11.[26] More recently, concurrent with completion of more construction at Walker's Bend and the beginnings of metrowide recovery in the housing market, prices have increased dramatically. According to Trulia, the average price per square foot for housing in Covington on June 14, 2013 was $71, an increase of 69 percent compared to the same period the previous year (and compared to the city of Atlanta's increase of 44 percent for the same period).[27]

Ironically, the long-term success of integrating Walker's Bend's subsidized affordable housing with market-rate housing may in fact depend on such further increases in local housing values. Private investment, whether in the form

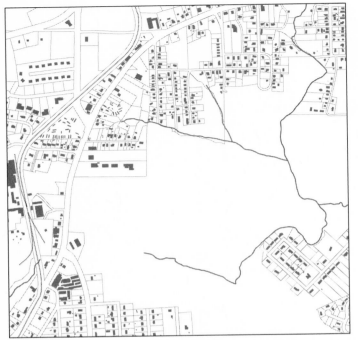

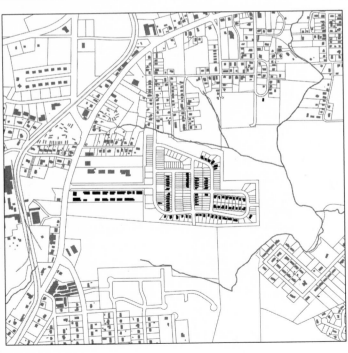

FIGURES 7.5A, 7.5B, AND 7.5C. Combined image of figure-grounds of Walker's Bend for 1987, 2007, and 2027. *Courtesy of Wesley Brown.*

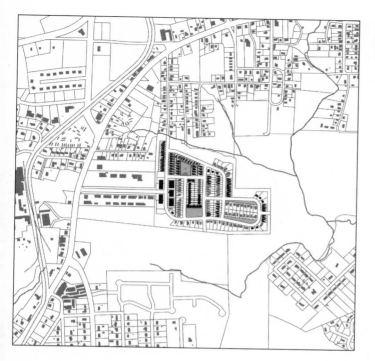

FIGURES 7.5A,
7.5B, AND 7.5C.
(continued)

of modestly priced Covington Cottages or more conventional homes, is unlikely until appraisal values rise. Is it possible that Walker's Bend will become
a ghetto of sorts, restricted to residents who meet low-income requirements?
Or, will the CRA and its partners' investments in quality placemaking and innovative financing succeed in providing the appropriate infrastructure for a truly
mixed-income TND? It's too soon to tell.

Beyond the financial return, Vinson believes his city now has a fuller ap-
preciation of both the value and the pace of community building. While he
expects that "in five years there will still be vacant lots in Walker's Bend," he also
believes citizens now understand that building a community requires more than
constructing single-family homes. The successes at Walker's Bend are building
"momentum [that] will allow the city to aid other redevelopments," said Vinson.[28] Covington is now much better positioned to accommodate the ambitious
growth goals set by Newton County's nationally recognized 2050 plan: absorb
88 percent of the future population on 30 percent of the county's land.[29]

Not every exurban zombie subdivision should be reinhabited and redeveloped. In fact, in rural places like Teton County, Idaho, where subdivisions were
excessively approved during the boom years, many are now being regreened
and having their entitlements vacated. Nor should every city take on the task
of master developer in order to stimulate suburban retrofits—although it has

also been used in strong markets like West Valley City, Utah.[30] Nor is Walker's Bend likely to ever be as connected or as pretty as Clark's Grove. The question is, how replicable is the retrofit of Walker's Bend for other communities struggling with near-in zombie subdivisions and increased needs for affordable housing (especially in the face of the dramatic rise in suburban poverty rates)?[31]

Walker's Bend illustrates how the public sector can leverage its patient capital and use the role of master developer to acquire and replat land (and take advantage of foreclosures to purchase the land at bargain prices). It shows the value of public-sector-led strategic partnerships that qualify for various forms of public financing. It also shows how Covington was able to use its role as master developer to improve the quality not just of affordable housing but of affordable living in a mixed-use, mixed-income community one mile from the downtown.

But it also reinforces the crucial importance of having both a strong vision—provided by the good New Urbanist plans that Covington invested in over the past eighteen years—and strong champions. The value of both Randy Vinson's broad talents and dedication to the project, as well as the catalytic role of the Arnold Fund, cannot be underestimated. Committed individuals and organizations who persevere through the political, financial, and societal challenges that retrofitting inevitably confronts make the difference between pretty projects on paper and realized change. As the public sector continues to step up its role in retrofitting suburbia, there will be just as much need for visionary planning and rezoning as there will be for savvy implementation, including understanding the role of the city as master developer.

NOTES

1. The phrase "zombie subdivision" began appearing in the popular and professional press in 2009 to describe stalled and abandoned partially built residential subdivisions. Approved and financed during the real estate boom of 2005–6, these subdivisions comprise thousands of acres of recently developed land across the United States with looping suburban roads, sewers, streetlights and, often, a few homes that went fallow and into foreclosure when the housing market crashed.

2. Ellen Dunham-Jones and June Williamson, *Retrofitting Suburbia: Urban Design Solutions for Redesigning Suburbs* (Hoboken, N.J.: Wiley, 2011).

3. Good examples of first-generation suburban retrofits include Belmar in Lakewood, Colorado (redevelopment of a dead mall into a new, green downtown); La Grande Orange in Phoenix, Arizona (reinhabitation of a strip mall with a gourmet grocery and restaurants that provide what sociologist Ray Oldenburg refers to as "third places"); and Ames Lake in Phalen, Minnesota (regreening of a dead strip mall by reconstructing the site's prior condition as a wetland—and creating lakefront property in the process that attracted the first new private development in over forty years to the low-income area).

4. The proportion of one-person households grew from 26 percent to 27 percent between 2000 and 2010. In 2000, 36 percent of all U.S. households included individuals under the age of 18. By 2010 that figure moved down to 33 percent. The number of households without children is expected to continue to rise. See Daphne Lofquist, Terry Lugaila, Martin O'Con-

nell, and Sarah Feliz, "Households and Families: 2010," *2010 Census Briefs*, Issued April 2012, U.S. Census Bureau.

5. See Center for Housing Policy and Center for Neighborhood Technology, "Losing Ground: The Struggle of Moderate-Income Households to Afford the Rising Costs of Housing and Transportation," October 2012. See also Todd Litman, "Smart Growth Savings: What We Know about Public Infrastructure and Service Cost Savings and How They Are Misrepresented by Critics," Victoria Transport Policy Institute, April 25, 2013.

6. Homes in the Philadelphia area in neighborhoods with New Urbanist characteristics lost 20 percent of their value during 2007–2012, while those in non–New Urbanist communities lost 54 percent. See Kevin C. Gillen, "The Correlates of House Price Changes with Geography, Density, Design and Use: Evidence from Philadelphia," Congress for the New Urbanism, October 2012, http://www.cnu.org/cnu-news/2012/11/cnu-releases-report -philadelphia-area-housing-prices.

7. Partnership for Sustainable Communities, "Three Years of Helping Communities Achieve Their Visions for Growth and Prosperity," http://www.epa.gov/smartgrowth /pdf/partnership_accomplishments.pdf.

8. The Blueprints report is online at http://www.georgiaconservancy.org/uploads/Blue prints/Covington.pdf.

9. The DPZ charrette team also included Gibbs Planning Group, Hall Planning and Engineering, and Home Town Neighborhoods. The DPZ team and plan was led by Galina Tachieva, author of *The Sprawl Repair Manual* (Washington, D.C.: Island Press, 2010).

10. This was paralleled by the addition of institutional capacity for directing growth at the county level. In 2002 the Center for Community Preservation and Planning was founded as a neutral place for discussions between citizens and elected officials. It was followed in 2005 by the establishment of the county's Leadership Collaborative helping the city and county work together. In 2007 the two organizations produced an ambitious new comprehensive county plan for 2050.

11. The team included developer Joel Embry, Tunnell-Spangler-Walsh and Associates, Jackie Benson Marketing, Whole Town Solutions, and Randy Vinson as the project manager. Phase Two began construction in 2008. For more info see www.clarksgrove.com.

12. Phase 2, across the street, started in 2007 before suspending further construction in late 2008 with 90 percent of the infrastructure in place. Vinson says they are waiting for appraisal values to return to a level that can justify new construction before building new homes again. Randy Vinson, interview, email correspondence with authors, June 20, 2013.

13. Vinson explained that because the city's revenues are largely based on utilities usage, not property taxes, Covington was somewhat cushioned from recessionary cutbacks. This helped to explain why the city council was able to loan funds to the CRA at a time when many other cities would not. Vinson, interview, email correspondence with authors, June 20, 2013.

14. "Walker's Bend Redevelopment," City of Covington website, http://www.cityof covington.org/COVINGTONCOTTAGES/NEIGHBORHOODS/Pages/WalkersBend.aspx.

15. Randy Vinson, interview with authors in his office, Covington, Ga., July 17, 2012.

16. Crystal Tatum, "Walker's Bend to be Revitalized," *Newton Citizen*, March 17, 2010.

17. Vinson, interview with authors.

18. This three-story building was funded through approximately $1.9 million in NSP3 funds; $750,000 loaned from CHA; and $500,000 contributed by Newton County from SPLOST. A fourth floor was value engineered out when efforts to secure additional funds were unsuccessful.

19. The ochre-toned watercolors of the Walker's Bend work by the UGA Metropolitan Design Studio is perhaps best seen at the website of the Fabric Urban Design Office, founded by one of the studio's graduates, Jacob Lindsey, http://fabricurbandesign.com/8700/142393/recent-work/walkers-bend-master-plan.

20. For more information, see http://www.cityofcovington.org/covingtoncottages/pages/default.aspx.

21. For the sake of comparison, RealtyTrac's June 2010 foreclosure research reported 1,868 foreclosed homes in Covington, Georgia. This equates to a foreclosure rate of 1 in every 165 housing units. Georgia had 1 in every 344 while the nation as a whole had 1 in every 411. This was reported in "A Market Conditions and Project Evaluation Summary of Village at Walker's Bend," Novogradac & Company LLP, July 16, 2010. A similar search on June 14, 2013 showed 1,200 foreclosures listed in Covington.

22. Walker's Bend Overlay Zoning District, available at http://www.cityofcovington.org/Departments/PlanningZoning/Housing%20Initiatives/Documents/Walker's%2end%20using%2rdinance.pdf.

23. Vinson, interview with authors.

24. Crystal Tatum, "Redevelopment Investment Totals $30M," *Newton Citizen*, May 14, 2012.

25. Ibid.

26. Data retrieved on June 14, 2013, from http://www.city-data.com/zips/30014.html.

27. Data retrieved on June 14, 2013, from http://www.trulia.com/real_estate/Covington-Georgia/. As is often the case, Trulia's data differ from that available on Zillow. Zillow.com shows more consistent downward trends in price and value from 2009 to 2012 and shows median value per square foot in April 2013 at $48.

28. Vinson, interview with authors.

29. Kaid Benfield, "A Rapidly Sprawling Community Tries to Save Itself," *The Atlantic Cities*, December 9, 2011, http://www.theatlanticcities.com/neighborhoods/2011/12/can-grassroots-planning-save-rapidly-suburbanizing-community/685/.

30. Will Macht and Christpher S. Blanchard, "City as Master Developer," *Urban Land*, December 2012, http://urbanland.uli.org/Articles/2012/Dec/MachtMasterDeveloper.

31. See Elizabeth Kneebone and Alan Berube, *Confronting Suburban Poverty in America* (Washington, D.C.: Brookings Press, 2013).

CHAPTER 8

Walking to the Strip Mall
Retrofitting Informal Pedestrian Paths
NICO LARCO

Key Points and Practice Takeaways

1. Pedestrian networks in suburbia are much more than just sidewalks along streets. They include sidewalks within private property, cut-throughs, the streets themselves, paved and unpaved bike paths, informal goat paths, makeshift gates in fences, and kickdowns.

2. There is a mismatch between designed suburban pedestrian networks and residents' desire for direct and convenient access to commercial strips.

3. Informal pedestrian networks are commonplace and greatly increase connectivity around suburban commercial strips. The widespread existence of these informal paths should be justification for creating more connected pedestrian networks in new developments and pushing for them as retrofits in existing developments.

4. Informal paths, while increasing connectivity, should not be considered an equivalent to formalized pedestrian paths. They are available to a limited population, can be unsafe, are not as regularly maintained, may not be permanent, and raise liability questions for property owners.

5. Planners must carefully consider how to address these networks so that they can guarantee their existence and provide maintenance and safety while not risking their closure due to increased costs and liability to owners.

An important aspect of fixing suburbia is increasing its walkability. As described by many—including contributors in this book—one of the most problematic aspects of suburbia is its current auto-dominated state and lack of a pedestrian-friendly environment. This has led to widespread calls for the creation of more compact, mixed-use, and well-connected developments.[1]

An important first step in creating more walkable and connected areas in suburbia is to better understand existing pedestrian networks and the range of path types that are being used by suburban residents. This chapter investigates the informal pedestrian paths that exist around commercial shopping strips and shows how they can be improved.

Promotion of walking in suburbia is a commendable goal as the benefits of active travel are far-reaching. An increase in active travel has been correlated with improved health, lower body-mass indexes, improved productivity, and increased independence.[2] If active travel trips substitute for auto trips and reduce vehicle miles traveled, the benefits extend to a reduction in greenhouse gas emissions, the amount individuals spend on transportation, and congestion as well as an improvement in the environment in terms of air quality.[3]

Numerous studies on walking and the built environment have coalesced around the "Seven D's" that play a key role in determining an individual's mode choice: density, diversity of land uses, design, distance to transit, destination access, demand management, and demographics.[4] When we think of typical suburbia, with its low-density housing, single-use patterns, and lack of destinations, it seems to embody the auto-dominated side of these criteria. This characteristic, however, does not describe all of suburbia. A number of studies have focused specifically on commercial strip areas and have shown a surprising amount of walking and biking actually occurring in suburbia.[5] Some of these studies counted pedestrians entering commercial strips in urban and suburban sites while others focused exclusively on the travel choices of suburban multi-family housing residents. Many of these studies showed that significantly more residents choose active modes of travel when they live in areas that are better connected to the commercial strip and therefore have reduced travel distances.

Connectivity is a measure of the general directness of routes between different areas. The actual distance between two locations is not determined by the straight-line distance from one to the other but, instead, by the in-network travel distance. In well-connected areas—such as gridded areas with small blocks— routes are generally direct with very small differences between straight-line distances and in-network distances.

This is not the case in most suburban areas where physical proximity often has little correlation with travel distance. Many suburban areas lack formal sidewalks that provide easy and direct access between different areas both within a development and between developments. Within single developments, when sidewalks do exist, they are often intermittent, may not connect to every destination and building entry, or have thin networks that lack robust internal connectivity and instead provide long, circuitous paths from one place to another.

Between developments, there is often a lack of direct connection as streets end at project edges and only connect directly to nearby arterials. Travel between developments often necessitates longer than necessary travel along arterials that have fast-moving traffic and limited or unprotected sidewalks. This lack of connectivity creates a condition where apparently close destinations are actually far away in terms of in-network travel (see figure 8.1). This is especially true in the design of developments that lie next to commercial strips, as these strips are typically walled off on all sides.

Ironically, these inaccessible commercial strips are pedestrian magnets. Neighborhood centers—as described by the International Council of Shopping Centers—are intended for day-to-day convenience shopping for residents in the immediate neighborhood, and have a catchment area of approximately three miles.[6] These centers typically include a range of potential pedestrian magnets including grocery stores, convenience stores, banks, restaurants, and dry cleaners. With approximately 32,000 of these centers throughout the country,[7] understanding and improving the walkability around them could have a major effect.

The potential of these centers to act as magnets is thwarted by the lack of designed pedestrian networks around them. Suburban commercial strips are typically designed with only the automobile in mind, featuring large parking areas situated between streets and continuous, sign-clad storefronts. All access

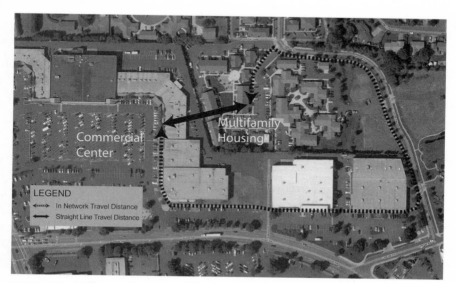

FIGURE 8.1. Walls around commercial strips make direct access impossible.
Illustration by author.

is considered to be from the street side, with the backs of developments—typically used for deliveries—fenced off from adjacent development. At first glance, if only looking at street networks or sidewalks, this would seem to create large, inaccessible areas alongside and behind commercial developments. What this overlooks, however, is the large number of informal pedestrian paths that greatly increase the connectivity of these areas.

Earlier pilot studies by the author of multifamily and single-family residents' travel patterns around commercial strips in Colorado Springs, Colorado, and Portland, Oregon, revealed a range of path types and the unexpected existence of numerous informal paths surrounding commercial strips. These additional paths can completely alter the connectivity of the pedestrian network and can have significant effects on trip length and mode choice. This chapter extends these earlier studies by looking at a range of suburban strip developments, identifying the different types of pedestrian paths that exist, and analyzing the degree to which these paths alter the overall connectivity of an area.

Methodology

To better understand the pedestrian paths in suburbia we documented the pedestrian networks around six commercial strips. Four strips are in the Portland, Oregon, metro area and two are in the Atlanta, Georgia, metro area. We chose these two metro areas specifically for the significant differences in their geographic locations, climates, and cultures of auto use. In a national ranking of the forty largest metro areas in the country, Atlanta ranked sixth in daily vehicle miles traveled per resident and Portland ranked thirty-fifth.[8]

For this study, we selected sites that were in suburban locations—defined as existing outside of central business districts, with auto-oriented commercial centers, single-use zoning, extensive parking areas in front of commercial spaces, and predominantly residential uses surrounding the commercial centers. Sites were along a single arterial, had full or near-full build-outs of adjacent properties, and had a grocery anchor with a minimum of 40,000 square feet of gross leasable space (GLSF). In addition, each site also had a range of other typical stores that might act as pedestrian magnets such as banks, restaurants, and dry cleaners.

The Oregon sites selected were: Oswego Town Center in Lake Oswego, Greenway Town Center in Tigard, and Meadowland Shopping Center and San Rafael Shopping Center in Portland. The Georgia sites were: Plantation Pointe in Smyrna and Candler-McAfee in Decatur. Information about each site is described in table 8.1.

For each site, we built pedestrian network maps in GIS using recent orthographic aerial photos, Google Street View, Bing Maps, and a Trimble GPS unit during on-the-ground site audits. The bulk of these networks were built

TABLE 8.1. Study site description

Site name	Gross leasable area	Number of stores	Type of anchor	2010 Median household income*	Single-family housing units†	Multifamily housing units†	Total housing units†
PORTLAND							
Oswego Town Center	105,062 sf	36	Supermarket	$83,318.00	505	835	1,340
Greenway Town Center	139,339 sf	27	Supermarket/ pharmacy	$65,226.00	810	1,336	2,146
Meadowland	163,819 sf	19	Supermarket	$54,340.00	572	1,443	2,015
San Rafael Shopping Center	142,495 sf	11	Supermarket	$55,658.00	978	326	1,304
ATLANTA							
Plantation Pointe	63,200 sf	21	Supermarket	$61,426.00	393	1,967	2,360
Candler-McAfee	175,272 sf	26	Supermarket	$45,394.00	593	56	649

* CoStar Realty Information estimates for households within a one-mile radius of LCA.
† Counts include all units within one-third mile of the commercial strip "as the crow flies."
Source: CoStar Realty Information Inc., CoStar Property Professional Database (Bethesda, Md.: CoStar, and GIS Data from Municipalities/Counties, 2010).

using the aerial photos and online maps/streetviews. Where foliage on aerials obstructed views, on-site audits were used to finalize network locations.

For the on-the-ground site audits, one to three researchers visited each site and traveled the pedestrian network by foot or on bike. Using base maps of the streets and pedestrian networks, we recorded additional formal and informal paths and connections that were not part of our street network data and not legible through the analysis of aerial photographs of the case study sites.

Since the study involved only six sites, it was not expected that the results would be absolutely generalizable to all development in the United States, but instead that they would give an educated snapshot of actual pedestrian networks, the variety of path types, and the extent of informal pedestrian paths.

Findings
Pedestrian Path Types

Our audits found a great variety of path types in suburbia—and not all paths are equal. Paths vary in their physical form, their ease of use, their maintenance, and their sanctioning (i.e., whether they are formally allowed and/or created by property owners). The largest distinction was between the category of formal paths (paths that are specifically designed for pedestrians by property owners or municipalities) and informal paths (paths that are not intended by planners, designers, or owners but clandestinely created by users, often simply through repeated use). Below is a listing of the different pedestrian path types and elements we found. The list is organized from the most formalized to the least. Images of these path types are shown in figures 8.2–8.11.

FORMAL PATHS/ELEMENTS

1. *Sidewalks along streets.* This is what is typically considered the norm for pedestrian travel—a continuous, hard and flat surface sometimes directly adjacent to the automobile realm and sometimes separated through medians or planted buffers.
2. *Sidewalks through private property.* This is most typically through larger properties such as commercial areas and multifamily housing developments. The connectivity of these sidewalks varies greatly in both internal and external connectivity. Some developments have robust internal networks while others have only a few continuous paths that create long, circuitous routes or don't connect to every building. External connectivity—or the degree to which the property connects to various, distributed points in adjacent developments— often is unrelated to internal connectivity. Some developments allow various links to adjacent properties on all sides, while others only link to adjacent arterials and have a large "access shadow" to all other adjacent developments.

FIGURE 8.2.
Sidewalks along
streets.
Author's photo.

FIGURE 8.3.
Sidewalks through
private property.
Author's photo.

3. *Sidewalks/cut-throughs between properties.* These are paths on public right-of-ways or easements that pass between private property and are independent from streets. These seem rare as we only found one example in all of our sites.

4. *Streets (without sidewalks).* In areas that do not have sidewalks, pedestrians often travel along roads themselves. This is especially true in low-traffic-volume residential streets.

5. *Gravel strips along streets.* These are unpaved areas beside roads that are often simply the extension of the leveled substrate material under the paved road. They provide little protection for pedestrians and often have uneven and unmaintained surfaces.

6. *Paved trails/bike paths.* These are paths through public property such as in parks, along utility easements, or occasionally along right-of-ways.

FIGURE 8.4.
Cut-throughs
between private
property.
Author's photo.

FIGURE 8.5.
Streets without
sidewalks.
Author's photo.

FIGURE 8.6.
Gravel strips along
streets.
Author's photo.

FIGURE 8.7. Paved trails.
Author's photo.

FIGURE 8.8. Unpaved trails.
Author's photo.

7. *Unpaved trails.* These are unpaved paths on public right-of-ways or easements but often with a soft, maintained surface such as bark chips or mulch. These are typically created and maintained by municipalities.

INFORMAL PATHS / ELEMENTS

1. *Goat paths.* These are informal, unpaved, often-uneven, and often-unsanctioned paths through private property. They vary greatly in their extent—from a simple shortcut through a corner of a lot to long, winding paths that cross multiple property lines.
2. *Gates.* These are formal pass-throughs in walls and fences typically inserted by residential property owners. While these can be considered formal elements (in that they are sanctioned and designed by property owners), they typically open onto commercial properties or parks without the explicit knowledge or approval from the commercial owners. Gates are often connected to surrounding properties by goat paths.
3. *Kickdowns.* These are informal, clandestine breaks in existing walls and fences. They range from cut holes or raised areas in fences to more carefully created openings that can include bridges and built-in edges.

FIGURE 8.9. Goat paths.
Author's photo.

FIGURE 8.10. Gates.
Author's photo.

FIGURE 8.11.
Kickdowns.
Author's photo.

Informal Paths

We were surprised by the number of sites that had a large number of informal paths and elements. These paths represented a range of conditions including brief short-cuts that linked parking areas to sidewalks, a large number of breaks or gates in fences, and longer meandering trails through wooded areas around commercial developments. The paths were equally pervasive through commercial property, on vacant land, around multifamily housing, and through private single-family yards (see figures 8.12A, 8.12B, 8.12C, 8.12D and 8.13).

FIGURE 8.12A, 8.12B, 8.12C, 8.12D. Examples of informal pedestrian paths.
Author's photo.

FIGURE 8.13. Informal connection at the rear of a commercial strip, Oswego Town Center. *Author's photo.*

Contrary to what might be expected, sites included informal paths irrespective of resident income. One of the sites with the largest extent of informal paths was located in the highest income category—the Oswego Town Center, with a 2010 Median HH income of $83,318.

The prevalence of these paths suggests two observations about suburbia and pedestrians. First, given the continuously worn nature of the informal paths we found, there seems to be a large amount of pedestrian activity in suburbia. This supports many of our earlier studies that found significant pedestrian activity around commercial strips. Second, the widespread number of these informal paths and the wide range of sites where we found them should serve as a striking indication of the persistent mismatch between residents' desire for well-connected pedestrian access and the existing, planned suburban built environment.

PEDESTRIAN NETWORK CONNECTIVITY AND INFORMAL PATHS

Where the designed pedestrian networks failed, informal paths sprouted in numerous locations. Informal networks were present in all the sites we studied and greatly increased the connectivity of the surrounding areas. As might be imagined, these connections occurred most often within *access shadows*, a term we coined to describe large expanses along the perimeter of a site that did not offer any access points to adjacent sites (see figures 8.14–8.16). These large, barren expanses are typical in suburban areas as developments rarely connect to each other directly, often only connecting to nearby arterials. The resulting thin and poorly connected networks caused such inconvenience that residents resorted to clandestine means for more direct access to adjacent sites. While access in our study sites was always possible through formal networks, because of the low connectivity, these networks often added significant distance to trips or necessitated uninviting walks along high-traffic arterials.

Informal paths were frequently created between multifamily housing sites and commercial strips or between two adjacent multifamily sites. Occasionally, these paths connected single-family-home neighborhoods to the commercial strip. This often occurred through wooded or abandoned sites and offered ac-

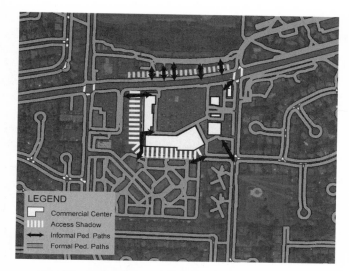

cessibility to entire neighborhoods that were largely isolated based on formal pedestrian networks.

In addition to paths that seemed to be accessible to anyone in the area, we found a few paths that were private or semiprivate. A number of paths and gates around commercial strips led to gates in fences that opened up to private yards. These were exclusively for the use of the families living in those homes. In one instance, however, a path traveled through a gated fence and through a single-family residence's yard. Discussion with the owners of this property revealed that only friends and close neighbors were allowed to use this path.

FIGURE 8.16.
Oswego Town
Center, Lake
Oswego, Oregon.
*Illustration by
author.*

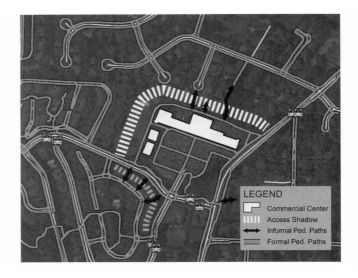

LEGEND

☐ Commercial Center
▥ Access Shadow
⟵ Informal Ped. Paths
═ Formal Ped. Paths

Gridded sites had lower frequencies of informal paths as the street organization inherently provided substantial connectivity and minimal access shadows. This existing connectivity within the formal network sufficiently served residents' needs, and in these sites we found only informal paths that cut out small corners.

It is interesting to note that the increased connectivity provided by the informal paths was beneficial not only for trips to commercial strips but also for trips to bus stops. Bus routes in suburbia are typically located along arterials and often include stops at commercial centers. With this, the increased connectivity created by the informal paths also increases the direct accessibility to these transit stops.

ISSUES WITH INFORMAL PATHS

While informal paths greatly increase the connectivity of an area, they are not equivalent to formalized and sanctioned paths. They differ in their accessibility, convenience, safety, permanence, maintenance, and liability. These differences are critical in that they limit the number of individuals who can and will use the paths and create uncertainty as to the paths' continued existence.

ACCESSIBILITY. While informal paths increase accessibility by offering a more direct connection between two points, the accessibility in terms of who can access these paths is often fairly limited when compared to formal paths. Because of their uneven surfaces and lack of maintenance, the paths are unusable by a wide range of populations such as the elderly or disabled. These paths often contain pools of water, soft mud, garbage, or ribbed surfaces that are barriers to wheelchairs, walkers, and individuals with less than sure footing. These conditions also make it difficult to travel with strollers or carriers for groceries or goods.

Informal paths are also occasionally limited in terms of who is allowed access to them. In one site, owners only opened the path through their yard that accessed a neighboring commercial area to friends and neighbors who they knew. This had previously been a more open access, but because of the number of strangers passing through and the accumulation of trash along the path, the owners preferred to minimize the traffic through their site.

CONVENIENCE. While informal paths do make more direct connections to destinations in terms of distance, these connections are not ideal in terms of convenience. Because these paths are often located on the backsides of commercial strips, the ways to access the strips are often awkward and unfriendly for pedestrians. Individuals typically have to walk around the length of the commercial strip along service roads used by large trucks and without easy access to stores' front doors.

SAFETY. The safety of many informal paths is an additional limitation and potential risk. Informal paths are often hidden between trees or bushes and are typically not well-lit. Because they are often on the backside of commercial developments, there is also limited "eyes-on-the-street" surveillance of the paths themselves and of travel along the service areas behind commercial strips. This creates a situation where the perceived and real safety of the path may be less than ideal. Vulnerable populations such as the elderly, women, and children might avoid these paths for these reasons or may only use the paths during daylight hours.

PERMANENCE. The permanence of these paths is also constantly in jeopardy. Paths can be blocked or eliminated by commercial property owners or by residential owners who no longer want the foot traffic through their property. We saw many examples of this around multifamily housing sites where fences seemed to be patched and broken through numerous times (figure 8.17).

This was also the case in a longstanding path through a single-family home property in Lake Oswego. New owners of the property were frustrated with how many youths passed through the area and the resulting trash that kept collecting in their yard, and they therefore erected a fence to cut off the path. As a testament to the strong desire to maintain convenient connections, the fence that was originally put up by the property owner was kicked down twice before a sturdier fence finally closed off the path for good.[9] The impermanence of these paths can have a significant effect on the mode choice and convenience for multiple residents.

MAINTENANCE. Because these paths are clandestine, they are typically not maintained by property owners and are often only given minimal attention and upkeep by users. In addition, because the paths are often hidden from view, there is little oversight and hence they can accumulate large amounts of trash

FIGURE 8.17. Patched fence in a multifamily housing development in Georgia. *Author's photo.*

(see figure 8.18). This affects both the ease of use of the path—based on how wet it is or the evenness of its surface—as well as its cleanliness and how inviting the paths are to residents. In our audits we found a substantially greater amount of trash and debris along the informal paths than along any of the formal paths.

LIABILITY. A significant issue for property owners is the liability they may be exposed to as a result of these informal paths. This is true for commercial property owners, single-family homeowners, multifamily property owners, and owners of vacant parcels. Because of all of the issues described above (uneven surfaces, lack of lighting, real or perceived safety issues, and lack of accessibility for disabled populations), owners carry substantial risk in allowing these paths to exist. In informal discussions with developers and planners about these types of paths, the paths were often unknown or were known but not formally acknowledged in order to limit the liability risk. Providing lighting or creating more even travel surfaces were not pursued in fear that doing so would prove the owner's knowledge of the paths and create future legal hardship.

PLANNING STRATEGIES

Informal paths are a compelling embodiment of the spatial mismatch between designated pedestrian networks and a latent desire for more convenient pedestrian access. There is a pent-up demand and interest by residents in having direct paths between residences and adjacent developments to minimize travel distances and increase pedestrian accessibility. While in many ways this desire is

FIGURE 8.18.
The maintenance
problems
of informal
connections.
Author's photo.

currently being addressed through the creation of informal paths, as described above, these paths are not equal to formalized paths. This leaves a number of unanswered questions as to the role planners should play in the creation or maintenance of informal paths. If the goal is to create more connected, convenient, and safe development, what should planners do? A few possible strategies are discussed below.

If safety, maintenance, and permanence are vital concerns, can and should planners push for the formalization of existing informal paths by property owners?

Formalizing previously informal paths would involve the paving, maintenance, and lighting of these paths by owners. This would ameliorate many of the problems currently associated with informal paths, such as their limited accessibility by some users, their safety, and their impermanence.

There are, however, substantial hurdles to doing this. First, it would require an acknowledgment of the paths by all surrounding property owners. This is a potentially complicated step as it would require coordination between owners as the paths often cross property lines. In addition, because of their current unmaintained state, the paths may require substantial modification—and cost—to bring them up to code standards.

Of concern to planners is the fact that formalizing these paths—or even shedding light on their existence—will also shed light on their potential liabilities. If this is not well managed, this could have the unintended consequence of a widespread closure of paths by property owners frightened by potential legal action and insurance concerns, as well as questions about the populations that are using the paths.

If legitimizing informal paths is the designated direction to move forward, substantial legal questions would need to be investigated as well as informal and discreet discussion with select property owners. Municipalities might also need to consider allocating funds to assist in the improvement of the paths in order to help motivate otherwise reluctant property owners.

Would it be possible for municipalities to take on the maintenance and liability of these paths? Or is shared maintenance and liability more appropriate— similar to the way street-side sidewalks currently function in suburban areas?

Having municipalities take on maintenance and liability for current informal paths could happen either through easements on the property or through the outright purchase of the portion of the property occupied by the path. This would guarantee the continued existence of the paths as well as a minimal level of maintenance.

While this option holds many benefits, it also creates challenges as cities are often averse to taking on additional legal and maintenance responsibilities and the financial burdens they entail. Not being part of an existing right-of-way— as sidewalks typically are—these paths might require a more complicated approach. The legal process could be burdensome in itself, as creating new easements or purchases of small slivers of a property is oftentimes difficult and could run into regulatory barriers. Most critically, property owners might be hesitant to accept an added easement for fear that it might limit future development options and hence property values.

This option will only be possible for municipalities who are able to take a long-term view of costs and benefits and, in the short term, are able to access funds and to leverage legal and planning support. Because of the complications involved, this direction might be best applied to priority paths—ones likely to have substantial impact on connectivity and resident access.

Could municipalities be more proactive in their planning and design of developments so that informal paths are not necessary?

A more proactive and less reactive approach might be to recognize that the existence of these informal paths proves a latent interest for more connected developments. If this is the case, how might planners and designers help foster new environments that attend to that desire? Should new development sites have pedestrian path connection requirements? And how can the unavoidable concern from residents about unwanted foot traffic be mitigated? (This may be a potentially irrelevant concern as informal connections seem to abound, regardless of the sanctioned connections.)

Planners and designers might proactively consider direct connections between developments in the planning and design process. This would require coordination between property owners, designation of path location and connection points, and internal site designs that accommodate arrival from various sides—especially in commercial development. While complicated, there are numerous examples of suburban commercial developments that have purposefully addressed pedestrian access from various locations and can serve as models for future development.[10]

One challenge to be addressed in this approach lies in the uneven nature of development timelines. Because development across adjacent sites rarely happens simultaneously, connection points and site design options would need to be considered while properties are in various stages of development—or not yet in development at all. As in areas that propose street stub-outs that will eventually connect to streets in yet-to-be-developed adjacent properties, the coordination among property owners may be a delicate process. Property owners are often reluctant to accept designations and easements that might limit their future development options.

Critical to the ability to have these conversations and to impose connectivity requirements is the existence of strong and documented community, city, and/or state planning goals that describe connectivity as a key desire. Without a clear designation of this desire, planners would be open to claims that they are inappropriately taking property rights and value.

Because of the potential safety liabilities surrounding informal connections and the difficulties in legitimizing and sanctioning these paths, is it more ethical and responsible to shut down the connections altogether?

Planners are responsible for the health, safety, and welfare of citizens. The difficulty in deciding what to do with informal paths is based on weighing the potential safety risks with the benefits of accessibility gained by residents who use them. On the one hand, eliminating the paths would also eliminate all of the many problems associated with these paths. On the other hand, eliminating the paths would drastically reduce the connectivity and accessibility of developments around commercial strips. This might significantly increase the hardship of residents as using the formal pedestrian network would increase trip length and would often include significant exposure to fast-moving traffic. This may not, in actuality, be safer for residents.

While the immediate reaction in a litigious society may be to shut down the paths and eliminate easily identifiable and assignable risks in favor of more amorphous ones, the potential benefits of eliminating informal paths may not be significant and in fact may reduce the overall quality of residents' travel experiences. This approach should be considered cautiously.

Maybe planners should simply do nothing?

Based on the range of issues described above, the unfortunate answer to the fate of existing informal paths might be simply to continue the status quo—allowing these paths to exist and to be used by numerous residents, but under the radar. The approach has some similarity to current efforts known as "tactical," "do-it-yourself," or "guerilla" urbanism.[11] The current state, while not ideal for its lack of maintenance, permanence, and safety, may actually represent a solution that manages to balance residents' desires for access and the obstinacy of liability concerns.

Even if informal paths are not directly addressed or legitimized in this scenario, planners should recognize that these types of paths are prevalent, and that they possess particular access, safety, and liability concerns. This should provide substantial motivation and justification to advocate for more connected future suburban development.

Conclusion

There is indeed a mismatch between suburban residents' desires for pedestrian access and the current status of pedestrian networks in suburbia. Pedestrian infrastructure is often not considered or included in suburban projects due in large part to a perception by planners, developers, and transportation engineers that the suburbs are predominantly if not solely the realm of the automobile.

This results in inadequate pedestrian environments that lack sidewalks altogether, have discontinuous sidewalks, lack direct connections between sites, or have street and parking configurations that preference the automobile and are hostile to pedestrians. The ubiquity of informal paths points to the need for a wholesale shift in our thinking about the demand for pedestrian networks in suburbia—and, ultimately, a shift in how these networks are designed.

This study has reviewed the character and complexity of informal pedestrian paths. While increasing connectivity, these types of paths present a number of challenges including ease of use, safety, maintenance, and liability. Because of this, addressing the existence of these informal paths is not a simple matter and involves legal, fiscal, and political issues. Cities have a diverse range of options to address these paths. Municipalities should consider ameliorative approaches while at the same time pushing for more connected pedestrian networks in future development so that informal paths are no longer necessary.

NOTES

1. R. Ewing, "Is Los Angeles-Style Sprawl Desirable?" *Journal of the American Planning Association* 63, no. 1 (1997): 107–25. S. Handy, "Smart Growth and the Transportation–Land Use Connection: What Does the Research Tell Us?" *International Regional Science Review* 28, no. 2 (2005): 146–67. Y. Jabareen, "Sustainable Urban Forms Their Typologies, Models, and Concepts," *Journal of Planning Education and Research* 26, no. 1 (2006): 38–52. Emily Talen, ed., *Charter of the New Urbanism* (New York: McGraw-Hill, 2013).

2. L. D. Frank, J. F. Sallis, T. L. Conway, J. E. Chapman, B. E. Saelens, and W. Bachman, "Many Pathways from Land Use to Health—Associations between Neighborhood Walkability and Active Transportation, Body Mass Index, and Air Quality," *Journal of the American Planning Association* 72, no. 1 (2006): 75–87.

3. R. H. Ewing, K. Bartholomew, S. Winkelman, J. Walters, and D. Chen, *Growing Cooler: Evidence on Urban Development and Climate Change* (Washington, D.C.: ULI, 2008).

4. R. Cervero and K. Kockelman, "Travel Demand and the 3DS: Density, Diversity, and Design," *Transportation Research Part D—Transport and Environment* 2, no. 3 (1997): 199–219. R. Ewing and R. Cervero, "Travel and the Built Environment," *Journal of the American Planning Association* 76, no. 3 (2010): 265–94. C. Lee and A. V. Moudon, "The 3DS+R: Quantifying Land Use and Urban Form Correlates of Walking," *Transportation Research Part D—Transport and Environment* 11, no. 3 (2006): 204–15. doi: 10.1016/j.trd.2006.02.003.

5. S. Handy and K. Clifton, "Local Shopping as a Strategy for Reducing Automobile Travel," *Transportation* 28, no. 4 (2001): 317–46. P. M. Hess, A. V. Moudon, M. C. Snyder, and K. Stanilov, "Site Design and Pedestrian Travel," *Transportation Research Record* 1674 (1999): 9–19. N. Larco, "Suburbia Shifted: Overlooked Trends and Opportunities in Suburban Multifamily Housing," *Journal of Architectural and Planning Research* 27, no. 1 (2010): 69–87. N. Larco, B. Steiner, J. Stockard, and A. West, "Pedestrian-Friendly Environments and Active Travel for Residents of Multifamily Housing: The Role of Preferences and Perceptions," *Environment and Behavior* (2011), doi: 10.1177/0013916511402061.

6. International Council of Shopping Centers, *ICSC's Dictionary of Shopping Center Terms*, 4th ed. (New York: International Council of Shopping Centers, 2014).

7. International Council of Shopping Centers, 2010, http://www.icsc.org/research/shopping-center-facts-and-stats, accessed October 10, 2014.

8. Federal Highway Administration, "Table HM-72—Highway Statistics 2008—Urbanized Areas," 2008, retrieved June 6, 2012, http://www.fhwa.dot.gov/policyinformation/statistics/2008/hm72.cfm.

9. R. Kalmeta and P. Kalmeta, personal communication with author, June 10, 2011.

10. E. Dunham-Jones and J. Williamson, *Retrofitting Suburbia: Urban Design Solutions for Redesigning Suburbs* (Hoboken, N.J.: John Wiley, 2009). L. S. Sobel, E. Greenberg, and S. Bodzin, *Greyfields into Goldfields: Dead Malls become Living Neighborhoods* (San Francisco: Congress for the New Urbanism, 2002).

11. J. Hou, *Insurgent Public Space: Guerrilla Urbanism and the Remaking of Contemporary Cities*, 1st ed. (New York: Routledge, 2010).

Imagined Possibilities

CHAPTER 9

Rethinking Residential On-Street Parking

MARC SCHLOSSBERG AND DAVE AMOS

Key Points and Practice Takeaways

1. Planners should conduct a simple block-by-block survey of parked cars and parking spaces on local suburban streets.

2. Older neighborhoods often need on-street parking, but local streets in neighborhoods built after 1950 are likely to have an excess of on-street parking spaces.

3. Unused parking is wasted space. Narrow streets can save money on construction and maintenance for housing developers and city public works departments. In addition, the land that would have otherwise gone to parking can be sold by developers to generate municipal tax income.

4. Much like cities have begun to rethink parking in dense urban areas via parklets, there may be creative reuse opportunities for underutilized suburban residential parking strips. Neighborhoods should be given permission to be creative and to repurpose some of the public space on their streets for gardens, games, murals, or storm water catchment.

5. Local street standards should be revised to reduce required right-of-way and curb-to-curb width standards for local streets, such that unnecessary parking lanes can be eliminated before they are built.

Residential streets serve a variety of uses. First and foremost, they provide access to homes alongside the street, but they also provide movement through neighborhoods. Within the roadway, however, a large amount of public space is often given to the parking of private automobiles. In a typical 34-foot curb-to-curb roadway, parking constitutes 14 linear feet (41 percent) of the paved space, assuming 7-foot parking lanes on each side of the street.

If residents and their guests use all of that parking space, then the developer or the municipality designed that street to the correct dimensions. If not, if some or even most of the parking spaces remain vacant, then original assumptions for the need for parking space were incorrect and need correction. Rewriting codes and standards for new streets can help future development get street proportions correct, but what opportunities exist to repurpose space on existing residential streets to make it more useful?

To better understand how residential on-street parking spaces are used and not used, a study of three neighborhoods from different development eras in Eugene, Oregon, was conducted to answer a very basic, but rarely asked, question: *Does the supply of on-street parking exceed the demand in low-density residential areas?* Intuitively for anyone who has lived in any single-family-home neighborhood, on-street parking is vastly underutilized because private homes always have their own private spaces. But what is the on-street vacancy rate? And is the vacancy rate such that portions of existing streets could be repurposed and new street design regulations offered? This study answers these basic, important questions.

The subject of parking has not traditionally been an area of robust study. There are no studies of residential parking design and utilization in suburban, low-density neighborhoods—the types of places where the majority of people live. Recently, the work of University of California–Los Angeles economics professor Donald Shoup introduced parking as an important research area, focusing on the supply and demand of parking in commercial areas, particularly in areas with parking meters like business districts. In his seminal work *The High Cost of Free Parking*, Shoup advocates for letting the market determine parking prices in places with high parking demand. Prices should be set at a level such that 85 percent of parking is occupied, leaving 15 percent so drivers can always find a space without searching.[1]

Shoup made city planners rethink downtown parking policies, but his work does not extend to low-density residential areas, where demand is low and parking is almost always free to residents. That doesn't mean residential parking is not worth studying. Residential streets are ubiquitous, so any attempts to optimize parking on residential streets can have a significant impact on the availability of developable land, the public costs of road construction and maintenance, and even the quality or livability of residential streets as public places for residents to use and experience.

Small changes to parking on residential streets may also positively impact other drawbacks associated with wide residential streets. These negative externalities can increase the rates of accidents and adversely impact the environment. For example:

- Wide streets encourage speeding and increase the frequency and severity of accidents. A typical 36-foot-wide residential street has 1.21 collisions/mile/year, while narrower 24-foot-wide streets have 0.32.[2]
- According to the Institute of Transportation Engineers, 70 percent of all accidents on local streets involve on-street parking made possible through wide streets. Nearly all of those accidents involve collisions with stationary vehicles, not cars attempting to park or unpark.[3]
- Wide streets pave over more pervious surface than necessary, increasing the severity of flooding and reducing water quality downstream.[4]

Clearly, even modest changes to residential streets can make a big difference. If wasted space exists on these streets in the form of unused parking, that space can be seen as an opportunity to fix some of the problems listed above.

Neighborhood Study Sites

Neighborhoods across the United States, particularly those composed of detached homes, consist of many common elements: front yards, garages, trees, sidewalks, and streets that tie everything together. Over time, housing, transportation, land use, and residential street design have changed. Historic neighborhoods may have skinnier streets and single-lane driveways because cars were less dominant and necessary. Neighborhoods of the 1950s and beyond began to be located further from city centers, were more dependent on car use, and consequently had more private space for vehicles in terms of both garages and wider driveways. Street widths in general increased.

This study looked at three neighborhoods in Eugene, Oregon, from three different eras to see how neighborhood parking design changed over time and what those designs mean for current on-street parking utilization (see figure 9.1).

South University Neighborhood (A)

The South University neighborhood, as the name suggests, lies south of the University of Oregon's campus. The university was originally established in 1876 on open land that at the time was outside the city center, but only a mile away. This neighborhood developed as the university grew. Streets and parcels were drawn up before 1912 and houses filled most lots by 1925.[5] The neighborhood was designed and built in the same period when the Ford Model T began driving down

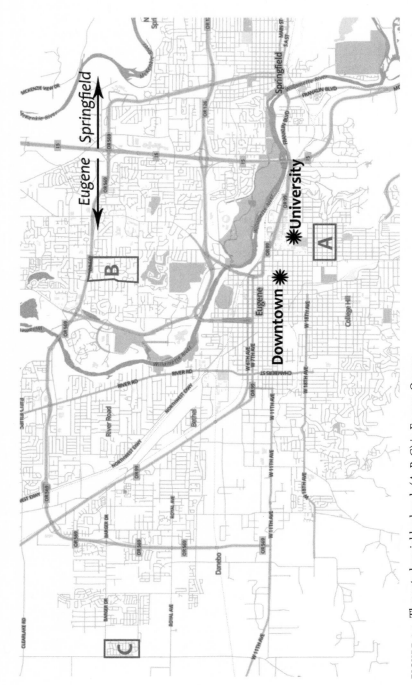

FIGURE 9.1. Three study neighborhoods (A, B, C) in Eugene, Oregon. Map by Dave Amos.

America's streets. The designers and surveyors of the neighborhood must have known that the automobile was more than a passing fad as they laid out mostly 34-foot-wide streets, with only a couple of exceptions both narrower and wider. The streets are laid out in a simple rectilinear grid that connects seamlessly with surrounding neighborhoods (see figures 9.2A, 9.2B, and 9.2C for photographs of typical street types in each neighborhood in the study).

More recently, the neighborhood's proximity to campus, coupled with its wide streets and on-street parking, attracted vehicles from students, faculty, and staff outside of the neighborhood looking for a parking space near the university without paying for campus parking. In 2012 neighbors complained to the city about "outsiders" using their on-street parking and the subsequent lack of available on-street parking spaces. In response to the complaints, the city created a permit parking zone in the area that allowed for two-hour parking only from 7:00 a.m. to 6:00 p.m. unless a vehicle had a residential parking permit, which allowed for unlimited on-street parking. The result was a noticeable drop in on-street parking use.

North Eugene Neighborhood (B)

In the postwar era, neighborhood and street design changed to make further accommodation for the automobile, which was becoming the dominant mode of personal transportation. This societal change manifests itself well in the North Eugene neighborhood, built in the 1970s and located 2.3 miles north of downtown Eugene.[6] This neighborhood's streets are typically either 28 feet or 36 feet wide, similar to that of the South University neighborhood. But unlike the South University neighborhood, the streets often do not include sidewalks and are not arranged in a strict grid that connects with other neighborhoods. Instead, streets bend and weave, occasionally ending in cul-de-sacs. Two primary streets bisect the area in an east-west direction, but no streets do so going north to south.

Builders placed the homes of this neighborhood farther back on the lot than the builders of the South University neighborhood. Homes are much more likely to feature two-car garages, wide and long driveways, and much more space between homes.

Northwest Eugene Neighborhood (C)

Real estate developers designed and built the Northwest Eugene neighborhood between 1999 and 2005.[7] This neighborhood represents more contemporary views on the role of the automobile on housing. In 1973 the Oregon legislature passed SB 100, a land use bill that required cities to create urban growth boundaries to limit urban sprawl and increase density.[8] The Northwest Eugene

FIGURE 9.2.
Neighborhood
types: South
University (*A*),
North Eugene (*B*),
and Northwest
Eugene (*C*).
*Photos by Dave
Amos.*

neighborhood symbolizes some of the goals of the legislation. It is located on the western edge of Eugene's urban growth boundary. Farms border the neighborhood immediately to the north and west, and the neighborhood features smaller lots with houses much closer together than those in North Eugene. The higher density of residential homes is likely a function of the developer maximizing the number of homes built on the land. Further outward expansion and building was not possible given the urban growth boundary.

The neighborhood lies six miles from downtown Eugene; a commute between the two takes 20–25 minutes by car. Despite the increase in residential density, no businesses exist within walking distance, and residents must rely on their cars for the vast majority of trips. Three-car driveways and two-car garages are the norm. Eugene's street design guidelines, last updated at the same time as this neighborhood was built, recommend 21- to 27-foot curb-to-curb measurements for residential streets.[9] Northwest Eugene followed this guidance and streets range from 19 to 28 feet, though most measure 25 feet wide. As a result, residents typically use only one side of the street for parking because parking on both sides would narrow the street such that two cars could not travel past each other. Parking is technically allowed on both sides, but local behavior staggers on-street parking to allow vehicles to move through streets comfortably. This condition and voluntary neighborhood parking behavior, coupled with few on-street spaces due to small lots and frequent and large driveway aprons, means the Northwest Eugene neighborhood provides residents with the fewest number of on-street spaces per block.

Methods

Together, these three neighborhoods represent many of the street conditions found in residential neighborhoods across the United States. Therefore, while this study focuses exclusively on Eugene, the results are likely widely transferable to single-family residential areas in communities of all sizes. Each study location consisted of:

- 45–50 blocks each, an area large enough to make broad conclusions about a neighborhood; and
- all, or nearly all, blocks in each neighborhood are designated R-1 zoning: low-density single-family housing. Any blocks with properties not designated R-1 (schools, parks, apartment buildings) were omitted from this study.

Once the neighborhoods and their corresponding blocks were identified, the blocks were surveyed via a walking audit. For each block, the following data were collected:

- total number of on-street parking spaces;
- total number of parking lanes in driveways;
- number of vehicles parked in on-street parking spaces;
- number of vehicles parked in driveways; and
- any parking restrictions.

Parking availability and use were surveyed visually by walking down each street and recording data digitally. Surveys were conducted between 5 p.m. and 7 p.m. on weeknights on weeks without any major holidays or other potentially disruptive events. Vehicles inside garages were not counted, and it was assumed that each driveway "lane" could accommodate only one vehicle. In essence, off-street parking spaces equated to one vehicle per driveway lane. While deep driveways could park more than a single vehicle, functionally this is impractical for daily use. Thus, this study errs conservatively in off-street parking availability by not including spaces inside the garage or the ability to park multiple vehicles per driveway lane.

Residential streets present somewhat of a challenge when calculating the number of parking spaces on a block because fixed spaces are not marked as they are in commercial areas. Parking spaces were thus estimated using visual cues (like the size of vehicles already parked on the street) and visual intuition based on firsthand experience. In general, if a street was very narrow, the parking capacity was counted for one side only, even if parking was legally allowed on both sides.

Findings: Many Spaces, Fewer Cars

The three neighborhoods were surveyed over seven evenings in March and April 2013. In total, 143 blocks, 1,019 homes with driveways, 4,356 parking spaces, and 1,189 parked cars were surveyed (see table 9.1). The key findings are as follows:

- Nearly 87 percent of on-street spaces were vacant across the three neighborhoods, and no neighborhood had greater than 21 percent of on-street parking occupied.
- Total parking provision (combined on- and off-street) in the South University (1920s) and Northwest (1990s) neighborhoods are quite similar, though parking shifted in provision from public on-street to private off-street.
- The 1970s North Eugene development pattern provided 55 percent more total parking per block than the more modern Northwest neighborhood and 45 percent more than the more historic South University neighborhood.

TABLE 9.1. Parking availability and utilization

	South University	North Eugene	Northwest Eugene
BASIC INFORMATION			
Blocks surveyed	49	46	48
Year platted/built	1912	1960s–1970s	1999
Parking restrictions	Permit only	None	None
Distance from downtown (miles)	1.3	2.3	6.0
Average block length (ft)	405.0	425.0	366.8
OVERALL CAPACITY			
Total driveways	298	398	323
Total driveway spaces	361	772	887
Spaces/driveway (avg.)	1.2	1.9	2.7
Total on-street spaces	965	1,041	330
Total on-street spaces/block	19.7	22.6	6.9
Total off-street spaces/block	7.4	16.8	18.5
Total spaces	1,326	1,813	1,217
Total spaces/block	27.1	39.4	25.4
OVERALL USE			
Total cars parked on street	204	66	38
Total street parking vacancy	79%	94%	88%

Off-Street Parking Surplus

Much of the data confirms conventional wisdom around the relationship between parking and housing through time. First, the number of driveway spaces per driveway increased from developments in the 1920s, 1970s, and 1990s. Rounding, one sees one-car-wide driveways in South University, two-car driveways in North Eugene, and three-car driveways in Northwest Eugene. In addition, South University homes typically have one-car garages, while North Eugene and Northwest Eugene homes have two-car garages.

On-Street Parking Surplus

The progressive increase in off-street, driveway spaces from South University to Northwest Eugene is not reflected in the trend of on-street parking. Interestingly, on-street parking provision decreased substantially between the 1970s and 1990s developments, as more recent development reflects more modern residential requirements of skinnier streets and smaller lot sizes. That said, these newer homes have bigger driveways and can accommodate more vehicles on private property without the need for public parking provision. In many ways, this shift in parking provision from public to private space reduces the public parking subsidy to private landowners and potentially reduces public costs for road maintenance by moving parking provision to a private, rather than public, good.

On-Street Vacancy

Perhaps most interesting is the actual utilization of on-street parking in the different neighborhoods. The highest occupancy rate occurred in the historic South University neighborhood, where homes typically only have single-lane driveways, and even in that case only 21 percent of on-street parking spaces were utilized. The low rate could partially be explained by a parking permit system only available to neighborhood residents. However, even in this area there exists a large amount of wasted space that is allocated for on-street parking but not utilized. (The other two neighborhoods are not as centrally located and are not destinations for parking, so the permit system in the South University neighborhood actually helps it emulate the other two neighborhoods in terms of local on-street parking demand.) In the North Eugene neighborhood (1970s), only 6 percent of on-street parking spaces were occupied. In other words, a whopping 94 percent of available parking was vacant.

Visual illustration of vacant on-street parking can be insightful as well. Figures 9.3A, 9.3B, and 9.3C show each neighborhood where less than 50 percent of on-street parking spaces are occupied, representing areas where parking could be removed on one side of the street and still have enough spaces to meet the demands of the neighborhood. As can be seen in figures 9.3A, 9.3B, and 9.3C, almost every street had less than 50 percent parking occupancy. This is an important threshold in neighborhoods with parking on both sides of the street, because if parking needs can be handled with parking on only one side of the street it becomes possible to conceive of alternative uses for the parking strip on one side of each block.

Discussion: Wasted Money and Wasted Space

The results of the parking survey show that parking supply significantly exceeds demand in residential neighborhoods. This has significant financial implications for both the public and the private sectors. City governments pay to construct and maintain parking, and real estate developers lose money by giving over land to parking that they cannot then otherwise sell to homebuyers. Table 9.2 estimates that the waste in financial terms for the excess parking in just these three Eugene neighborhoods is almost $11 million when road construction, maintenance, and land costs are considered.

On-Street Parking Occupancy Rates, South University Neighborhood

FIGURE 9.3.
On-street parking
utilization (less
than 50 percent
occupancy means
parking availability
on one side of the
street is adequate to
handle all on-street
parking needs):
South University
(*A*), North Eugene
(*B*), Northwest
Eugene (*C*).
*Illustrations by
Dave Amos.*

On-Street Parking Occupancy Rates, North Eugene Neighborhood

On-Street Parking Occupancy Rates, Northwest Eugene Neighborhood

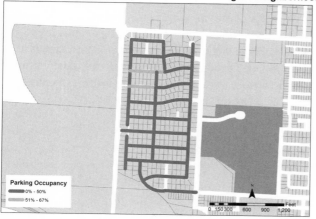

TABLE 9.2. Financial costs of unused parking, study areas only

	All parking	Unused parking
Construction	$6.2 million	$5.4 million
Maintenance (every 20 years)	$1 million	$0.9 million
Land	$5 million	$4.4 million
Total cost	$12.2 million	$10.7 million

Construction Costs

There is not a constant cost estimate for new suburban streets that can be applied universally nationwide; each project is different and material costs and location costs vary. As a result, per-mile estimates are rare and differ widely. One estimate from Florida's Department of Transportation (FDOT) in 2012 places the cost per centerline mile, not including contingency, of a new two-lane urban street at $4,279,236.[10] This cost includes the roadway, storm sewer system, and sidewalks. To determine the cost of additional paving, which does not affect the storm sewers or sidewalks, one can look at the cost of building a wider street. FDOT places the cost of a four-lane roadway at $6,040,559. By using the difference between these numbers, it is possible to estimate a square-footage cost of just the roadway surface. By doing so, one can estimate the cost to build a standard 22-foot-by-8-foot parking space to be $2,668.67. In the three Eugene neighborhoods, the 2,336 parking spaces included in the survey areas would therefore have cost just over $6.2 million. Given that only 308 on-street spaces were in use (13 percent), the construction cost for unused spaces can be estimated at $5.4 million.

Maintenance Costs

A typical asphalt roadway on a residential street lasts for 15–20 years before resurfacing is required. Using the maintenance costs from the Florida Department of Transportation, the cost to mill and resurface one mile of a two-lane urban street is $425,742, which translates to $443 for the average-sized on-street parking space. Multiplying that cost per space for resurfacing against the vacant on-street parking spaces in the study areas means that every 15–20 years the City of Eugene will pay about $900,000 to resurface unneeded and mostly unused parking. (Note that this analysis does not account for more routine maintenance like street sweeping and crack sealing.)

Land Costs

Construction and maintenance costs are the public costs for on-street parking, but there are private costs as well, especially in areas where land is scarce.

Across all three surveyed Eugene neighborhoods, 9.4 acres of public land (on-street parking) is used for parking cars. With only 13 percent of that land actually used, 8.2 acres of public land is lying fallow in just those three neighborhoods. As with construction and maintenance costs, estimating the exact value of that land is highly variable; however, using the existing real estate market can help provide an estimate. Using a 0.11-acre vacant property only a few blocks from the North Eugene study area,[11] in May 2013 at a market price of $58,000, we can determine the cost of one acre of developable residential land in Eugene at $527,273. Multiplying the cost per acre of developable land by the acres of unused on-street parking, nearly $5 million of developable land has been lost. That is, land that could have been sold to homebuyers (and generate public revenue as well) was used to build unnecessary on-street parking instead.

Strategies for Design and Redesign

Given that residential streets in many, if not most, communities are often too wide due to underutilized on-street parking, and that wide streets are costly to city government and private developers, the question is what to do next. In particular, what can be done to retrofit the many miles of existing local streets across the United States?

Unlike the blank canvas of a new subdivision, existing neighborhoods present challenges to planners and engineers who seek to reduce street width and parking capacity. In dense, urban environments, where parking is at a premium, parking is increasingly being repurposed for uses such as bike lanes, dedicated transit lanes, or mini public spaces or "parklets." But in lower-density residential areas, repurposing opportunities may seem less obvious or impactful. However, when thinking about a 6–8-foot-wide, block-long length of space block after block, it quickly becomes apparent that an opportunity for significant reuse may be present. Two potential ideas include adapting the space to perform environmental services or turning acres of underutilized land into opportunities for urban agriculture.

From Parking to Environmental Services

In cities that see significant rainfall, like those in the Pacific Northwest, officials are trying to find cost-effective and sustainable ways to deal with stormwater runoff, a negative externality of impervious street paving. In Seattle, for example, city engineers are redesigning streets to manage nearly 100 percent of all stormwater to eliminate the burden rain places on expensive treatment facilities. One strategy is to drastically reduce on-street parking, narrow the roadway, and use the extra space for rainwater capture.

- SEA Street (Street Edge Alternatives) was built in 2001 with these features:
- SEA Street provides eighteen on-street parking spaces in an angled configuration spread throughout the street. This total is approximately half of a conventionally designed street.
- Stormwater runoff is reduced by 98 percent compared to nearby conventional streets.
- This approach to managing stormwater is 25 percent less expensive than a traditional roadside system.
- SEA Street features 11 percent less pervious surface than typical streets.
- The winding design of the street calms traffic and creates a welcoming shared space for pedestrians and bicyclists.
- The roadway is narrow, at 14 feet wide with 2-foot curbs on either side. The 2-foot flat curbs make the road wide enough for emergency vehicles but create a narrow feeling for drivers.
- Over 100 evergreen trees and 1,100 shrubs add beauty to the right-of-way.[12]

In terms of cost, a similar Seattle project (the Broadview green grid) cost $280,000 per block to construct compared with costs of $520,000 for a conventional street with traditional drainage.[13] Rethinking the initial design of streets thus deserves serious consideration even in places without stormwater capacity issues. The lower initial cost, narrower street design, improved traffic safety, and added curb appeal are all strong selling points, especially if on-street parking is less necessary than previously assumed.

In Portland, Oregon, the city's Bureau of Environmental Services (PBES) instituted a Green Streets program to begin to address impervious surface stormwater issues and excessive on-street parking provision (see figure 9.4). Rather than retrofitting an entire block, the Portland program repurposes parking spaces into "pocket swales" to treat and slow rainwater before it moves into the traditional stormwater system.[14]

The three initial projects were built on NE Siskiyou (2003), SE Ankeny (2004), and NE Fremont (2005), and replaced two to four parking spaces on residential blocks. As noted above, the cost to build a parking space on a new street is estimated at $3,868. In this Portland program, pocket swales range from $4,000 to $8,200 (the NE Fremont project included extra work that inflated the cost relative to the other two projects) (see table 9.3). Thus pocket swale projects are not expensive relative to the alternative traditional design technique. Of course, replacing an existing parking space with a pocket swale doubles the initial cost, but it could be price competitive if built into street design initially, and may still be financially worthwhile if reduction in municipal stormwater costs are considered.

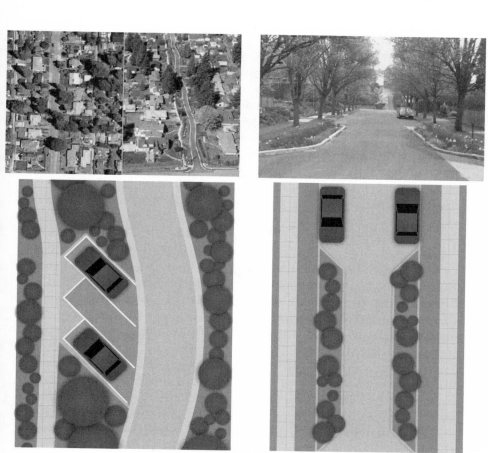

FIGURE 9.4. Street stormwater redesigns in Seattle, Washington (*left*), and pocket swales in Portland, Oregon (*right*).
Illustrations by Dave Amos.

TABLE 9.3. Cost breakdown for Portland Green Streets program projects

Street	Year	Total cost	Spaces displaced	Cost per space displaced
NE Siskiyou	2003	$17,000	4	$4,250
SE Ankeny	2004	$12,000	3	$4,000
NE Fremont	2005	$16,400	2	$8,200

Perhaps a more radical idea of repurposing underutilized public land that is currently allocated as unused on-street residential parking is to farm it. In this study, almost all surveyed blocks had more than twice as many on-street parking spaces as needed, thus potentially opening up an entire strip of land on one side of the street for urban farming. In this study alone, there were 8.2 acres of unused parking space. As a hypothetical thought experiment, table 9.4 shows potential yields for carrots, tomatoes, and squash, three common Oregon vegetables, if they were grown and cultivated on this fallow public land.[15] Farming the unused on-street parking spaces in this study could yield $583,000–$786,000 in market prices and enhance local food and sustainability opportunities.

Some obvious caveats exist as these numbers assume an open field with adequate sun. In addition, some efficiencies of a farm may be lost working along the side of the road, and there will need to be some consideration of how to eliminate runoff contaminants from the roadway. However, even at half of those yields, parking farms could provide a bountiful harvest to the community, to adjacent homes, or to a larger market. The main point is that there is a vast untapped opportunity for a new type of urban farming that utilizes existing and inefficiently utilized public land.

Who might farm such an unorthodox field? Adjacent residents are the most likely caretakers, as the planted buffers between sidewalks and streets are already public land that residents maintain. In addition, in the Portland Green Streets program, routine maintenance is done by nearby residents. If a resident does not want to tend to this land, however, the city could lease the space to a farmer. This turns a wasted resource into a small source of income for the city, all while improving access to locally grown food and, ultimately, the health of residents. In Portland, there is a business model already in place that works similarly. Farmers farm the yards of residents for a fee ($1,675 in 2009) and the residents receive all of the vegetables farmed.[16] Instead of charging a fee, farmers could simply pay a small land fee and keep all of the vegetables to sell.

TABLE 9.4. Potential unused parking space crop yields

Crop	Yield per acre (in pounds)	Total yield (in pounds)	Price per pound (19)	Total market price
Carrots	50,000	410,000	$0.43	$176,300
Tomatoes	23,000–27,000	188,600–221,400	$1.31	$247,066–$290,034
Squash	15,000–30,000	123,000–246,000	$1.30	$159,900–$319,800
Total				$583,266–$786,134

Source: United States Department of Agriculture, "National Fruit and Vegetable Retail Report: Advertised Prices for Fruits & Vegetables at Major Retail Supermarket Outlets 07/13 to 07/25," 2013, accessed July 25, 2013, http://www.ams.usda.gov/mnreports/fvwretail.pdf.

Farming parking spaces is just one idea to repurpose underused parking space. One can imagine a neighborhood shuffleboard court, flower garden, bike rack, bench, or storage shed for shared tools occupying underused parking spaces. Each option turns wasted space into a neighborhood asset and may reduce some of the negative externalities associated with wide streets.

Play the Parking

There are many other imaginative ideas for how to repurpose a 7–8-foot-wide, block-long stretch. For example, some neighborhood blocks could dedicate the strip to games—large chess sets, shuffleboard, basketball, etc. Other blocks could be painted with murals, taking advantage of the street-based "canvas." Seating areas, observatories, book exchange kiosks, or community tool-lending libraries are all additional ideas that could take advantage of the otherwise unused residential street space. Perhaps a national neighborhood competition to unleash such creativity could inspire a complete rethinking of these sprawl spaces, much like parklets are repurposing dense, urban street space.

Streets in the United States are often taken for granted. Recently, local governments, urban designers, and traffic engineers have been rethinking busy arterial streets, but little attention has been paid to the ubiquitous residential street. Without much thought for the real and societal costs, residential streets across the country have been built far wider than they need to be.

This study surveyed three Eugene neighborhoods built in different eras of automobile ownership. In each case, on-street parking supply exceeded demand by large margins. This indicates that streets can be designed with less parking in the future, and existing streets can be retrofitted with amenities like pocket swales that mitigate impervious surface-water runoff, agricultural land to provide local food, or other creative uses with public benefit.

Costs to private developers as a result of underutilized land are substantial, and the costs of maintenance to local government are equally high. Streets are public spaces, and while they may have been overbuilt over the last eighty years—mostly with good intentions—there is no reason to maintain the status quo if such spaces are no longer needed. This study has documented the extent of the waste of residential street construction and provided several creative ways to repurpose this public land for greater neighborhood and community benefit.

NOTES

1. Donald C. Shoup, *The High Cost of Free Parking*, vol. 7 (Chicago: Planners Press, American Planning Association, 2005).

2. R. Ewing and E. Dumbaugh, "The Built Environment and Traffic Safety: A Re-

view of Empirical Evidence," *Journal of Planning Literature* 23, no. 4 (2009): 347–67. doi:10.1177/0885412209335553.

3. P. C. Box, "Curb Parking Findings Revisited," *Transportation Research e-Circular*, 2000.

4. L. Chester Arnold Jr. and C. James Gibbons, "Impervious Surface Coverage," *Journal of the American Planning Association* 62, no. 2 (1996): 243.

5. "Eugene," 1912, Eugene, Oregon: Sanborn Map Company, http://sanborn.umi.com.

6. "Brewer Park," 2013, Eugene, Oregon Website, accessed May 25, 2013, https://www.eugene-or.gov/facilities/Facility/Details/44.

7. "Eugene," 1994–2005, Eugene, Oregon, Google Earth.

8. "Oregon Department of Land Conservation and Development History of Oregon's Land Use Planning," 2013, accessed May 26, 2013, http://www.oregon.gov/LCD/Pages/history.aspx.

9. "Design Standards and Guidelines for Eugene Streets, Sidewalks, Bikeways and Accessways," 1999, Eugene, Oregon: City of Eugene, www.eugene-or.gov/Document Center/Home/View/5737.

10. "Roadway Costs Per Centerline Mile," 2012, Florida: Florida Department of Transportation, http://www.dot.state.fl.us/planning/policy/costs/costs-D7.pdf.

11. "Piper Ln, Eugene, OR 97401—Zillow," 2013, Real Estate Listing, Zillow.com, accessed May 5, 2013, http://www.zillow.com/homedetails/Piper-Ln-Eugene-OR-97401/2116015692_zpid/.

12. Hiroko Matsuno and Selina Chiu, "SEA Street" (Seattle, Wash.: Seattle Public Utilities, 2001).

13. Steve Wise, "Green Infrastructure Rising: Best Practices in Stormwater Management," *Planning* (September 2008).

14. "Green Streets. The City of Portland, Oregon," 2013, accessed April 22, 2013, http://www.portlandoregon.gov/bes/45386. *NE Siskiyou Green Street Project*(Portland, Ore.: City of Portland Bureau of Environmental Services, 2005).

15. "Carrots—Western Oregon Department of Horticulture, Oregon State University," 2013, accessed May 20, 2013, http://horticulture.oregonstate.edu/content/carrots-western-oregon-0. "Tomato, Fresh Market. Department of Horticulture. Oregon State University," 2013, accessed May 20, 2013, http://horticulture.oregonstate.edu/content/tomato-fresh-market. "Squash, Zucchini and Summer, Department of Horticulture, Oregon State University," 2013, accessed May 20, 2013, http://horticulture.oregonstate.edu/content/squash-zucchini-and-summer.

16. Adrianne Jeffries, "Down and Dirty," *Oregon Business*, July 2009, http://www.oregonbusiness.com/articles/62-july-2009/1872-down-and-dirty.

CHAPTER 10

Spaces of Indeterminacy
From Thresholds to Ecotones in Retrofitting Sprawl

GABRIEL DÍAZ MONTEMAYOR AND NABIL KAMEL

Key Points and Practice Takeaways

1. Suburban sprawl is both a social and a spatial phenomenon consisting of uneven urban development that especially burdens marginalized social groups.

2. The everyday lived reality of marginalized communities in sprawl locations includes nonsanctioned, opportunistic, and vernacular activities that function as a form of retrofit. We refer to these activities as "everyday tactics" or "retrofit tactics."

3. Retrofit tactics take advantage of the ill-defined, indeterminate spaces that characterize suburban sprawl. These spaces are analogous to "ecotones," a term used to define a transitional area between two biological environments.

4. Everyday tactics merge public and private spaces and create opportunities for retrofitting sprawl.

5. Tactics include deprogramming urban space for local needs, such as appropriating sidewalks for economic exchange, extending objects onto public land, and walking over vacant private land for pedestrian access.

This chapter discusses the possibilities of an approach to retrofitting sprawl in which the spaces between public and private realms are conceived as "ecotones." The ecotone condition of suburbia is analogous to the interstices, thresholds, and indeterminate spaces of urban form. In retrofitting sprawl, ecotones can be used to promote an intense relationship between single-family detached houses and the surrounding public realm.

Since the very first sprawling suburban development in the postwar United States, iconized by Levittown, New York, urban sprawl and the suburbs have been criticized from numerous perspectives.[1] These critiques have traditionally suggested two types of solutions. The first addresses sprawl by redressing its design and architectonic features; these solutions range from comprehensive multiscalar design solutions[2] to more situated solutions at the local and micro levels.[3] The second type aims to redress urban sprawl through policies, controls, and formal governance instruments. These solutions range from market-oriented mechanisms[4] to policies for regulating and collectivizing development and various form-based "smart" codes.[5]

In this chapter, we explore a third avenue for finding sprawl retrofit solutions. We examine ground-up practices of retrofitting sprawl and propose a framework for understanding and implementing these retrofitting tactics. The entry point for this approach is understanding the "sprawl problem" as essentially a matter of rigidity manifested at various levels. For example, from an economic viewpoint, the dependence of sprawl on predictable, stable, and large-scale demand runs against the current economic conditions of uncertainty, dynamic and diverse household and lifestyle needs, rapid and intense boom-and-bust cycles, repeated bouts of fiscal austerity, and cuts in social and physical infrastructure expenditures. Culturally, one-size-fits-all generic design is the materialization of the tyranny of the lowest common denominator in terms of taste, culture, and lifestyle. It represents a parochial, closed imaginary of urban life that runs counter to change, adaptation, and diversity. The rigidity of sprawl also has a political dimension. Despite being promoted as a place of freedom and shared values, the political climate in sprawl communities masks an obsession with property rights that runs against liberal and communal values. Finally, and most relevant to this chapter, is the problem of the physical rigidity of sprawl. With its simplistic and formulaic layout, along with the relative longevity of the built environment, sprawl is ill-suited to respond to economic, demographic, and lifestyle changes intrinsic to urban evolution and development.

In this chapter, we sketch how the communities locked in a sprawl development are able to circumvent these rigidities by renegotiating the parameters of urban space and thus create opportunities to redefine its meaning. We apply the concept of ecotones as an analytical tool to describe a specific urban environment. Ecotones offer a way to loosen up the rigid spatial delineations of sprawl. Traditionally, the term "ecotone" is used to describe a transitional area between two biological communities or environments, such as forest and grass-land or forest and desert. We apply the term "ecotone" in the urban context to describe spaces of activities that transgress and redefine established sociospatial boundaries—functionally, institutionally, and materially. For example, ecotones in an urban context can be public spaces that contain private activity, residential spaces that perform commercial functions, or spaces where multiple layers of meaning coincide.

What enables these transgressions in certain spaces of urban sprawl is the dual condition of having, on one hand, an urban design that prescribes a rigid overdetermination of urban space and, on the other hand, a lived urban space that is characterized by a high level of indeterminacy. While the rigidity of urban design restricts the formal use of urban space, it also engenders creative solutions for the necessary bypassing of such restrictions. Similarly, indetermi-nacy, a condition of incomplete urbanization in older and neglected sprawling suburbs, provides opportunities for redefining the meaning and use of urban space. Finally, it is important to note that ecotones, as spaces of coexistence, diversity, transition, and transformation, are not static environments. Rather, they are spatially and temporally dynamic and respond to changing conditions in an opportunistic way.

Spatial Indeterminacy

In a well-functioning urban environment, it can be assumed that inhabitants enjoy a proliferation of multiple relationships between the public and private realms. In the built environment, this applies both to architecture and urbanism. Multiple relationships happen because of, and in spite of, attempts to control or limit architecture and urban design, as in the case of sprawl or suburbia. In American suburban areas, control is manifested in the continuity, repetition, and protection of architectural and urban models that largely isolate or limit the relationship between public and private realms in deep and large transitional areas in the form of front, side, and backyards that organize the single-family detached housing typology. This urban form does not foster the necessary quantities and qualities of interaction between people, particularly those in need or in disenfranchised communities.

Nonetheless, sprawl gradually loses its rigidity and ability to control. People living in decaying or aging sprawl conditions, often belonging to lower-income and minority groups, introduce a culture of survival and adaptation. This cul-tural capacity arises in spaces where the limits between the public and the pri-vate, and between properties, have been blurred by physical or behavioral ad-aptations in a condition of spatial indeterminacy. In such indeterminate spaces, the life cycle of sprawl is extended in what otherwise would be expendable, short-term architectures and urbanisms.

Designers and planners can be sensitized to this social and urban phenomenon. Adaptations provide lessons to rethink suburban environments and the potential to reuse the elements of sprawl.

Thresholds

The disciplines involved in the construction of the built environment provide various interpretations of the concept of indeterminacy. While most applicable for the purposes of sprawl retrofit might be those directly related to architecture and urbanism, other disciplines, such as ecology and geography, also provide valuable definitions, revealing opportunities for sprawl that are "hidden in plain sight."

A condition of indeterminacy is found, for example, in the concept of a threshold. This spatial type performs the transition between the outdoors and the indoors. When going through a threshold, there's a change from one spatial condition to another. As a person advances, one spatial condition decreases and the other increases. The closer you are to the exterior when moving out from the interior, the more you are outside. Likewise, the closer you move toward the interior, the less you are outside. By belonging to neither a fully exterior nor fully interior condition, the threshold enjoys a quality of spatial indeterminacy. These spaces are also called "interstices."

Thresholds also contain a crucial cultural value. Porches, hallways, vestibules, entrances, and porticos are all related to how people communicate with each other. In sprawl, the most prevalent threshold architectural element is the porch. A similar function is performed by *zaguanes*, which are built passages running from the front door near the street toward the central patios (see figure 10.1); these are found in many places throughout the world, but for purposes of this chapter the focus is particularly on South and Central America and the southwestern United States. In old town vernacular architecture, often found in small agricultural towns where a large percentage of the Latino immigrant population comes from, these provide a transition between the zero-lot-line interior of the building and the street.

The expanded threshold in suburbia, and another crucial element in the assemblage of the single-family detached house, includes the front yard. This mostly empty space provides additional space for the threshold function of the porch, thickening the transition between public and private property. The single-family detached house is separated by open outdoor spaces also in the back and sides. The side yards transition between different private properties, and the backyard often does so as well, although it is sometimes related to a semi-public-access alley in older forms of suburbia. These suburban dwellings are surrounded, in other words, by thresholds with a capacity for spatial indeterminacy.

FIGURE 10.1. *Zaguan* housing typology in Parral, northern Mexico. *Photos by Gabriel Díaz Montemayor.*

Yards are a main cultural signifier of American suburbia. As such, these remain as spaces where adaptive intervention is often not culturally acceptable. In the book *Re: The American Dream,*[6] architects and educators surveyed the diverse suburban forms of Los Angeles and concluded that they were evidence of an adaptive suburban housing stock, one with the capacity for higher densities that multiply the number of transitions, thresholds, and units. While this interpretation of the American Dream is mainly about rethinking the core of urban blocks and their capacity to absorb larger populations and provide new access points between properties through backyards, side yards, and alleys, the projects leave the front, that is, the perimeter of the block, relatively untouched.

In a context similar to that of *Re: The American Dream*, James Rojas explores the intensification of relationships within suburban fabrics by conducting studies on "enacted spaces" in East Los Angeles.[7] Unlike *Re: The American Dream*, however, Rojas concentrates on front yards and the spaces in between, where social interaction and activity are most evident. But Rojas also puts forward the indissoluble relationship of the unit to the street, and he analyzes the ways in which social activity spills over from the private to the public, and vice versa.

Urbanists with a social interest work to strengthen intensive, dense, and multiple relationships between public and private domains. In the case of the Charter for the New Urbanism, for example, principle number 19, the first one at the scale of "the block, the street, the building," reads: "A primary task of all urban architecture and landscape design is the physical definition of streets and public spaces as places of shared use."[8] In this view, architecture and landscape are the shapers of shared or public space. If this concept were to be instrumental, it would lead to an urban form more likely to foster community ties, place making, and diversity; to define identities; and to concentrate investment in the public domain. This is conceived as a more just and therefore sustainable form of urbanism.

Unfortunately, the current cultural and economic construction of society provides no legal framework for operationalizing indeterminacy. The urban form of most American cities provides evidence that society is founded more on private than on public property. American architecture and landscapes are not about the shaping of shared public spaces but rather the shaping of private interests. As such, the economy of debt and investment security relies on the fixed edges of territorial units.

This may need to change. Before the recession, which began in 2008, little thought was put into the resilient capacity of suburban form. Today, with abandoned subdivisions and people finding alternative ways to support their income, there are growing practices that contravene the control and fixity of sprawl. The economic downturn has prompted the emergence of new typologies for retrofitting sprawl, demonstrating the obsolescence of the simple threshold.

Ecotones

An ecotone is a region where characteristics of two ecosystems or biomes coexist through transitions. Because of the diversity of their flora and fauna, ecotones are among the most valuable of all ecological regions. It is in these spaces that two different conditions are in tension. Ecotones are edges, or margins of larger areas, defined sometimes by wide strips of variable form—sometimes one biome scatters into another causing patches of different scales—but at other times the contrast between regions is more highly defined. Spatially, ecotones are indeterminate as they do not contain one biome or the other but rather both (see figure 10.2). Since these spaces are unstable and flexible, they shift depending on larger environmental conditions such as drought, seasons, and climate change.

Given the value of these environmental areas, decision makers in the fields of landscape architecture and planning have begun to place investment and effort not into the center of regions but rather at their edges. Furthermore, in cases where resources are limited, protecting a region where two conditions are served is a more efficient investment, as opposed to serving only one. This expenditure protects a region more efficiently when it serves two conditions as opposed to one.

In the discipline of landscape architecture, one of the fundamental ways to achieve a harmonious and sustainable relationship between the ecological and human realms is precisely the opening of areas or spaces of access, interaction, and overlap. This approach has been applied in the fields of landscape urbanism and ecological urbanism, which explore the possibilities of merging the human, cultural, and urban with the ecological. These proto-disciplines avoid

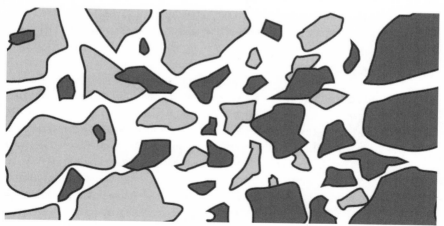

FIGURE 10.2. Hypothetical biome transition or ecotone. Ecotones are unstable and flexible.
Source: Ecological Society of America.

solely concentrating on natural and cultural systems related to open space, and focus instead on a wider array of issues, including urban form. The result of the multiple overlays becomes naturally ambiguous and indeterminate.

However, the few built projects that belong to this hybrid approach perform more as a formal metaphor of ecology than as systems that incorporate both urban and natural ecologies. An example of this would be the Flowing Gardens project in Xian, China.[9] If the coexistence of two opposing conditions is to be sought, then the form that results from it should operate as an ecotone, eventually no longer resembling one form or the other. It should begin to resemble something in between, where the most important considerations are the interactions or relationships between urban and natural systems, or in our case, private and public systems. Given the nature of urban ecology, it may be useful to think of the existing interactions between the public and the private in suburban sprawl as facilitated by the spatial conditions of an ecotone.

Practices such as Mexico City's *Taller de Operaciones Ambientales* (TOA), meaning "Environmental Operations Studio," have been put forward in public, private, and community-based work.[10] This practice attempts to merge a biological understanding with architectural and urban issues in response to the needs identified in local populations, often belonging to low-income rural or indigenous communities, through field research. In the case of TOA, the approach involved a partnership between a biologist and an industrial designer.

The recent emerging hybrid disciplines speak to the need to progressively embrace practices where clearly and strictly determined spaces evolve into a dynamic condition of flows, interactions, and overlays. This is likely to happen in territories that resemble the natural condition of the ecotone while keeping the basic, but evolving, foundations of contemporary society as represented by private and public property. The long-term sustainability of sprawl cannot take place without reflecting the diversity that exists in the contemporary city.

A Diverse Sprawl

Sprawl is indeterminate, but its indeterminacy is radically different from that found in compact, older forms of urbanism. Sprawl is possible only in a culture where respect for the property of others is paramount. While in many foreign urban contexts and cultures the idea of having an open lawn or space with virtually no physical barrier to separate public from private would be impossible, in the United States the culture of law, free markets, and fear provide a foundation for the continuation of sprawl. In a typical suburban neighborhood, relationships between the private and the public and between neighbors are negotiated by open spaces that are occupied by green lawns, shrubs, and trees. These are largely devoid of human activity, and their most important spatial quality is openness. The wide-open thresholds of the front yards taken together become a collective assemblage of front lawns mirrored on both sides of the street. These lawns act as a community offering, yet normally do not host or foster any community activities.

The embedded quality of indeterminacy in the open yards of sprawl is one that is simultaneously and immediately suppressed by American cultural behavior. This suppression favors the fixed, determinate condition of open spaces around and between dwellings and is reflected by immobility and lack of change. This is particularly apparent in recent or new subdivisions in middle- to high-income areas, but in depressed neighborhoods the relationship between private and public in open spaces has both positive and negative implications. On the one hand, the unifying trust that made the open quality of suburbia so successful in an earlier era has become distrust. On the other hand, the indeterminate capacity of open space in these neighborhoods can be leveraged to ameliorate the absence of social, economic, and recreational amenities. This is the case for immigrant Latin American populations that often concentrate and cluster in the inner ring of old sprawl areas. While the shift from the original form of sprawl in these neighborhoods is not radical, it is visible. Gardens and front yards demonstrate such cultural adaptations, including architectural elements, such as fences, altars, and decks, as well as diverse objects, such as sculptures, furniture, and junk. The activities happening in the yards frequently jump over the fence or the property line into the public realm and vice versa. The open front lawn becomes more of a *zaguan*, transformed into a narrower and thicker strip of land where interactions are culturally facilitated. This creates a sense of protection that eases the fear of transgression of the boundaries between the public and the private. The shortened distances humanize sprawl. The scattering of elements of use and outdoor activity happening in the yards are often mirrored by the public shared space—that is, the sidewalk or the street—bringing the private into the public. The result is a diagram not so different from that of the ecotone, consolidating a shift from a simple spatial threshold transition to an urban ecology that relies on living, animated, and dynamic systems.

The first factor for sprawl adaptation located within inner-ring sprawl is cultural. The second has to do with the passing of time, as the city grows and extends toward newer rings of development. This gradual process is made particularly visible by the insertion of large infrastructures and the process of the decay of single-family detached homes.

If the common property lines in sprawl (i.e., the most ubiquitous) are those that separate private properties, in the case of decaying sprawl, the postdevelopment insertion of infrastructures of various types provides new boundaries that diversify and affect the original subdivision. One of the most critical new spatial additions to inner-ring sprawl are the numerous wasted spaces and parcels of land created as interstices between an older urban fabric, the original sprawl, and the new infrastructures, including freeways and the rights-of-way associated with these. There is a contemporary fascination with these spaces, which suggests the potential capacity of these territories for urban, ecological, cultural, and economic recovery. It is also no surprise that these spaces have become release valves for artistic and cultural expression.

These *drosscapes*,[11] alternatively called "wasted landscapes," *terrain vague*,[12] or "diffuse indeterminate spaces," are most often denied maintenance because it is unclear who owns them and why these spaces deserve attention. These spaces are beyond sprawl's notion of control. The very fact that only one new condition of public property—the off-limits, "city property: trespassers will be fined," nonaccessible condition—multiplies new relationships in sprawl is telling of the capacity of such a regular, repetitive, and formulaic system to easily accept new programs and uses in the thresholds between the public, the private, and the off-limits. New large infrastructures cut through suburbia loosening rigidity and activating indeterminate spaces. In these cultural contexts, some of these otherwise wasted spaces offer opportunistic fields that are occupied by nonsanctioned tactics of economic and cultural survival.

Spatial Indeterminacy in Sprawl: Case Study in Phoenix, Arizona

As part of a recent grant provided by the Phoenix Urban Research Laboratory (PURL) of Arizona State University, a team of researchers led by Kristin Koptiuch, Nabil Kamel, and Gabriel Díaz Montemayor explored the capacities to "learn from the margins" in the inner growth rings of the city of Phoenix. These areas were developed in the suburban model dating back to the mid-twentieth century. Today, these areas are largely inhabited by immigrant populations and minorities. The clue that makes it possible to understand how sprawl had been adapted and retrofitted by cultural and economic practices was the presence of informal, nonsanctioned, street and front-yard vendors. In this area of Phoenix, such practice is common, particularly on weekends. In order to discover why this practice was happening, the project delved beyond the cultural and economic explanations. This included an analysis of the physical conditions of where these practices happen and how the opportunistic behavior was facilitated by often invisible conditions found in the physical infrastructure of the neighborhood. The practices that retrofit sprawl were understood as tactics. These are activities that are not planned but arise spontaneously in response to the often unfavorable social conditions of suburbia in order to provide more intensive social and economic interactions.

The explorations found that, besides the operationalization of front yards, public space and rights-of-way were also being frequently used for informal economic activities. Both practices retrofit sprawl by providing additional economic and even recreational means that the community and its infrastructure formally lack by operating according to the very same logic as formal conventional capitalist marketing—namely, identifying opportunities for appropriate spatial functions and high visibility.

The physical conditions of the identified tactic sites were organized and approached on two scales: a large-scale macro-analysis to provide a broad urban and historical context, and a smaller-scaled spatial analysis to examine the micro-adaptations of the tactic. The former was analyzed to reveal the large-scale infrastructure insertion and neighborhood deterioration. The latter was studied to understand cultural adaptive practices.

Both scales of analysis were developed in part by using publicly available prerecorded data, particularly the information provided by the county, which included parcel and property lines, owners, streets, and, most critically, historical aerial imagery. The tactics, however, were identified through on-site reconnaissance. The work relied on field visits to tactic sites throughout the year of the project's development (2011–2012) to record how these operated. In all cases, there were multiple visits, on each of which photographs and sketches were recorded. Researchers used information taken on site to draw and diagram the relationship between movements of tacticians, customers, and passersby. These flows were also mapped differentiating pedestrians from vehicles.

The large-scale context analysis is relevant to understand the historical development of the areas in question. The Maricopa County website provides aerial photographs, at five- to ten-year intervals, covering the period from 1930 to 2010. In order to understand the evolution of urban form in areas of old sprawl—that is, predominantly post–World War II sites developed before the completion of the central freeway system in the late 1980s—critical historical junctures that influenced development in and around the tactic sites were investigated. Five historical moments for the metropolitan area of Phoenix were identified in the urban form of the tactic locations: (1) the pre-urban condition, predating World War II and largely visible by agricultural practices already following the parcel lines later converted into urban form; (2) the introduction of sprawl development, post–World War II, when most of the inner ring was developed; (3) the evolution/consolidation of the sprawl fabric, mainly during the 1960s and 1970s, and its decay; (4) the construction of freeway systems in the late 1980s; and (5) present-day conditions.

The identified tactic sites suggested a particular condition of activated spatial indeterminacy. The sites were often close together, occupying spaces directly affected first by the decay of sprawl and second by the construction of a freeway. This discovery was made visible by the mapping of changes in urban form over time and on aerial photographs. The analysis of historical aerial imagery evidenced the economic process of gain of value, followed by the loss of value and the eventual replacement of the original demographics by a new population.

At the large scale, what is particularly important for the adaptation of the original suburban patterns is the insertion of the freeway. Being a hard and impenetrable barrier, its presence reconfigured a wide corridor along its path where many local streets had to be adapted into dead-end streets. The neighborhoods lost connectivity—streets with continuity—with the rest of the city. Houses that used to have a mirror unit in front of them now had the impenetrable right of way of the freeway. There was also a loss of accessibility—distances having to be covered to reach places—through these neighborhoods. The inner-city ring is now a region surrounding the downtown area of Phoenix that can be avoided by jumping onto the freeway. This modification converted the area into an almost natural depository of disenfranchised communities. The definition of an inner ring confined by hard boundaries between the city core and the outer ring of newer suburban development provided a space of indeterminacy in a favorable, if blighted, location close to both the center and the periphery.

A cultural socioeconomic activation of spatial indeterminacy was found in a smaller-scale site-specific analysis. Initially, all of the physical elements of the area around the tactic were drawn as identified on-site. This included property lines of both public and private properties. Also included were building footprints and all of the outdoor elements found in the front, side, and backyards, including pavers, paths, sidewalks, fences, exterior walls, furniture, and vegetation. Different states of ownership were identified based on levels of public and private use, access, and legal ownership. Publicly owned spaces were identified in four different spatial subtypes defined as follows: (1) public spaces fully accessible to cars and pedestrians, such as streets and sidewalks; (2) restricted public spaces, such as rights-of-way, embankments for infrastructures, and service areas; (3) freeways; and (4) lots of land acquired by local and state governments. This mapping reflected a much more complex mixture of the spatial property regime than what otherwise would be understood as a binary system of public and private land. This multiplied the kinds of transitions or interstices between the street and the private lot.

With the mapping of property lines, it was revealed that not all of these were following the expected repetitive parallelism and frontal continuity typical of suburbia. Some of the properties intruded into the expected continuity of the street's edge, while others were reshaped in adaptation to the geometry of the freeway and the discontinuity of cut-off local streets. The property limit variations produced by later insertions of infrastructure created spaces ripe for nonsanctioned practices.

The tactics were then mapped in a diagrammatic logic (see figure 10.3). First, the internal movements of the tacticians were drawn, moving in and out of the house, through the front yard, and taking supplies from the street into the tactic site. Drawn second was the location of the ephemeral infrastructure put in place to make the tactic happen, including canopies, shades, adapted fences and vertical elements as displays, large items for sale, tables for small items, and chairs for both vendors and customers. Drawn third were the flows of cars in and out, approaching and leaving the tactic.

One tactic became of particular interest due to the presence of factors pertaining to large-scale infrastructural insertions, decay over time, and small-scale tactical practices. The tacticians were of Latin American descent and Spanish-speakers, and they referred to their yard sale as a "yarda" sale. The house sits in what was a continuous local street until the arrival of the freeway. The neighboring buildings in front and to the north were demolished, and this building would probably have been demolished as well, but it was made accessible by an extension of the local street to provide car and pedestrian access and a front to the home. The street extension involved infrastructure and land ownership extruding the front yard of the tactician's home over the sidewalk and the street (see figure 10.4). Although it is not a yard but a street serving only one owner, the vendors occupy that space, set up their yard sale, and enjoy full visibility as the axial visual relationship of the street looking north ends in their sale with the freeway as backdrop. This location does not disrupt any neighbor's accessibility since their home is the only one accessible by the extended street. Customers typically advance into the cul-de-sac, park, and walk into the sale. If they come on foot, they simply stroll over the empty strip of private land neighboring the tactician's site immediately to the south. The tacticians have even placed a couch in front of their empty neighbor's land to lure people in toward the core of the sale in front of the dwelling. The shifting and pulling of property limits and infrastructure provided these dwellers with an extended and more capable, if casual or random, environment. The location of the tactical elements, such as tables, items for sale, cars, and shades, suggest a constellation of private things for sale, originating from the home outward, into and over the different conditions of public, shared space. The overflow of private activities over public land can be separated into five movements: (1) occupying the front yard as part of the sale; (2) jumping the property limit onto the sidewalk, extending objects and activity into public land; (3) extending into the street; (4) using public rights-of-way for parking; and (5) walking over vacant private land for pedestrian access. The front yard, the sidewalk, the street, rights-of-way, and private vacant land act as an ecotone where public and private merge.

Through the interviewing of the tacticians, it became clear that these non-sanctioned activities respond to a very instinctive and intuitive understanding of spatial conditions. For them, spatial analysis is an aspect of everyday life. In this view, the ecotone concept is of greater accuracy as it incorporates and explains the coexistence of the two basic biomes: the public biome manifested by abandonment, lack of maintenance and activity, and variable degrees of accessibility; and the private biome manifested by the opportunistic tactics that retrofit sprawl and society.

FIGURE 10.3.
"Yarda" sale
tactic—areas
of spatial
indeterminacy
acting as ecotones.
*Drawings by Gabriel
Díaz Montemayor
and Adam Atkins.*

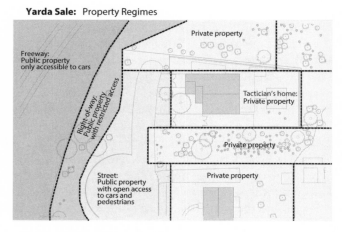

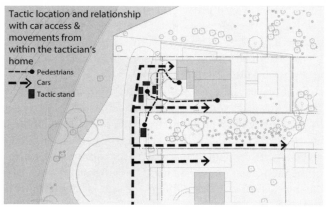

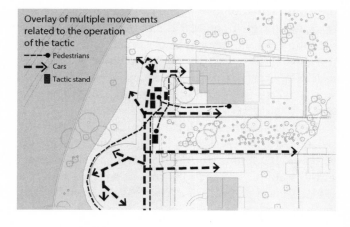

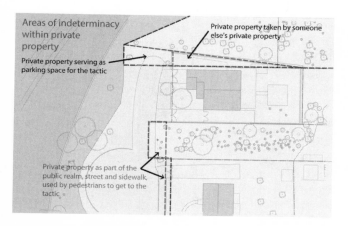

Areas of indeterminacy within private property

Private property serving as parking space for the tactic

Private property taken by someone else's private property

Private property as part of the public realm, street and sidewalk, used by pedestrians to get to the tactic

FIGURE 10.3. (*continued*)

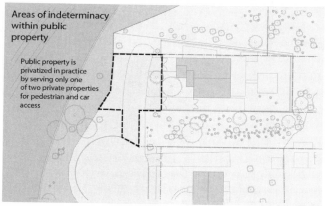

Areas of indeterminacy within public property

Public property is privatized in practice by serving only one of two private properties for pedestrian and car access

From Thresholds to Ecotones

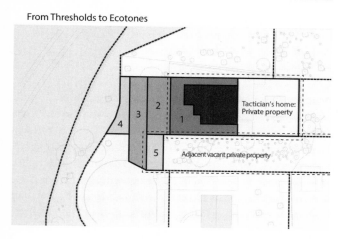

Tactician's home: Private property

Adjacent vacant private property

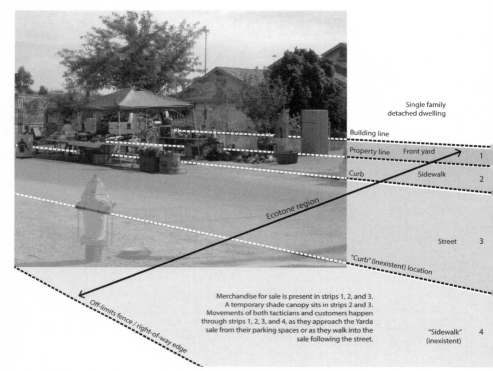

FIGURE 10.4. "Yarda" sale ecotone photo analysis. Merchandise for sale is present in strips 1, 2, and 3 (from lower left to upper right). A temporary shade canopy sits in strips 2 and 3. Movements both of tacticians and of customers happen through strips 1, 2, 3, and 4, as they approach the Yarda sale from their parking spaces or as they walk into the sale following the street.
Montage by Gabriel Díaz Montemayor, photos by Nabil Kamel and Rafael Fontes.

From Thresholds to Ecotones

The disciplines concerned with the built realm and ecology coincide in providing a qualitative value to areas where opposite or complementary conditions merge or interact. Widened, active, and even aesthetically pleasing thresholds and interstices are preferred in the architectural and urban shaping of our cities. The presence and quality of areas of transition between biomes provides a richer environment of coexistence, particularly in light of the contemporary relevance of the idea of diversity and resiliency, so critical for the retrofit of suburban sprawl. Unfortunately, the formulas exhausted by suburban sprawl retrofit have been based on precisely the opposite presumption: control and clear limits, or a form-based approach as opposed to a systems or ecological approach. In view of environmental, economic, and social crises, the question is not whether the quality of indeterminate space is necessary but how to find ways to embed it into preexisting and future urban areas. As demonstrated by a small sample of urban phenomena in the metropolitan area of Phoenix, these spaces exist in invisibility until a pressured social group comes in and leverages the opportunity that these provide not just for economic improvement but also for social enhancement.

The spaces between the public and the private can be included in urban form from the start in order to provide flexible and adaptive capacities. The rights-of-way can be relabeled, and reregulated, into rights to the city. The linear front edges of the ubiquitous rows of sprawling single-family detached houses can be allowed to advance into underutilized sidewalks, parking lanes, vacant properties, rights-of-way, and public spaces to provide for the creation of a porous and thickened edge where niches for interaction become part of the outdoors. The ecology of indeterminacy can be more fully established as a vital factor of urbanism.

Spatial indeterminacy in architecture and urbanism is a fundamental program for social, economic, and ecological sustainability. It is the ecotone that sprawl must embrace in order to transition into a viable architectural and urban model for the twenty-first century. Sprawl retrofit has to move to the front yard and toward the public; it needs to shift from a physical formal approach to one where living resilient systems determine form.

The analysis of the *actual* retrofit of spaces of urban sprawl through the lens of ecotones provided several important lessons for urban design practice and thought. This chapter shows that urban form is in a constant state of flux, that—for better or for worse—the regulations and boundaries that define urban space are constantly challenged and transgressed, and consequently that urban space is constantly redefined and appropriated by local actors. Ecotones and indeterminate spaces provide an environment that facilitates such redefinition and reappropriation of urban space. It is in such spaces that sprawl is actually being retrofitted organically to address the changing and unmet needs of local residents. This is especially the case in older and neglected suburbs where erosion by time, public and private disinvestment, and destruction by new freeway construction blurred the previously unambiguous urban spatial demarcations and rendered them more porous to invading activities. Existing elements of the built environment are creatively repurposed with minimal costs to replace the stale form of sprawl with a more vibrant and active urban environment. Rigid definitions of public versus private space, and of permissible uses of urban space, are subtly renegotiated. The basis upon which sprawl retrofit takes place in ecotones thrives through the deprogramming of urban space and the insertion of locally produced spatial practices that are initiated by the local community in order to meet their needs.

Urban design practitioners can benefit from analyzing the ways in which their designs and programs are transgressed, transformed, and appropriated to actually fit the lives of residents. Similarly, in their urban design plans, practitioners ought to account for and incorporate spaces that enable the local production of urban space. As seen in this chapter, as well as in the work of Gehl, Koolhaas, and others, such activities take place in spaces that tend to be less determined and programmatically open to the coincidence of multiple activities, meanings, and definitions.

NOTES

1. Andres Duany, Elizabeth Plater-Zyberk, and Jeff Speck, *Suburban Nation: The Rise of Sprawl and the Decline of the American Dream* (New York: North Point Press, 2000).

2. Galina Tachieva, *Sprawl Repair Manual* (Washington, D.C.: Island Press, 2010).

3. Ellen Dunham-Jones and June Williamson, *Retrofitting Suburbia: Urban Design Solutions for Redesigning Suburbs* (Hoboken, N.J.: Wiley, 2011).

4. William A. Fischel, *Sprawl and the Federal Government* (Washington, D.C.: U.S.A. CATO Institute, 2000); see also Jan K. Brueckner, "Urban Sprawl: Diagnosis and Remedies," *International Regional Science Review* 23, no. 2 (2000): 160–71.

5. Andres Duany, Jeff Speck, and Mike Lydon, *The Smart Growth Manual* (New York: McGraw-Hill, 2007).

6. Roger Sherman, *Re: The American Dream. Los Angeles, CA, U.S.A.* (New York: Princeton Architectural Press, 1995).

7. James Rojas, "The Enacted Environment: The Creation of 'Place' by Mexicans and Mexican Americans in East Los Angeles," master's thesis, Massachusetts Institute of Technology, 1991.

8. Emily Talen and the Congress for the New Urbanism, *Charter of the New Urbanism* (New York: McGraw-Hill, 2013), 181.

9. Groundlab, "Flowing Gardens in Xian, China," retrieved on April 15, 2013, http://groundlab.org/portfolio/groundlab-project-flowing-gardens-xian-china/.

10. Emiliano García and Juan Rovalo, "Collaboration," lecture presented at the Design School of Arizona State University, February 27, 2013, Tempe, Az.

11. Alan Berger, *Drosscapes* (New York: Princeton Architectural Press, 2006).

12. Ignasi De Sola-Morales, "Terrain Vague," in *On Landscape Urbanism*, edited by Dean Almy, 108–13 (Austin, Tex.: Center for American Architecture and Design, 2007).

CHAPTER 11

Retrofitting the Cul-de-Sac in Suburban Arizona
A Design Proposal

BENJAMIN W. STANLEY, AARON GOLUB, MILAGROS ZINGONI, WHITNEY WARMAN, AND CHRISTIAN SOLORIO

Key Points and Practice Takeaways

1. The suburban cul-de-sac presents a unique opportunity to develop a dense, diverse urban node serving as a mixed-use center for productive activities and community interaction.

2. Our design intervention transforms seven private single-family properties into thirty-one varied residential units surrounded by a range of shared community facilities and spaces, organized along a continuum from public to private spaces.

3. The productivity and resilience of retrofitted urban communities are enhanced when indoor and outdoor spaces are designed to be flexibly configured and adaptable on both hourly and yearly time scales.

4. Sustainability is encouraged by implementing closed-loop metabolisms of food, water, waste, and energy on-site.

5. Retrofitting cul-de-sacs can not only reduce transportation energy expenses but also introduce new ways to generate local economic growth. On-site production of human, social, natural, and financial capital in flexible built environments can provide a new growth trajectory.

The notion that urban development involves the "irrigation of territories with potential" has long been an aspect of urban planning and design practice, but it seems especially relevant to the growing necessity to retrofit sprawling suburban environments.[1] In this chapter, comprehensive design improvements to a suburban cul-de-sac in Avondale, Arizona, are proposed to show how the emergent ideal of retrofitting can be congruent with specific notions of sustainable urban development. Four exogenous factors elevate the importance of redesigning and retrofitting peri-urban environments in twenty-first-century American cities: the coming demographic transition; increasing energy costs; future climate change policies; and economic restructuring (already begun), resulting in stagnant or declining incomes for most households.

Sustainable urbanism centered around design retrofits holds promise for tackling these challenges. Here we will focus upon initiatives currently integral to the existing retrofitting movement—such as increasing the density, diversity, and walkability of suburban places—as well as upon a novel approach to encouraging place-based economic development through the design of flexible and adaptable spaces that can "irrigate," or squeeze more value out of, existing urban configurations.[2] By encouraging "import-replacement" through the facilitation of on-site human, social, natural, and financial capital production, a retrofitted design of the cul-de-sac's existing physical capital can simultaneously promote urban sustainability and economic development.

A wide variety of reasons have been cited to support the retrofitting of suburbia: public health issues related to the sedentary lifestyles of automobile-based urbanism; the ongoing shift to a postindustrial city, where an emphasis on services and telecommuting means that "the qualities of individual places matter more in locational decisions"; a growing disconnect between the homogeneity of suburban housing stock and the increasing diversity of households, workplaces, and needs; rapidly aging inner suburban properties and fears of urban blight; and "edge city" congestion problems coupled with the "underperforming asphalt" of these automobile-dominated areas.[3] While the generalized framework of the retrofitting suburbia and New Urbanism movements represents our starting point, the design presented in this chapter is specifically oriented toward the bioregional, cultural, and socioeconomic character of peripheral Arizona subdivisions.

Our vision of sustainable urban development derives from the contemporary paradigm of Fordist economic growth that for many decades has driven public policy in American cities and in Arizona in particular. By emphasizing how our sustainable design interventions will specifically encourage cooperative local economic development—instead of sustainability approaches rooted in communal and antigrowth sentiment—we hope to adhere to Arizona's growth-obsessed culture while extending the long-term viability of vulnerable suburban neighborhoods.

Our specific design proposal extends strategic urbanism to sprawling peripheral neighborhoods representing a large proportion of American suburbia. We will begin with a discussion of the growing pressures on suburbia resulting from four exogenous trends in the society and economy at large. Our general approach to retrofitting sprawl builds on existing work in this important arena. Finally, we present our design and use proposal for an example cul-de-sac in suburban Arizona and end with some concluding thoughts.

Exogenous Trends Addressed by Retrofitting Suburban Arizona

Four exogenous trends pose significant challenges to the current configuration of suburbs nationally and in Arizona. Our design and reuse proposal is intended to address these challenges.

The Demographic Transition in American Cities

The changing demographics of the United States will have a significant impact on future housing needs. In the 2013 book *Reshaping Metropolitan America: Development Trends and Opportunities to 2030*, Arthur C. Nelson estimates that by 2030 only about a quarter of American households will be raising children. Nelson also translates projected numbers of households (by type) into housing-type demand in 2030. He estimates that the typical detached suburban home will be in oversupply by about 30 percent—that is, about 30 percent of the now-existing suburban homes will not be needed in 2030. Furthermore, marketers have found that the generation born between 1979 and 1996 will incur a new type of housing demand, as the majority state a preference for walkable, mixed-use communities. Of this group, 77 percent plan to live in a more urban environment than most suburban offerings, and 70 percent do not anticipate a move to suburbia upon having children. In addition, older households in the baby boom generation prefer to age in place, and 71 percent would prefer to live within walking distance of transit.[4] These statistics confirm planners' concerns that the paradigm of zoning for low-density, single-family housing in auto-dependent neighborhoods may soon seriously constrain the housing choices of many American consumers.

Rising Energy Prices

The Phoenix metropolitan area has been one of the fastest-growing areas in the United States since World War II primarily due to low-cost, low-density subdivision development on the urban fringe. The viability of this model of dispersed and cheap housing rested for decades on a delicate balance of interlocking public and private policies that have created a steady supply of cheap petroleum for U.S. consumers. This model is no longer dependable for a variety of interrelated reasons, including cost, geology ("peak oil"), and geopolitics, alongside the emergence of additional demands on the international petroleum supply system from economies like China and India. Indeed, the average inflation-adjusted price of gasoline in the United States more than doubled between 1998 and 2010, and it has continued to rise dramatically in the past few years.[5] The U.S. Energy Information Agency's "reference" (i.e., most likely) case projects 2035 oil prices to be around 50 percent higher than current prices; their "high" price is twice that of today's.[6]

Emergent Climate Change Policy

While retrofitting projects aimed at combating climate change can be justified on various grounds (e.g., ethical), future shifts in public policy will likely make such planning reforms an economic imperative as well. For example, California's Sustainable Communities and Climate Protection Act of 2008 (State Bill 375) specifically incentivizes planning practices that can decrease greenhouse gas emissions, especially from automobiles. The bill requires each of California's eighteen metropolitan planning organizations to prepare a "sustainable communities strategy" that will use "integrated land use, housing and transportation planning" to meet the greenhouse gas reduction targets specified in AB 32.[7] Although the bill attempts to reduce emissions through a combination of regulations and market-based initiatives, it specifically provides incentives for developers to produce dense, mixed-use, and walkable urban environments. Although the Arizona legislature is currently opposed to such regulation, a combination of demographic turnover and the increasing effects of climate change in a precarious desert ecosystem will almost certainly lead to similar policy shifts in the coming decades.

The Economic Growth Paradigm in Urban Arizona

Phoenix's suburban development epitomizes the national Fordist integrated economic development paradigm based on the confluence of: (1) high wages linked closely with improved economic productivity; (2) mass production managed by large firms integrated into noncompetitive sectors (such as petroleum, defense, housing, automobiles, durable goods, etc.); (3) mass consumption patterned into bundles reflecting the same cartelized production sectors (petroleum, automobiles, etc.); and (4) the set of public policies (fiscal and monetary management and infrastructure investments) that facilitate the mass consumption and production cycle. Fordism, named after one of the famous originators of mass production, is the systemic Keynesian response to the instabilities (e.g., the Great Depression) arising during periods of low to zero growth in capitalist economies; it reinforces the ideal of a "self-sustaining feedback process" of urban growth.[8] The suburb, the single-family home, the freeway, and the automobile became the centerpieces of Fordist economy. Like many other American cities, but perhaps to an extreme, the economy of the Phoenix metropolitan area has been shaped by the Fordist growth economy.[9] Unlike urban economies based on technology development, manufacturing, or resource extraction, Phoenix's economy relies on the process of growth itself. As Patricia Gober notes, "as the region urbanized, growth at the fringe became the central driving force underlying the regional economy and prosperity."[10] When financial crisis driven by speculative housing markets emerged in 2007, Phoenix's economy was thus hit especially hard. Lenders foreclosed on 70,000 homes, housing values fell by 50 percent, and half of the state's homeowners owed more than their houses were worth.[11]

Fordism was linked to the incredible manufacturing capacity of the U.S. economy, along with the supply of inexpensive oil, conditions that have changed drastically over the past forty years. For a variety of reasons too complex to address here, the articulations between wages and productivity and between production and consumption inherent in the Fordist regime have weakened, replaced by systems of lower wages, wage stagnation, and debt for most households. Inequalities in wages and wealth then arose, even as productivity per worker grew, since wage growth no longer tracked with productivity. From its peak, automobile manufacturing and those other sectors at the heart of the articulated economy are now much smaller.

In sum, these four urgent challenges facing the United States call for a drastic rethinking of its existing consumption patterns—especially those of its housing and neighborhoods. Addressing these challenges will mean retrofitting both the physical design as well as the use of suburban neighborhoods and houses. We now discuss our approach to this retrofitting process.

The Transition from Scalar Growth to Sustainable Development

The theoretical distinction between "growth" and "development" becomes important when conceiving of alternatives to existing Fordist growth patterns. Herman Daly describes growth as an inherently quantitative process, increasing the scale of resource consumption, while development is a qualitative "improvement in the structure, design and composition of the physical stocks of wealth that result from greater knowledge."[12] Sustainable development discourses often imply that a wholesale shift from growth to development is critical because the environmental resource base and population-carrying capacity of the earth are both finite.[13] Here, development is often conceived as locally and bioregionally generated, in tandem with a knowledge-driven economy in which local urban cultures become vital generators of economic development.[14] Jane Jacobs was the first to expound a coherent philosophy of urban economic growth based on local development.[15] Her fundamental observation is that economic development generates novel goods and services from existing, emplaced economic activity in dynamic cities—"new work" derived from "old work"—instead of traditional economic foci on the efficiency of business and scale-expanding growth. The idea of "import-replacement," whereby local businesses arise to produce items formerly imported, represents the critical moment of development, where novelty, specialization, and growth all expand in a feedback loop.[16] The idea that socioeconomic success can be generated from within cities, through novel innovations and cultural production, is crucial for sustainable development since the existing Fordist paradigm of scalar urban growth is often linked to the functional decline of natural ecosystems.

Beginning with Jacobs's vocal defense of vibrant urbanism, and continuing in the smart growth movement, support for dense, walkable urban environments has been further strengthened by various calls for sustainable urban design.[17] Dense, well-designed urban neighborhoods can decrease the energy costs associated with housing and transport while increasing the social synergies of cooperative communities. Sustainable urban planning often centers on efficiency improvements in the provision of ecoservices, involving shifts from Fordist centralized, fossil-fuel based energy and food production to decentralized, local renewable energy production; from linear systems of water and goods provision to circular systems in which recycling methods allow for the reuse of "waste"; from cookie-cutter housing designs, wasteful of energy and ignorant of the specificities of place, toward more bioregionally and culturally specific designs promoting energy efficiency and carbon reduction; and toward transit systems emphasizing pedestrian and mass transit options.[18] Local food production is often linked with sustainable urban design (e.g., in suburban retrofitting), as it promises to lower the transport energy use of capitalist food systems and to increase local self-sufficiency and resilience.[19]

Merging sustainable development practices with neighborhood design holds potential for locally generating social, human, natural, and financial capital and encouraging import-replacement. Many sustainable design ideas promote local economic development by realizing potential efficiencies, such as in physical capital (energy-efficient architecture and transportation) or social capital (dense urban environments that promote social cohesion). Other ideas focus on novel sources of economic development, such as producing natural capital (local energy generation and food production) or developing human capital (educational attainment and local cultural production). Development strategies based on efficiency and novelty help transcend the Fordist scalar-growth paradigm by refocusing social investments into existing urban communities and generating place-specific economic success.

Sustainable design can further promote development when household and neighborhood spaces are designed for short-term flexibility in temporal use and long-term adaptation to changing circumstances. The notion of "adaptive management" emphasizes that disruptions and change are natural aspects of social-ecological systems and that human institutions must be flexible enough to manage under changing circumstances.[20] Norton emphasizes how adaptive management entails the maintenance and growth of "options and opportunities" for future generations.[21] These sustainability notions share many similarities with planners and designers who emphasize the importance of adaptive infrastructures. Landscape urbanism, for example, promotes the strategic design of urban spaces so that ecological, social, and economic infrastructures are inherently flexible and preserve future development potential, creating "a kind of urbanism that anticipates change, open-endedness, and negotiation."[22] Urban sustainability theorists tend to merge these ecology- and planning-based notions, emphasizing that good planning practices promote "diversity, adaptiveness, interconnectedness, resilience, regenerative capacity, and symbiosis."[23]

Ultimately, flexible and mixed-use urban spaces can generate economic development, as new efficiencies in the temporal use of space allow increased capital production, but they also can increase the long-term socioeconomic resilience of communities. Especially when anticipating energy price volatility, climate change, and the upcoming demographic transition, designing a more locally controlled, flexible, and productive urban metabolism is essential for sustainability.

Revisioning the Cul-de-Sac: A Retrofitted Design

Our approach to retrofitting draws upon notions of sustainable urbanism and flexible design to improve the urban environment of a peripheral Phoenix cul-de-sac without wholesale redevelopment. Yet the cul-de-sac urban form is widely criticized in New Urbanism and retrofitting literature due to its lack of pedestrian and traffic connectivity. "Connecting the cul-de-sacs" to create more travel flexibility and street traffic represents the extent to which the retrofitting movement has addressed the cul-de-sac form.[24] Retrofitting is also seen as most effective when applied to large-scale development in inner suburbs close to urban cores, with preexisting or planned transit accessibility; peripheral low-density suburbs might be considered a low priority for retrofitting. Although these points are clearly valuable, we emphasize the cul-de-sac's potential for community and economic development. As a predesigned node of houses surrounding a shared community space, this form has much potential for encouraging place-based development of social and natural capital. Furthermore, these types of far-flung neighborhoods may be the most vulnerable to upcoming energy, climate, and demographic challenges and most in need of design interventions. Thus we argue that smaller-scale retrofitting projects focused on place making within smaller "urban nodes," such as the cul-de-sac, can be valuable additions to the retrofitting movement.

Like most Sun Belt cities, the Phoenix metropolitan area primarily consists of low-density, automobile-dependent residential areas dominated by large single-family homes. The urban problems motivating the suburban retrofit movement are plainly apparent across Phoenix. For example, Arizona added fossil fuel pollutants faster than any other state between 1990 and 2007, a rate three times greater than the national average.[25] Opportunities for community-based social development may have been subsumed by the rapid proliferation of homogeneous subdivisions. For example, the percentages of Phoenix residents that work with neighbors to solve community problems or that participate in a group are both below national averages.[26] Maricopa County is nationally ranked close to the bottom in an index of social capital formation.[27]

Our design intervention focuses on a specific subdivision in Avondale, Arizona, a town lying about twenty miles west of downtown Phoenix. Avondale was founded as a farming settlement, but like many metro-area towns, it rapidly developed into a series of housing subdivisions in the last thirty years. This development was predicated upon homogeneous mass-construction techniques employed by large development companies, where initial cost is emphasized over durable construction and energy efficiency. The market for these houses has been based on cheap energy prices, with little incentive for building higher-cost, more efficient infrastructure. This rapid development has led to a loss of farmland and Avondale's agriculture-based identity, often replaced by a free market mentality emphasizing home ownership as a lucrative financial investment. Since the 2008 collapse of the housing market, the town has been hurt by high residential foreclosure and vacancy rates.

Our retrofit design is based on one particular Avondale cul-de-sac: 2200 South 112th Drive. The site is positioned in the heart of the West Valley's I-10 residential corridor, located far from major employment centers; at a smaller scale, it lies about one mile from both old downtown Avondale and the Avondale civic complex. The site occupies a relatively central position in relation to the larger subdivision, and has walking accessibility to a major public park and two schools. The site itself includes seven large single-family homes surrounding a large paved cul-de-sac. Like most suburban places, this cul-de-sac lacks many aspects of "good" urbanism, such as pedestrian and traffic connectivity, transit and commercial service accessibility, residential density, and pedestrian shade. It is notable, however, that this cul-de-sac is very short and thus not excessively removed from cross streets, allowing a stronger connection to the adjacent street.

The cul-de-sac encompasses 78,250 total square feet of surface, split between seven walled properties and public street space; the majority of this area is private space. It includes four two-story houses with 3,561 square feet of indoor space and three one-story houses with 2,696 square feet (both including garages), providing a total of 22,332 square feet of indoor space on top of 19,797 square feet of building footprints. Many features of the indoor and outdoor spaces in these houses are duplicated among houses, such as appliances and pools, and all orientations and floor plans follow a homogeneous template regardless of specific lot position.

Ellen Dunham-Jones and June Williamson argue that "single-family houses may be remodeled to respond to modern lifestyles, nontraditional family structures, and aging boomers," and they note that Arthur C. Nelson "predicts that the enormous houses being built on large lots in exurbs will in the future be subdivided into multifamily units."[28] The following redesign of 2200 South 112th Drive is based upon these prescient views, but it also extends beyond them to revision the cul-de-sac as a site for sustainable urban development and use.

Design Overview

Our design began with a number of a priori rules derived from a focus on sustainable, flexible, and productive urbanism. All architectural redesign is channeled into existing housing footprints to maximize adaptive reuse and preserve open spaces. The orientation of structures is reconfigured based on site-specific climatic variables and toward the generation of walkable urbanism and social interaction, and existing open spaces are designed for multiple uses and community development in a detailed spatial transition from public to private spaces. The resulting design increases residential density and the flexible use of indoor and outdoor spaces while decreasing the amount of space used for vehicle parking, ornamental landscaping, and private activities. Figure 11.1 shows the transformation from individual parcels to a more connected and integrated space encompassing the entire cul-de-sac, and figure 11.2 interprets this transformation into changes in the public, semipublic, semiprivate, and private realms.

The seven houses on site were converted into thirty-one residential units averaging 548 square feet, ranging from studio spaces at 274 square feet to two- and three-bedroom units up to 1,133 square feet, all within previous building footprints. The number of dwelling units was increased 440 percent and the number of bedrooms was increased 150 percent, while the overall amount of private living space was diminished 24 percent. Figure 11.3 shows the proposed site layout for the ground floor and second floor.

The proportions of the various units were based explicitly on the expected demographic transition away from traditional families and toward singles, se-

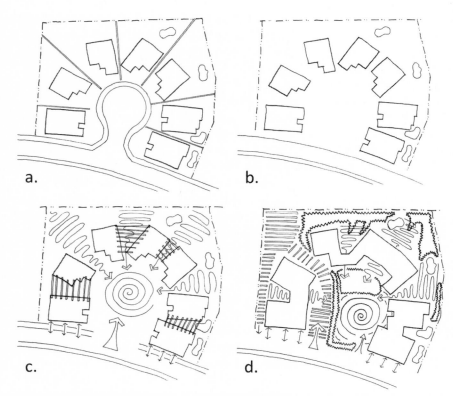

FIGURE 11.1. Site transformation from individual parcels to an integrated space.
Drawings by Whitney Warman, Christian Solorio, and Milagros Zingoni.

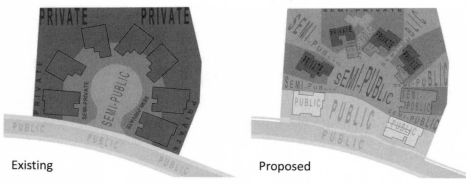

FIGURE 11.2. Balance of public and private space, including semipublic and semiprivate spaces.
Drawings by Whitney Warman, Christian Solorio, and Milagros Zingoni.

Ground Level

Second Level

FIGURE 11.3. Proposed site plan with building types A and C identified; the remaining are type B.
Drawings by Whitney Warman, Christian Solorio, and Milagros Zingoni.

	Existing	Proposed
PRIVATE SPACES		
Number of units	7	31
Number of bedrooms	28	42
4 bed, 2.5 bath	3	0
4 bed, 3.75 bath	4	0
Studios	0	8
1 bed, 1 bath	0	14
2 bed, 1 bath	0	3
2 bed, 2.5 bath	0	4
3 bed, 2 bath	0	2
Total indoor private space (sf)	22,332	16,984
Average unit size (sf)	3,190	548
Unit size range (sf)	2,016 to 2,791	274 to 1,133
Total garage space (sf)	5,120	0
COMMERCIAL AND MULTIUSE SPACES		
Flex space (sf)	NA	1,693
Educational kitchen (sf)	NA	593
Workshop (sf)	NA	856
Pottery lab (sf)	NA	309
Office spaces and classrooms (sf)	NA	202 to 315
Hair and nails (sf)	NA	611
Café (sf)	NA	812
Laundry (sf)	NA	292
Bike shop (sf)	NA	311
Daycare center (sf)	NA	1,125
PARKING		
Shared-car spaces	NA	6
Onsite residential	14 (2/driveway)	8
Street parking	NA	20

niors, and non-child families.[29] Thus 74 percent of units are oriented toward either single-person occupancy or couples/roommates without dependents (one-third are placed at ground level in secluded zones to facilitate senior living), while only 26 percent of units are designed for larger families with children. Table 11.1 shows the types and numbers of each unit.

A variety of flexible, community-oriented indoor spaces are provided to supplement individual living spaces, to allow for a range of group activities, and to encourage on-site telecommuting and continuing education. Three community living spaces totaling 1,601 square feet are included in building B to provide additional living space for residents with small apartments and to allow for group interaction. One larger community "flex space" was included in the design, adaptable for a range of activities like exercise classes, daycare, community meetings, and performances. Closely connected to this flex space is a community kitchen allowing residents to share use of special appliances, as well as opening the possibility that community cooking clubs or educational cooking seminars could organically arise from residents' initiative. A laundry room is similarly provided to allow sharing of costly and energy-intensive appliances. Flexible work-oriented spaces are provided for building maintenance and income generation, including a community workshop for on-site construction projects, a pottery/arts studio, and five adaptable office/classroom spaces allowing for both daytime telecommuting and nighttime education.

Indoor space intended for commercial sales is included in buildings A and C. The design provides four leasable spaces for a variety of storefront businesses, perhaps including a café, medical office, nail salon, bike shop, or other light commercial businesses needed in a residential neighborhood. Commercial space for a daycare center is provided near the community flex space, educational kitchen, and children's pool, allowing for daytime utilization of these spaces by the center (see figure 11.4).

Outdoor space is fully transformed from its existing private, walled-off, and ornamental character to a progressive spectrum from more public to more private spaces. A host of design elements are used to provide clearly delineated but visually permeable borders between these semipublic spaces. Like with our indoor spaces, outdoor spaces are designed to squeeze more economic and social value from existing space. Additions include a public lawn for recreational and social use, productive gardens and a livestock pen to augment food supply, semiprivate patio and pool spaces, youth-oriented spaces for small children (attached to the daycare center) and teens (surrounding a pool converted into a skate park), and both semipublic and private balconies. A dedicated parking lot with unique, fire-code-accepted, one-way entry and exit lanes was designed with seventeen parking spaces to allow most households to own a car but to reduce per-capita parking spaces. This parking area includes sustainable transport features, such as an electric vehicle–charging station and space designed for community vans/vehicle-sharing programs. Eight parking spaces for commercial customers are also provided, and these spaces can be flexibly used by residents during non-working hours. Overall the design provides twenty-five on-site parking spaces, while about twenty more parking spaces will be available on the street.

Finally, a host of sustainable design improvements incorporating green, bioregionally specific technologies are included wherever possible (see figures 11.5 and 11.6). These include an array of photovoltaic solar panels on south-facing roof pitches, ideally connected to vehicle-charging stations; rainwater catchment cisterns doubling as public benches, ideally connected to productive agriculture and aquaculture; the adaptive reuse of two in-ground pools for aquaculture production; a recreational skateboard park; and a general design oriented to-

FIGURE 11.4. Street view of the proposed design. Buildings are designed to accommodate a variety of uses. *Image by Whitney Warman, Christian Solorio, and Milagros Zingoni.*

FIGURE 11.5. View of central spaces incorporating sustainable design improvements. *Model and photo by Whitney Warman, Christian Solorio, and Milagros Zingoni.*

FIGURE 11.6. A community garden in the design's common space. *Image by Whitney Warman, Christian Solorio, and Milagros Zingoni.*

ward energy-efficient cooling in the desert, with no unshaded windows facing southwest.

The Continuum of Public, Communal, and Private Spaces

A central focus of this design intervention was the reordering of indoor and outdoor spaces to move away from the suburban preoccupation with private space toward a more urban vision where public, communal, and private spaces coexist (see figures 11.7 and 11.8). Jacobs was the first to emphasize the importance of delineating public and private urban spaces, noting that traditional urban blocks allow a certain visual permeability that encourages public safety and selective social contact.[30] Recent authors continue to emphasize this concept:

> City building therefore is partly a boundary setting exercise, subdividing space and creating new functions and meanings, establishing new relationships between the two sides. The way boundaries are established, articulated and related to the private or public spheres often has a major impact on the character of each side. . . . A porous and highly elaborate boundary which acknowledges and protects individual and collective interests and rights is what distinguishes a sophisticated urban environment from a harsh one.[31]

Our design explicitly recognizes the importance of carefully constructed boundaries, especially for human and social capital formation. Fully public spaces exist

FIGURE 11.7. Balconies and walkways connect houses.
Model and photo by Whitney Warman, Christian Solorio, and Milagros Zingoni.

FIGURE 11.8. The overall plan invites guests into community spaces.
Model and photo by Whitney Warman, Christian Solorio, and Milagros Zingoni.

on the edges of the cul-de-sac, represented by the sidewalk and main circulatory paths, the commercial spaces, and front parking. Communal-public spaces represent a way to welcome outsiders into the community while also signaling a shift in use and meaning: the front lawn, front garden, and indoor flex space used for community functions all are examples. Communal-private spaces are delineated from more public spaces by design features signaling more privatized territory, often through spatial bottlenecks between housing units. Community patio spaces, the back garden, and indoor communal spaces communicate the ownership of cul-de-sac residents by their obscured nature. Purely private spaces such as private patios or balconies are further delineated by raised platforms and semitransparent borders.

Although our unique, dense design immediately signals a border between the cul-de-sac and surrounding subdivision, aesthetic and social continuity between the two populations is encouraged. The cul-de-sac is intended to function simultaneously as a socioeconomic node for the wider subdivision as well as a semiprivate space for cul-de-sac residents. The availability of commercial and informal services is intended to consistently draw outside residents into the cul-de-sac and foster social interaction; dropping children at daycare, tending a community garden plot, or attending public meetings are some possible examples. Yet the cul-de-sac is not intended as a self-sufficient community, and it is expected that residents will need to travel daily to outside places for commercial services, employment, schools, and park use—again fostering cross-border interaction. We hope that the small size and relative socioeconomic heterogeneity of the cul-de-sac will prevent the types of exclusionary, parochial behavior sometimes linked with planned developments.

Generating Capital Assets and Site-Specific Economic Development

While many design improvements were specifically motivated by the upcoming transition to new demographic and energy regimes, the generation of economic development was also a central goal. By attempting to engender natural, physical, human, social, and financial capital within the confines of our design site, we hope to illuminate a new, more sustainable path forward in the everlasting American quest for economic growth.

Perhaps the clearest source of development potential inherent to the existing cul-de-sac is untapped natural capital. Although situated on highly productive former farmland, the site's existing open space is primarily occupied by paved spaces, ornamental vegetation, and small tracts of grass lawn. Although these uses do have an economic impact (e.g., landscaping businesses), they are economically limited. Our design intends to generate natural capital in the form of agriculture, horticulture, and livestock as well as through solar energy and rainwater technologies. Local natural capital is key for local economic development, especially if energy and food prices rise in the coming decades.

Economic development is also generated by a variety of physical capital improvements that increase the efficiency of existing community functioning. By reducing the amount of private space used by each person, and eliminating types of space duplicated among houses, efficient development is spurred. For example, living rooms, lawns, pools, and patios are included for communal use and imply squeezing more value out of existing space. Sharing of certain vehicles and appliances, such as Flexcars and ovens, can also eliminate duplication to enhance efficiency and save money. The application of green practices and technologies also represent physical capital upgrades tied to development: increases in the quality, durability, and energy efficiency of the housing stock; implementation of solar PV and electric vehicle technology; and aquaculture technology linked with agricultural productivity. In many situations where green technologies are used to facilitate agricultural or energy-generation productivity, physical and natural capital improvements intertwine to induce efficient development.

Aspects of our design oriented toward generating human capital can also aid economic growth, especially through the novel development of residents' skills and consumption identities. We argue that the more skills and interests are held by residents (e.g., from professional skills like air conditioning repair to a diversity of interests in various activities and hobbies), the more intense the economic activity generated. Here, the latent potential for development lies in replacing the one-size-fits-all consumption identities encouraged by homogeneous suburbia with individuals who participate in a more dynamic array of activities supported by a more diverse collection of industries. Good urbanism has long been cited as a source for economic innovation.[32] But it is less often recognized that urban places are also crucial for the cultural production that supports many industries.[33] Increasing the experiential and mental complexity of daily life is the first step in this direction, and so our design includes spaces conducive to ongoing learning and development of personal identities. Ultimately, "the challenge in design is to develop ways of working that can support and represent a multiplicity of spatial identity."[34] Thus our design includes flexible communal space supporting activity classes (e.g., yoga, arts) and skill development (e.g., bike repair classes); communal kitchen space for formal cooking classes and informal knowledge sharing; outdoor spaces that support other types of activities (e.g., gardening, sports); and classroom/office rental space for more traditional educational activities (e.g., youth tutoring, professional development, continuing education). These spaces are designed for flexible use to encourage the highest possible diversity of initiatives to develop human capital over time.

Social capital, one of the primary goals of our retrofit design, both facilitates the generation of other types of capital and represents economic development itself. In many existing subdivisions, place-based social network connectivity is relatively low and places are governed more by formal legal frameworks, like homeowners' associations and municipal regulations, than informally by residents. The ideal behind social capital is that informal social norms and networks can provide the same regulatory and communicative functions at a much lower cost, generating efficient development. Our design attempts to encourage social capital formation in specific ways, like encouraging car-sharing and community cooking clubs. The design of communal living, patio, and pool spaces also allows informal socialization generating more ephemeral benefits. Although our design is intended to generate social capital, it also protects individual privacy by providing clear distinctions between public and private spaces. Social capital emerges from shared interests and identities that can be aided by shared spaces, but it cannot be forced or attributed solely to design; we simply hope to provide an open-ended environment where an optimal level of social connectivity can naturally emerge. In turn, this social connectivity may be able to enhance the collective action needed for food production, building maintenance, and disseminating knowledge.

Finally, the newly designed cul-de-sac can directly generate financial capital through the commercial provision of neighborhood services. Commercial spaces related to daycare, food service, professional offices, and other services may be able to generate significant income and employment opportunities for residents. Yet augmenting natural, physical, human, and social capital can also lead to financial returns when the efficiency of existing practices are increased. Efficient forms of development (e.g., energy efficiency savings) only represent economic growth, however, if the financial savings are actively reinvested in the novel and efficient development of the community's capital assets.

Adaptability and Flexible Space

Our design promotes adaptability and flexibility—key for community resilience as well as ongoing development—by designing infrastructure with multiple configurations and uses. Rainwater catchment, for example, represents the most obvious way in which we have designed for multiple uses. Roofs are designed to funnel rainwater downward into pipes and ground-level cisterns, which double as public benches in community spaces. One of the community's pools, normally intended as a skate park, can be used for rainwater catchment during monsoon seasons if cisterns are filled. These systems create a local stock of water, providing a degree of independence from municipal sources and enhancing resilience.

The variety of indoor and outdoor communal and commercial spaces are also intended for flexible use based on daily, seasonal, and long-term timescales. This flexibility can allow for more diverse development opportunities as well as allow adaptive management under changing conditions. For example, indoor flex space can be partitioned at will and used as activity space for classes (morning), spillover space for the daycare center (afternoon), and as community meeting space (evening). Lawn space can be combined with or separated from the flex space, allowing a variety of community events from movie screenings to sports. Classroom/office spaces allow resident professionals to rent individual offices during the day, then transform to tutoring spaces at night. Even the front parking lot can be flexibly used, morphing from daycare dropoff in the morning, to commercial parking during business hours, to an extension of community lawn space in the evening, and finally to overnight parking for resident commuters.

Certain spaces can also accommodate flexible use on a monthly or seasonal basis. Garden space is the most obvious example here, since it can allow productive agriculture during growing seasons and other uses when fallow. Some commercial spaces, however, could also be rented on a flexible, month-by-month basis if congruent with market demand. For example, a professional space could be shared weekly by entrepreneurs, allowing a nail salon on Mondays, a chiropractor on Wednesdays, and yard sales on Fridays. Such spaces could also be rented on a seasonal basis, in line with the bioregional specificity so often mentioned in the sustainable design literature. For example, one commercial space could sell community garden produce in October, provide tax management services right before the federal deadline in April, and become a gallery for local artists in July.

The flexibility of community space is also an asset and an opportunity for development in long-term perspective. The existence of flexible space allows future adaptability to changing socioeconomic or ecological conditions that is sorely lacking in contemporary development. For example, in thirty years, the indoor flex space could evolve into a highly specialized activity space, with a number of permanent class instructors and more permanent infrastructure, if the community contains a growing upper middle class contingent with high demand for such services; on the other hand, if economic hardships or natural disasters become more common, this space could also become a temporary shelter for displaced people or homeless populations. The possibility of both outcomes is real, and only adaptable space with adaptive management will be equipped for all possibilities. Furthermore, if certain spaces are underused in practice, the community could democratically decide to sequentially develop them into new residential units for mutual benefit. The balance of residential, commercial, and communal spaces could be constantly shifted based on future conditions and needs, and economic development could be generated through both flexible use and onetime development.

Conclusion: The Semantics of Community

The retrofitted cul-de-sac design presented here shares many similarities with the "ecovillage" concept emerging out of urban sustainability.[35] Although ecovillages are diverse in practice and accommodate a range of visions, the concept has roots in longstanding ideals related to cooperatives and co-housing, permaculture and self-sufficiency, bioregional design, and a skeptical attitude toward the contemporary global economy. Like in ecovillages, our design places emphasis upon the decentralized generation of natural capital through physical capital improvements. Yet we attempt to avoid this terminology and its connotations because it does not seem appropriate to the middle-class suburban culture of Phoenix's peri-urban sprawl. Just as sustainability theorists emphasize designs that mesh with bioregional specificity, our design attempts to cohere with a regional culture shaped by the Fordist growth paradigm. Instead of labeling the retrofitted cul-de-sac as an "ecovillage," perhaps it is better described as a "neighborhood growth corporation," where community members enter into a specific set of financial and social obligations for mutual profit. Using "corporate" instead of "cooperative" terminology helps emphasize how sustainable design can pragmatically prepare a neighborhood for the upcoming demographic, energy, and climate transitions. In doing so, it avoids sociopolitical preconceptions about the ecological movement and its holistic ideals of communal living.

Ultimately, our retrofitted cul-de-sac is intended to enhance the options and opportunities lying at the core of sustainable communities as well as American definitions of freedom. This redesign should be viewed less as a new paradigm of urbanism and more as a market niche that should be available to consumers looking to "purchase a lifestyle" from the relatively homogeneous selection provided by Phoenix's twentieth-century sprawl. A more cooperative lifestyle could be framed as a radical break from American values, but it could be equally portrayed as an expansion of the market and American freedom more generally; like in politics, semantics are increasingly crucial. While we propose the "neighborhood growth corporation" as a cultural selling point, our design is intended to allow residents to define and continually redefine the meaning and function of their community over time. We hope that the open-ended nature of our design would allow the neighborhood to evolve in a variety of ways, and that in fifty years there might be equal probability that the cul-de-sac will be populated by communal ecological radicals, conservative urban professionals, a diverse mix of senior citizens, or a combination of all three groups.

NOTES

1. Rem Koolhaas, "Whatever Happened to Urbanism," in *S, M, L, XL*, edited by R. Koolhaas and B. Mau, 959–71 (New York: Monacelli, 1995).

2. Ellen Dunham-Jones and June Williamson, *Retrofitting Suburbia: Urban Design Solutions for Redesigning Suburbs* (Hoboken, N.J.: John Wiley, 2011).

3. Ibid.

4. Ibid., 19.

5. United States Energy Information Administration (U.S. EIA), "Annual Energy Review: Retail Motor Gasoline and On-Highway Diesel Fuel Prices, 1949–2010," 2011, retrieved March 1, 2012, http://www.eia.gov/totalenergy/data/annual/showtext.cfm?t=ptb0524.

6. United States Energy Information Administration (U.S. EIA), "Annual Energy Outlook 2012 with Projections to 2035," 2012, retrieved February 15, 2013, http://www.eia.gov/forecasts/aeo/pdf/0383%282012%29.pdf.

7. California Environmental Protection Agency, Air Resources Board (CA EPA ARB), "Sustainable Communities and Climate Protection Act of 2008 (SB 375)," 2008, retrieved March 1, 2012, http://www.arb.ca.gov/cc/sb375/sb375.htm.

8. Herman E. Daly and Joshua Farley, *Ecological Economics: Principles and Applications* (Washington, D.C.: Island Press, 2003).

9. Bradford Luckingham, *Phoenix: The History of a Southwest Metropolis* (Tucson: University of Arizona Press, 1989); Andrew Ross, *Bird on Fire: Lessons from the World's Least Sustainable City* (Oxford: Oxford University Press, 2011).

10. Patricia Gober, *Metropolitan Phoenix: Place Making and Community Building in the Desert* (Philadelphia: University of Pennsylvania Press, 2006), 137.

11. Ross, *Bird on Fire*, 57.

12. Herman E. Daly, *Beyond Growth: The Economics of Sustainable Development* (Boston: Beacon Press, 1996), 6.

13. Ibid.

14. Michael Storper, *The Regional World: Territorial Development in a Global Economy* (New York: Guilford, 1997); Peter Newman and Isabella Jennings, *Cities as Sustainable Ecosystems* (Washington, D.C.: Island Press, 2008).

15. Jane Jacobs, *The Economy of Cities* (New York: Random House, 1969).

16. Ibid.

17. Jane Jacobs, *The Death and Life of Great American Cities* (New York: Random House, 1961); Andres Duany, Jeff Speck, and Mike Lydon, *The Smart Growth Manual* (New York: McGraw Hill, 2010); Newman and Jennings, *Cities as Sustainable Ecosystems*; David Owen,

Green Metropolis: Why Living Smaller, Living Closer, and Driving Less Are the Keys to Sustainability (New York: Riverhead, 2009).

18. Peter Newman, Timothy Beatley, and Heather Boyer, *Resilient Cities: Responding to Peak Oil and Climate Change* (Washington, D.C.: Island Press, 2009).

19. See Rob Hopkins, "The Food Producing Neighborhood," in *Sustainable Communities: The Potential for Eco-Neighbourhoods*, edited by H. Barton, 199–215 (London: Earthscan, 2000); Newman and Jennings, *Cities as Sustainable Ecosystems*.

20. Gary P. Kofinas and F. Stuart Chapin III, "Sustaining Livelihoods and Human Well-Being during Social-Ecological Change," in *Principles of Ecosystem Stewardship: Resilience-Based Natural Resource Management in a Changing World*, edited by F. S. Chapin III, G. P. Kofinas, and C. Folke, 55–75 (New York: Springer Verlag, 2009).

21. Bryan Norton, "Ecology and Opportunity: Intergenerational Equity and Sustainable Options," in *Fairness and Futurity: Essays on Environmental Sustainability and Social Justice*, edited by A. Dobson, 118–51 (New York: Oxford University Press, 1999).

22. James Corner, "Terra Fluxus," in *The Landscape Urbanism Reader*, edited by C. Waldheim, 21–33 (New York: Princeton Architectural Press, 2006), 31.

23. Newman and Jennings, *Cities as Sustainable Ecosystems*, 92.

24. Dunham-Jones and Williamson, *Retrofitting Suburbia*, 19.

25. Ross, *Bird on Fire*.

26. Corporation for National and Community Service (CNCS), "Current Population Survey," Civic Engagement Supplement, Nov. 2010, United States Department of Commerce, Bureau of the Census, United States Department of Labor, Bureau of Labor Statistics, retrieved March 6, 2012, http://civic.serve.gov/rankings.cfm.

27. Anil Rupasingha, Stephan J. Goetz, and David Freshwater, "The Production of Social Capital in U.S. Counties," *Journal of Socio-Economics* 35 (2006): 83–101.

28. Dunham-Jones and Williamson, *Retrofitting Suburbia*, 19.

29. Arthur C. Nelson, *Reshaping Metropolitan America: Development Trends and Opportunities to 2030* (Washington, D.C.: Island Press, 2013).

30. Jacobs, *Death and Life of Great American Cities*.

31. Ali Madanipour, *Public and Private Spaces of the City* (London: Routledge, 2003), 240–41.

32. Jacobs, *Economy of Cities*; Edward Glaeser, *Triumph of the City* (New York: Penguin, 2011).

33. Storper, *Regional World*.

34. Linda Pollak, "Constructed Ground: Questions of Scale," in *The Landscape Urbanism Reader*, edited by C. Waldheim, 125–38 (New York: Princeton Architectural Press, 2006), 128.

35. Newman and Jennings, *Cities as Sustainable Ecosystems*; Newman, Beatley, and Boyer, *Resilient Cities*.

CHAPTER 12

Occupy Sprawl, One Cul-de-Sac at a Time

GALINA TACHIEVA

1. Sprawl should be repaired but it will happen incrementally, slowly, at a microscale, one element at a time. There is a need to challenge outdated regulations, bringing more flexibility, adaptability, and enterprise to subdivisions and cul-de-sacs.

2. The successful repair of the cul-de-sac may have a catalytic effect on the broader reformation of sprawl.

3. A first strategy involves the insertion of a Complete-the-Neighborhood Module. A small grouping of buildings and uses are proposed to rebalance sprawling residential enclaves, adding some of the missing elements.

4. A second strategy employs the Supportive Living Module and creates opportunities for senior living within a single-family subdivision.

5. A third strategy, which is a version of the second, includes the Semi-Independent Living Option, which would provide intensive care and assisted living close to family and friends. The strategy is focused on a transition from the megascale of nursing homes amid sprawl to a smaller, neighborhood-based model.

Sprawl has been a major source of our economic troubles, including the mortgage meltdown, our dependence on cars and oil, pollution, and waste of resources. But we have invested so much in sprawl—resources, finances, human energy, and dreams—that we cannot abandon it. We need to reform and reuse sprawl. Essentially we need to "occupy" it and change the sprawl-supporting system—the physical pattern, laws and regulations, and financing mechanisms—in the same way that occupiers of Wall Street demand systemic changes in our society.

This occupation will most likely happen one sprawl element at a time, from office parks, strip malls, and shopping centers (see figure 12.1) to wide arterials and cul-de-sacs. In this chapter, I focus on the case of the cul-de-sac. Prevalent within hundreds of thousands of single-family subdivisions in the United States, the cul-de-sac not only is emblematic of sprawl but also has become one of the most widespread development patterns in the world. The creation of successful strategies for the transformation of these patterns may have a catalytic effect on the broader reformation of sprawl.

This chapter will demonstrate strategies that can improve cul-de-sacs through slow, incremental interventions, upgrading the quality of life in and around their single-family subdivisions. The process is called "Micro Sprawl Repair." It includes connecting cul-de-sacs through pedestrian and bike lanes in places where it is possible to attain easements. In some rare cases it may be feasible to puncture streets through cul-de-sacs, stitching together the suburban fabric. But the most innovative and transformative intervention is to create new centers of activity. Single-family subdivisions are not complete, self-sustaining entities: they lack the most elementary daily services such as corner stores, dry-cleaners, and places for gathering and socializing. The idea is to repair cul-de-sacs by inserting a "package" of buildings and uses that will rebalance sprawling residential enclaves by adding some of the elements they lack.

These examples should be seen as part of the larger effort to repair and retrofit sprawl. Resources for this effort have expanded significantly in the past decade. Practitioners, municipalities, and private developers can now make use of the strategies documented in *Retrofitting Suburbia*, the toolkit of the *Sprawl Repair Manual*, the creative interventions of the Tactical Urbanists, the ideas behind Incremental Sprawl Repair and Planned Densification, the common sense of the Original Green and the CNU Sprawl Retrofit Initiative, the sustainability of Rainwater-In-Context and Light Imprint, and the SmartCode and other techniques for rezoning sprawl found in the Center for Applied Transect Studies website.[1]

From Occupy Wall Street to Occupy Sprawl

The idea of occupying sprawl was inspired by the recent popular discontent passionately expressed by occupiers of Wall Street. One important lesson to

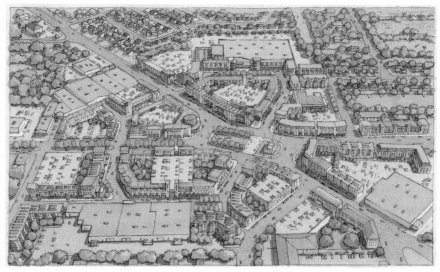

FIGURES 12.1A AND 12.1B. A typical shopping center transformed into a mixed-use, walkable town center.

come out of the Occupy Wall Street movement was the fundamental importance of public space and its role in facilitating the democratic process. What enabled the outpouring of political protest was a supportive public realm: the streets and squares of Lower Manhattan that provided plenty of places to gather. Good urbanism requires good spaces for assembling and protesting. In contrast, sprawling suburbs are devoid of such places. There are very few public venues where people can gather in a spontaneous way, whether to express discontent or collective celebration.

Might it be possible to "occupy" sprawl in the same way that protesters occupied Wall Street? The metaphor of occupation might serve us well in the quest to reform sprawl. What is needed is a dramatic overhaul—of the physical pattern, regulations, and financing mechanisms that have created, supported, and encouraged sprawl for decades. The sprawl system needs a radical intervention, in the same way that occupiers are now demanding systemic changes on Wall Street.

And there is much to occupy in sprawl, a multitude of empty, unproductive, wasteful spaces: overscaled parking lots, empty big boxes, dead malls, vast front lawns, foreclosed McMansions, massive cul-de-sacs, and underperforming golf courses. All of these spaces can be reimagined. Suburban strip corridors can become Main Streets and boulevards, malls can incubate much-needed town centers, deserted McMansions can house students and seniors, and parking lots can be transformed into productive community gardens.

There is also a more technical and less metaphoric connection between Wall Street and the future redevelopment of sprawl. A few years ago, Christopher Leinberger identified nineteen real estate categories or standard product types preferred by Wall Street that are having a direct role in perpetuating the worst sorts of sprawl patterns and building types. He also showed the need to provide new alternatives that are walkable, diverse, and more resilient. Leinberger put it succinctly and unambiguously: "We can stay outside the world of Wall Street–dominated real estate finance, discuss, and (occasionally) design and build precious, expensive alternatives. Or we can work hard to develop new product types that the mainstream can understand, accept, and prosper by developing and owning."[2] Newly formulated building types will be the new products in the Wall Street toolbox. Fortunately the market is already shifting toward more intelligent, human-scale urban patterns and Wall Street is paying attention. In the economic context of sprawl repair, Walkscore is becoming a Wall Street underwriting tool.[3]

The occupation of sprawl with new building types will not be immediate or ubiquitous. We cannot occupy or reform sprawl in one sweeping gesture. Rather than the instant and total overhaul of communities, as promoted so destructively in American cities half a century ago (during the urban renewal period), occupy sprawl should be a strategy for incremental and opportunistic improvement, starting in the places where the most opportune circumstances converge. These include areas where the crisis is most acute—where traffic congestion, falling real estate values, outdated infrastructure, and lack of public amenities have become unbearable—as well as places with regional importance and manageable ownership patterns.

Priority areas should be delineated at the regional level in consideration of the larger context—existing infrastructure, thoroughfare connectivity, potential for transit, and goals for preservation and regeneration of natural systems. The objective is to analyze transportation, other infrastructure, and natural areas as a complete system and to identify the nodes best suited for repair. Parts of suburban sprawl have the potential to be transformed into desirable urban nodes because they contain employment concentrations and have potential for economic growth. Ideal examples, such as shopping malls and large office parks, are located along thoroughfare networks that support transit or can be repaired to accommodate it.

Within these priority areas, residents can begin to implement repair strategies and occupy sprawl.

Occupy the Cul-de-Sac: An Example of Micro Sprawl Repair

As a quintessential element of sprawl, the cul-de-sac has become a predictable target for critique and attack.[4] Loved by suburbanites for its presumed safety, privacy, and even exclusivity, the cul-de-sac has been blamed for many of the ills of sprawl: disconnected street networks, overloading of suburban thoroughfares, lack of walkable block structures, residual open spaces, and the inability to accommodate more than a single building type or single use. Prevalent within single-family subdivisions, the cul-de-sac has become in the past sixty years one of the most widespread planning patterns around the world.

Of all the types of sprawl patterns, residential subdivisions, where cul-de-sacs proliferate, are the most difficult to change, for many reasons. One is that they consist of multiple properties. In addition, single-family houses are usually the largest investment of homeowners, and thus they might be especially fearful of any change that they believe will negatively impact this investment. NIMBYism, ironically itself the result of sprawl, is another obstacle. Homeowner associations and their restrictions are often the most powerful impediments to sprawl repair.[5]

How can cul-de-sacs be transformed into something more useful than dead-end patches of asphalt? Can they be "occupied" in more meaningful ways? Our proposal involves a slow, incremental transformation. This is likely to be the only viable option, as it is not realistic to assume a more sweeping retrofitting process, at least not in the near term.

The process can be defined as "Micro Sprawl Repair." It may include connecting cul-de-sacs through pedestrian and bike lanes in places where it is possible to attain easements. In some rare cases it may even be feasible to puncture streets through cul-de-sacs, stitching together the suburban fabric. These straightforward techniques are explained in the *Sprawl Repair Manual*.[6]

But the most innovative and transformative intervention is to create new centers of activity. Single-family subdivisions are not complete, self-sustaining entities: they lack the most elementary daily services such as corner stores, drycleaners, and places for gathering and socializing. We propose the insertion of a Complete-the-Neighborhood Module, a package of buildings and uses that will rebalance sprawling residential enclaves by adding some of the missing elements. An expandable, flexible grouping of structures can be made to fit within and between existing houses or replace abandoned or outdated housing stock to provide much-needed amenities.

Figures 12.2–12.6 show the incremental replacement of three houses with new structures. First, the house on the left is replaced by a flex building—a recycling/learning center that includes a workshop and market where people can build or repair and then sell such things as furniture, appliances, and electronics. A recycling drop-off station and compactors for plastic and aluminum are in the back; a greenhouse is attached on one side, with a compost drop-off spot behind it.

The house on the right is replaced by a cooking school and a small restaurant that can be used as a banquet room by the residents and seniors. A dry cleaner, hairdresser, or small daycare can occupy the middle portion that joins the two structures. The new buildings face the street and form an attached plaza that can later be replicated on the other side of the entrance street. The plaza can be used

FIGURE 12.2.
An existing cul-de-sac before insertion of a Complete-the-Neighborhood Module.

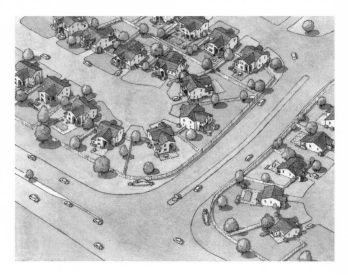

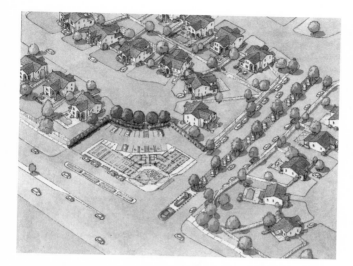

FIGURE 12.3.
Replacement of
two houses with
a new Complete-
the-Neighborhood
Module.

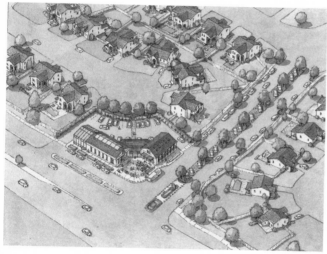

FIGURE 12.4.
A Complete-the-
Neighborhood
Module consisting
of a recycling center
to the right; a dry
cleaner, hairdresser,
or small daycare
in the middle; and
a cooking school
and a restaurant to
the left.

for outdoor eating and games for the elderly. The parking is hidden behind the structure, but it is conveniently accessible from two sides, and a path connects it to the cul-de-sac.

The next step is the replacement of the third house by six live-work units with an average footprint of 1,000 square feet or less (figures 12.5 and 12.6). They represent valuable real estate that could pay for the acquisition of the houses and construction of the additional amenities. Senior housing is an alternative to the live-work units that could allow retired residents to remain in the neighborhood.

This transformation is the beginning of a Main Street for the single-family

FIGURE 12.5.
Live-work units are
added to replace
one more house on
the cul-de-sac.

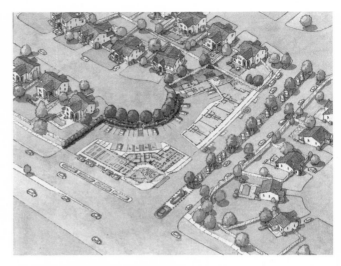

FIGURE 12.6.
The redevelopment
is potentially the
beginning of a new
Main Street.

subdivision. It may undergo further and more substantial changes if there is support from the residents. This technique can be applied not only to the cul-de-sac but also to other places around a sprawling neighborhood in need of repair. Similar ideas for the redevelopment of an entire single-family subdivision are illustrated in the *Sprawl Repair Manual*.[7]

Aging in Place on a Cul-de-Sac

Another strategy for upgrading a cul-de-sac is to employ the Supportive Living Module and create opportunities for senior living within a single-family subdivision. Aging in place—growing old and retiring in the community where a person lives—is an important issue, and one that has been exacerbated by sprawl. Nursing homes are currently separated from neighborhoods because they are treated as commercial or medical land uses. They suffer from gigantism, similar to other nonresidential uses in sprawl such as malls, big box retailers, and educational, medical, or even penitentiary facilities, and they tend to be concentrated in mega-structures. The isolation and large concentrations of patients in these places often lead to depression and alienation, while the long distances preclude regular visits by friends and family.

Cul-de-sacs have become easy targets for criticism and even ridicule by an up-and-coming generation of newly minted urbanites and activists. Cul-de-sacs are symbols of a past trend—sprawling, far-flung suburbs, isolated and boring. An essential issue is whether cul-de-sacs appropriately serve the older generations who were originally drawn to them. Once considered the safest place for children to play and for families to have peace and quiet, cul-de-sacs have now become a problem for the aging population. Far away from everything, they are islands of remoteness and loneliness when an older person can no longer drive.

For older residents, the choices are to (1) move to an all-inclusive senior facility far from town; or (2) move to a place in the city that is closer to daily needs. Unfortunately, the latter option is problematic for many seniors because it is unlikely to be affordable. This is exacerbated by the fact that the demand for houses in the exurbs is decreasing. If aging residents are not able to sell their large homes, they will have little option but to remain in their existing subdivisions.

With this aging population in mind, our proposal is to transform car-dependent residential subdivisions with cul-de-sacs into something that proactively supports the needs of older residents.

The Supportive Living Module, shown in the progression of figures 12.7–12.10, is in the form of a traditional two- or three-story building where seniors can receive skilled, community-based assistance. The structure can be accommodated on two lots. Because the building is small, with approximately ten units per floor, it is easy to manage, and its scale is appropriate for a residential subdivision. Its volume can easily blend with the surrounding single-family houses.

If the building is located at an entrance to a subdivision or next to an existing amenity, it is possible to assign its ground floor to mixed uses: a corner store, a daycare, a hairdresser, a post office, or a small diner with a kitchen that could also provide food to senior residents. The upper one or two floors consist of bedrooms for residents, with common living quarters as well as a caretaker's suite.

A second option includes attached, single-story cottages for Semi-Independent Living (see figures 12.11 and 12.12). The L-shaped structures form private courtyards, with the interior consisting of a bedroom, a spacious living

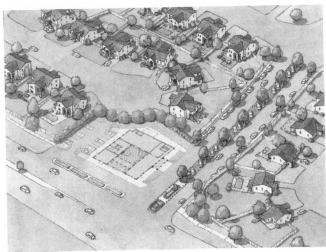

room, and a kitchenette to be used by residents or their visitors. A common facility building in the middle contains offices, rooms for medical exams and procedures, and potential living quarters for one or several caretakers, as well as a kitchen to supply meals to the residents. This central building may be connected to the cottages by a corridor to be used on rainy days. There is also common courtyard space between the cottages and the facility building.

This semi-independent module would be well integrated within the community and would provide the opportunity for intensive care and assisted living close to family and friends. The strategy is to transition from the mega-scale of nursing homes in sprawl to a smaller neighborhood-based scale,

FIGURE 12.9.
The courtyard
building housing
the supportive
living facility
frames the cul-de-
sac's corner.

FIGURE 12.10.
The Supportive
Living Module
accommodates
community services
on the ground floor.

in which financing, construction, maintenance, and operation can happen in smaller increments, providing jobs close to home and allowing residents to age in place.

The separation and isolation associated with sprawl that once was considered a virtue has now become a problem. In response, communities need to take control of their own destinies and implement creative sprawl repair strategies. They must challenge their outdated governing regulations and rebalance their single uses, bringing more flexibility, adaptability, and enterprise to subdivisions and cul-de-sacs.

Without a proactive, "occupy sprawl" response, millions will be stuck in de-

FIGURE 12.11.
A Semi-Independent
Living Module
replaces the two
corner houses.

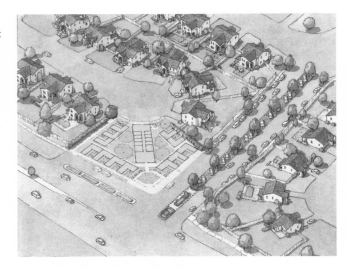

FIGURE 12.12.
Courtyard cottages
with a common
facility building
comprise the Semi-
Independent Living
Module.

clining, impoverished suburbs.[8] Economic factors will make it difficult for some of the younger residents moving out and will prevent seniors from selling their large homes and mortgages when they wish to retire. This will create an urgent need to change the existing arrangement.

This chapter has presented several ideas for one type of transformation. While some subdivisions with fossilized governing documents will be frozen by inaction and left to decline, unable to service the growing needs of their population, others will gather the collective strength needed to make changes that will benefit not only everyone around the cul-de-sac but also the wider community.

The drawings for this chapter were developed together with Chris Ritter and Eusebio Azcue and are based on ideas and designs from DPZ's Lifelong Communities charrette conducted for the Atlanta Regional Commission, in collaboration with Lew Oliver. For more on the topic of urbanism and senior living, see M. Scott Ball, *Livable Communities for Aging Populations: Urban Design for Longevity* (Hoboken, N.J.: Wiley, 2012).

1. CNU, "Rainwater-in-Context," Congress for the New Urbanism, 2011, retrieved April 20, 2013, http://www.cnu.org/rainwater. Ellen Dunham-Jones and June Williamson, *Retrofitting Suburbia: Urban Design Solutions for Redesigning Suburbs* (Hoboken, N.J.: John Wiley, 2008); Brian Falk, "The Center for Applied Transect Studies (CATS)," 2008, retrieved April 20, 2013, http://www.transect.org/index.html. Caitlin Ghoshal, "Sprawl Retrofit," Congress for the New Urbanism, 2011, retrieved April 20, 2013, http://www.cnu.org/sprawlretrofit. ISR Working Group, "Incremental Sprawl Repair Working Group," 2011, retrieved April 18, 2013, http://isrworkinggroup.posterous.com/. Thomas E. Low, *Light Imprint Handbook: Integrating Sustainability and New Urbanism* (Charlotte, N.C.: Island Press, 2010); Mike Lydon, Dan Bartman, Ronald Woudstra, and Aurash Khawarzad, *Tactical Urbanism*, vol. 1, retrieved April 20, 2013, http://www.scribd.com/doc/51354266/Tactical-Urbanism-Volume-1. Planned Densification, "Planned Densification and Urban Betterment," 2013, retrieved April 19, 2013, http://www.planneddensification.com/. Steve Mouzon, "Original Green: Common Sense, Plain Spoken Sustainability," 2013, retrieved April 21, 2013, http://www.originalgreen.org/. Galina Tachieva, *Sprawl Repair Manual* (Washington, D.C.: Island Press, 2010).

2. Christopher B. Leinberger, "The Need for Alternatives to the Nineteen Standard Real Estate Product Types: Creating Alternatives to the Standard Real Estate Types," *Places* 17, no. 2 (2005), retrieved April 20, 2013, http://escholarship.org/uc/item/00f0r5kn.

3. Adam Ducker, "A Market and Economic Context for Thinking about Suburban Sprawl Repair," RCLCO.com, 2011, retrieved April 19, 2013, http://www.rclco.com/generalpdf/general_Jun320111220_6–3–11_Ducker_-_Congress_for_the_New_Urbanism.pdf.

4. Emily Badger, "Debunking the Cul-de-Sac," *The Atlantic*, September 19, 2011, retrieved April 20, 2013, http://www.theatlanticcities.com/design/2011/09/street-grids/124/.

5. Aron Chang, "Beyond Foreclosure: The Future of Suburban Housing," Places. DesignObserver.com, 2011, retrieved April 21, 2013, http://places.designobserver.com/feature/beyond-foreclosure-the-future-of suburban-housing/29438/.

6. Galina Tachieva, *Sprawl Repair Manual* (Washington, D.C.: Island Press, 2010).

7. Ibid., 75–92.

8. Tami Luhby, "Poverty Pervades the Suburbs," CNN.Money.com, 2011, retrieved April 21, 2013, http://money.cnn.com/2011/09/23/news/economy/poverty_suburbs/index.htm.

Contributors

Dave Amos is an associate planner at Mintier Harnish, an urban planning consulting firm based in Sacramento, California. He coauthored *Rethinking Streets: An Evidence-Based Guide to 25 Complete Street Transformations* (2014). His professional interests include complete streets, urban design, and land use planning.

Aviva Hopkins Brown holds a master's in community development from the University of Maryland, College Park. She is currently a consultant at Vantage Point Economic and Transportation Development Strategies where her work focuses on economic development strategies for public-sector transit oriented development projects.

Wesley Brown is a project manager for Central Atlanta Progress (Atlanta's Downtown Improvement District) and is responsible for managing capital projects and planning efforts. He received a B.S. in landscape architecture from North Carolina State University and an M.S. in urban design from the Georgia Institute of Technology.

David Dixon, FAIA, leads Stantec's Urban Places Group, one of the world's largest architecture/engineering firms. His work focuses on implementation of walkable, mixed-use, and diverse communities. He is the coauthor of *Urban Design for an Urban Century: Shaping More Livable, Equitable, and Resilient Cities* (2014).

Ellen Dunham-Jones, AIA, is a professor at the Georgia Institute of Technology where she coordinates the M.S. in Urban Design program. She is coauthor with June Williamson of *Retrofitting Suburbia: Urban Design Solutions for Redesigning Suburbs* (2009). She lectures widely and continues to build her database on successful, sustainable suburban retrofits.

Aaron Golub, Ph.D., is an associate professor at Arizona State University in the School of Geographical Sciences and Urban Planning and the School of Sustainability. His research focuses on the environmental and social impacts of transportation policies. He has worked extensively in Africa and South America on projects related to urban bus system policy and planning.

Nabil Kamel, Ph.D., is an assistant professor in the Department of Environmental Studies at Western Washington University. His research and teaching deal with critical urban theory, planning theory, housing, urban design, and the production of urban space. His work connects the political economy of urbanization, urban form, and social and environmental justice.

Gerrit-Jan Knaap, Ph.D., is director of the National Center for Smart Growth, associate dean for research and creative activity, and a professor in the School of Architecture, Planning, and Preservation at the University of Maryland. He is the author or coauthor of seven books and more than a hundred academic journal articles. He serves on the State of Maryland's Smart Growth Subcabinet and Sustainable Growth Commission.

Julia Koschinsky, Ph.D., is an associate research professor at Arizona State University's School of Geographical Sciences and Urban Planning (SGSUP) and the research director of SGSUP's GeoDa Center for Geospatial Analysis and Computation. Her research addresses questions at the intersection of spatial data analysis and application areas in urban planning, housing, crime, and health.

Nico Larco, AIA, is an associate professor in the Department of Architecture and codirector of the Sustainable Cities Initiative at the University of Oregon. His research focuses on sustainable urban design, street design, and how urban design affects the sustainability of buildings. His latest book is *Site Design for Multifamily Housing: Creating Livable, Connected Neighborhoods* (2014).

Rebecca Lewis, Ph.D., is an assistant professor in Planning, Public Policy and Management at the University of Oregon. Her research broadly focuses on land use policy, growth management, local comprehensive plan quality, and measuring urban form. She is a faculty affiliate of the National Center for Smart Growth Research and Education at the University of Maryland.

Gabriel Díaz Montemayor, ASLA, is an assistant professor of landscape architecture at the University of Texas at Austin. His research focuses on the border region between the United States and Mexico, dealing with public space, green infrastructure, and landscape urbanism. His work has been published in *Landscape Architecture Magazine, Arquine,* and *Aula Journal,* among others.

Matthew Salenger, AIA, is an artist, architect, and associate faculty at Arizona State University's Design School. He cofounded colab studio, llc in 1999, which has won over twenty-five major design awards for residential and commercial architecture, as well as public art. He cofounded Citizens for a Vibrant Apache Corridor in 2014, dedicated to improving thriving downtown areas in Arizona.

Brenda Case Scheer, FAIA, FAICP, is a professor in the College of Architecture + Planning at the University of Utah. She was dean there during 2002–2013. She specializes in the study of urban morphology, especially comparing contemporary places with more historic fabric. Her most recent book is *The Evolution of Urban Form: Typology for Planners and Architects* (2010).

Marc Schlosserg, Ph.D., is a professor of city and regional planning and codirector of the Sustainable Cities Initiative at the University of Oregon. His research focuses on sustainable neighborhood design with an emphasis on retrofitting for better bicycle and pedestrian transportation options. His most recent book is *Rethinking Streets: An Evidence-Based Guide to 25 Complete Street Transformations* (2014).

Christian Solorio is a graduate of the Design School at Arizona State University. He served as a research assistant for the Retrofitting Suburbs: Re-Visioning the Cul-de-Sac research project that was presented at the Phoenix Urban Research Laboratory in 2012. Christian now works in the architectural field specializing in twenty-first-century learning environments in K–12 education.

Benjamin W. Stanley, Ph.D., is a postdoctoral research associate in the School of Human Evolution and Social Change at Arizona State University. His research focuses on comparative urban history and the political economy of sustainable urban development. He has published articles in *Urban Geography*, *Urban Studies*, *Journal of Urbanism*, and *Journal of Urban History*, among others.

Galina Tachieva is a partner at Duany Plater-Zyberk & Company in Miami. She is a founding member of the Congress for European Urbanism, a leader of the Sprawl Retrofit Initiative of the Congress for the New Urbanism, and author of the *Sprawl Repair Manual* (2010). She oversees projects throughout the world, including regional plans, environmental conservation, new communities, resort towns, and urban infill.

Emily Talen, Ph.D., FAICP, is a professor at Arizona State University in the School of Geographical Sciences and Urban Planning and the School of Sustainability. Her research is devoted to urbanism, urban design, and social equity. Her books include *Design for Diversity: Exploring Socially Mixed Neighborhoods* (2008), and *City Rules: How Regulations Affect Urban Form* (2012).

Whitney Warman has a master's in architecture, master's in urban design, and a bachelor's in landscape architecture from Arizona State University. Her research at the university focused on cyclo-centric urban infill within auto-centric cities, with the intent of revitalizing "third places" through the unexpected social encounters of cyclists. She is now an architectural associate in Scottsdale, Arizona.

June Williamson, RA, is an associate professor of architecture and urban design at the City College of New York/CUNY. She is author of *Designing Suburban Futures* (2013) and coauthor of *Retrofitting Suburbia: Urban Design Solutions for Redesigning Suburbs* (2009). She organized the Build a Better Burb: Be Bold and ParkingPLUS design competitions for Long Island, New York.

Milagros Zingoni is an assistant professor in the Design School at Arizona State University. She is originally from Argentina, where she received her professional degree and license in architecture from the Universidad de Flores. She has volunteered in many public projects and her design studios are about how education in design can serve the public good in underrepresented communities.

Index